I0234811

Translation and Multilingual Natural Language Processing

Editors: Oliver Czulo (Universität Leipzig), Silvia Hansen-Schirra (Johannes Gutenberg-Universität Mainz), Reinhard Rapp (Hochschule Magdeburg-Stendal), Mario Bisiada (Universitat Pompeu Fabra)

In this series (see the complete series history at https://langsci-press.org/catalog/series/tmnlp):

7. Hansen-Schirra, Silvia, Oliver Czulo & Sascha Hofmann (eds). Empirical modelling of translation and interpreting.

8. Svoboda, Tomáš, Łucja Biel & Krzysztof Łoboda (eds.). Quality aspects in institutional translation.

9. Fox, Wendy. Can integrated titles improve the viewing experience? Investigating the impact of subtitling on the reception and enjoyment of film using eye tracking and questionnaire data.

10. Moran, Steven & Michael Cysouw. The Unicode cookbook for linguists: Managing writing systems using orthography profiles.

11. Fantinuoli, Claudio (ed.). Interpreting and technology.

12. Nitzke, Jean. Problem solving activities in post-editing and translation from scratch: A multi-method study.

13. Vandevoorde, Lore. Semantic differences in translation.

14. Bisiada, Mario (ed.). Empirical studies in translation and discourse.

15. Tra&Co Group (ed.). Translation, interpreting, cognition: The way out of the box.

16. Nitzke, Jean & Silvia Hansen-Schirra. A short guide to post-editing.

17. Hoberg, Felix. Informationsintegration in mehrsprachigen Textchats: Der Skype Translator im Sprachenpaar Katalanisch-Deutsch.

18. Kenny, Dorothy (ed.). Machine translation for everyone: Empowering users in the age of artificial intelligence.

ISSN: 2364-8899

Machine translation for everyone

Empowering users in the age of artificial intelligence

Edited by

Dorothy Kenny

language
science
press

Dorothy Kenny (ed.). 2022. *Machine translation for everyone: Empowering users in the age of artificial intelligence* (Translation and Multilingual Natural Language Processing 18). Berlin: Language Science Press.

This title can be downloaded at:
http://langsci-press.org/catalog/book/342
© 2022, the authors
Published under the Creative Commons Attribution 4.0 Licence (CC BY 4.0):
http://creativecommons.org/licenses/by/4.0/ ⓒ ①
ISBN: 978-3-96110-348-5 (Digital)
       978-3-98554-045-7 (Hardcover)

ISSN: 2364-8899
DOI: 10.5281/zenodo.6653406
Source code available from www.github.com/langsci/342
Errata: paperhive.org/documents/remote?type=langsci&id=342

Cover and concept of design: Ulrike Harbort
Proofreading: Amy Amoakuh, Annika Schiefner, Bianca Prandi, Brett Reynolds, Felix Kopecky, Jeroen van de Weijer, Juan Antonio Pérez, Liam McKnight, Jean Nitzke, Oliver Czulo
Fonts: Libertinus, Arimo, DejaVu Sans Mono
Typesetting software: X∃LATEX

Language Science Press
xHain
Grünberger Str. 16
10243 Berlin, Germany
http://langsci-press.org

Storage and cataloguing done by FU Berlin

Freie Universität ⬤ Berlin

Contents

Contents

Acknowledgments

This book has been written with the support of the European Union's Erasmus+ strategic partnership programme, as part of the project known as "MultiTraiNMT: Machine Translation training for multilingual citizens" (project ID: 2019-1-ES01-KA203-064245).

Introduction

Dorothy Kenny

Dublin City University

> In this Introduction I set out the rationale for this book and suggest ways in which readers might approach the material it contains.

1 Why this book?

Multilingualism is a foundational value of the European Union. In practice, it depends on multiple pillars, including language learning and translation. In recent years, both of these pillars have been profoundly affected by the continued development of machine translation. Machine translation, if used wisely, can serve to support language learning efforts. It can provide access to more texts, originally written in more languages, to more users than ever before. And it can help professional human translators to work more productively, given the right circumstances. There is a danger, however, that uncritical use of the technology could set back individual efforts to learn languages. It could also be used in ways that gloss over potential problems with the output it produces, so that consumers don't realize when texts they are reading contain machine-translation induced inaccuracies or biases. And if excessively hyped, it could discourage new blood from entering the translation profession.

In order to harness the benefits of machine translation without jeopardizing other valuable pillars of multilingualism, we take the view, following Bowker & Ciro (2019), that good multilingual citizenship and professional translation must be underpinned by *machine translation literacy*. Different levels of machine translation literacy will be appropriate for different people. Bowker & Ciro (2019) are concerned with the international research community, for example. Here we target two main constituencies: more "occasional" users of machine translation – those who use the technology for *ad hoc* information gathering purposes, or even unwittingly when they consume machine translated text without realizing it, or

Dorothy Kenny. 2022. Introduction. In Dorothy Kenny (ed.), *Machine translation for everyone: Empowering users in the age of artificial intelligence*, v–viii. Berlin: Language Science Press. DOI: 10.5281/zenodo.6759972 casually in language learning contexts; and people who are either already working as translators or training to become translators. We take the view that all users of machine translation should have some basic understanding of why the technology is important, and where it fits into the maintenance of multilingual regimes. And all users should have some basic understanding of how the technology works, so they can use it intelligently and avoid common pitfalls. Some users, who may wish to engage more deeply with the technology, may benefit from knowing how to get the best out of machine translation, for example, by writing texts in a way that makes them easier to translate by machine. The same users might also be interested in ways to improve machine translation outputs. Those working in, or about to join, the translation industry, will have a particular interest in evaluating machine translation output, in order to gauge whether it is "fit for purpose". They might even get involved in integrating machine translation into the workflow of their company or need to know how to customize machine translation so that they can better serve the needs of particular clients. They will also be interested in how machine translation might impact on their working conditions. Such readers require more in-depth knowledge of the technology itself, and of the techniques and tools they can use to implement it. All users should have some basic knowledge of the ethical issues that arise when we use machine translation, for different reasons. Some users may be concerned about the possibility of cheating: in what cases might the use of machine translation constitute a breach of trust in educational environments, for example? Others, mainly professional translators, may have to consider how the use of certain types of machine translation might constitute a breach of contract. And everybody has to be concerned these days about protecting the privacy and data rights of others. Contemporary machine translation is also one of the many technologies that can be implicated in processes that degrade our natural environment. And it has been known to produce biased outputs, preferring male to female forms, for example. Like all communication technologies, it can be used for nefarious causes or positive humanitarian purposes. These are issues that concern us all.

2 How to use this book

In this book we attempt to guide readers through all of the above issues. We do not assume any prior knowledge of either translation in general or machine translation in particular. When we do move on to the more technical aspects of machine translation, and especially neural machine translation – a state-of-the-art translation technology based on artificial neural networks – we first describe these technologies without recourse to mathematical concepts that may not be familiar to readers. We attempt to use insightful explanations, and especially metaphors, that will help readers understand the general concepts that inform the area. In so doing, we provide a gentle introduction to the contemporary world of machine learning. We gradually build up a rich picture of machine translation. In general, readers will find the earlier chapters less specialized than the later ones, and earlier sections of later chapters less specialized than subsequent sections. Some readers may be able to skip some chapters completely, but even machine translation specialists might benefit from reading "non-technical" chapters, for example, on machine translation and ethics.

3 The structure of this book

This book opens with Olga Torres-Hostench's discussion in Chapter 1 of multilingualism, what it means, and how it is operationalized, in particular in the European Union. She makes the case for the considered integration of machine translation into both language learning and translation. In Chapter 2, Dorothy Kenny discusses translation in general and machine translation in particular, aiming to dispel some myths about translation before gently introducing the reader to the basic concepts behind contemporary approaches to machine translation, including artificial intelligence and machine learning. Chapter 3, by Caroline Rossi and Alice Carré, brings us into the world of machine translation evaluation, an area of considerable scientific and economic importance. In Chapter 4, Pilar Sánchez-Gijón and Dorothy Kenny address the ways in which we can make translation easier for machines before the fact, while in Chapter 5, Sharon O'Brien guides us through approaches to after-the-fact improvement of machine translated texts through the activity known as *post-editing*. Chapter 6, by Joss Moorkens, discusses the many ethical issues that arise in contexts where machine translation is used. Chapter 7 is the most technical chapter in the book. In it, Juan Antonio Pérez-Ortiz, Mikel Forcada and Felipe Sánchez-Martínez explain how neural machine translation works, covering the basic techniques that are most commonly used in contemporary systems. Gema Ramírez-Sánchez's guide to custom neural machine translation follows in Chapter 8. The volume closes with a chapter dedicated to machine translation and language learning, written by Alice Carré, Dorothy Kenny, Caroline Rossi, Pilar Sánchez-Gijón and Olga Torres-Hostench.

Dorothy Kenny

Accompanying resources

Each chapter of this book is accompanied by a set of interactive activities accessible through the MultiTraiNMT website at http://www.multitrainmt.eu/. A permanent link to these activities can be found at https://ddd.uab.cat/record/257869. Most of the activities can be completed on a self-access basis, although some will benefit from the guidance of a teacher.

A special pedagogical platform known as MutNMT has also been created as part of the MultiTraiNMT project. It is designed to help users learn how to train, customize and evaluate neural machine translation systems. It is accessible through the MultiTraiNMT website, and will be of particular significance to readers of Chapters 7 and 8 of this book.

References

Bowker, Lynne & Jairo Buitrago Ciro. 2019. *Machine translation and global research*. Bingley: Emerald Publishing.

Chapter 1

Europe, multilingualism and machine translation

Olga Torres-Hostench
Universitat Autònoma de Barcelona

This chapter explains multilingualism as a foundational principle of the European Union, describing how it is put into practice and supported through language learning and translation. Taking the university campus as a case study, it argues that machine translation can be used to foster multilingualism in this context.

1 Introduction

The European Union's motto "united in diversity" is said to symbolize "the essential contribution that linguistic diversity and language learning make to the European project" (European Commission 2021). But European Union (EU) policy on multilingualism is mostly built upon language learning and mobility, both time-consuming activities. And human language learning presents particular challenges. After all, there is a limit to the number of languages the average EU citizen can learn. The aim in this chapter is to suggest answers to these questions by arguing that machine translation can contribute to the promotion of multilingualism in Europe and thus to European linguistic diversity.

2 A multilingual EU

It is ... an open secret that the EU's supposedly humane multilingualism is but an illusion. (House 2003: 561)

ISO 639-3 is a set of codes developed by the International Organization for Standardization (ISO) that defines three-letter identifiers for all known human

Olga Torres-Hostench. 2022. Europe, multilingualism and machine translation. In Dorothy Kenny (ed.), *Machine translation for everyone: Empowering users in the age of artificial intelligence*, 1–21. Berlin: Language Science Press. DOI: 10.5281/zenodo.6759974 languages. As of 30 January 2020, the standard contained entries for 7,868 languages (Wikizero 2020), around 600 of which are spoken in Europe, and 24 of which are official languages of the EU. These are: Dutch, French, German, Italian (since 1958); Danish, English (since 1973); Greek (since 1981); Portuguese, Spanish (since 1986); Finnish, Swedish (since 1995); Czech, Estonian, Hungarian, Latvian, Lithuanian, Maltese, Polish, Slovak, Slovene (since 2004); Bulgarian, Irish, Romanian (since 2007) and Croatian (since 2013).

Linguistic diversity is part of Europe's cultural heritage. In Europe, there are languages with official status at state level, and indigenous regional and/or minority languages with different degrees of recognition. The 1998 European Charter for Regional or Minority Languages is the European convention for the protection and promotion of languages used by traditional minorities. It was reformed and strengthened by a monitoring mechanism in 2019. The Charter covers 79 languages used by 201 national minorities or linguistic groups (Council of Europe 2020). They are presented in alphabetical order in Table 1.

According to the Charter, some of these languages are to be protected in just one country, such as Skolt Sami in Finland, whereas others should be protected in several countries, such as Slovenian in Austria, Bosnia and Herzegovina, Croatia and Hungary. Beyond the Charter, there are other languages with different levels of recognition. For instance, Sardinia, an autonomous region of Italy, recognizes the Sardinian language as an official language, and Romansh Ladino, Cimbrian and Mocheno, spoken in certain communes of the mountainous North of Italy, also have local recognition.

The European Charter for Regional or Minority Languages, however, guarantees the rights only of regional minority groups, and not of migrant groups. What's more, the Charter has noteworthy absences, such as Breton, spoken in the North West of France, although a Breton language agency was created by the Region of Brittany in 2010 to promote daily use of the language.

Multilingualism in Europe is also enhanced by immigration and mobility. There have been intra-European migrations, leading, for example, to Portuguese being spoken in Andorra and Polish in Ireland, alongside languages traditionally spoken outside the EU, such as Mandarin Chinese or Arabic. In the Multilingual Cities Project (Extra & Yagmur 2005), home language surveys amongst pupils both in primary and secondary schools were collected in Brussels, Hamburg, Lyon, Madrid, The Hague and Göteborg. The list of collected languages was the following: Romani, Turkish, Urdu, Armenian, Russian, Serbian/Croatian/Bosnian, Albanian, Vietnamese, Chinese, Arabic, Polish, Somali, Portuguese, Berber, Kurdish, Spanish, French, Italian, English, German. The authors of the study reached an obvious but provocative conclusion:

Table 1: Languages covered by the European Charter for Regional or Minority Languages

Albanian	Finnish	Lemko	Sater Frisian
Aragonese	Franco-Provençal	Leonese	Scots
Aranese	French	Limburgish	Scottish-Gaelic
Armenian	Frisian	Lithuanian	Serbian
Assyrian	Gagauz	Low German	Skolt Sami
Asturian	Galician	Lower Saxon	Slovakian
Basque	German	Lower Sorbian	Slovenian
Beás	Greek	Lule Sami	South Sami
Belarusian	Hungarian	Macedonian	Swedish
Bosnian	Inari-Sami	Manx Gaelic	Tatar
Bulgarian	Irish	Meänkieli	Turkish
Bunjevac	Istro-Romanian	Moldovan	Ukrainian
Catalan	Italian	North Frisian	Ulster Scots
Cornish	Karaim	North Sami	Upper Sorbian
Crimean Tatar	Karelian	Polish	Valencian
Croatian	Kashub	Romani	Vlach
Cypriot Maronite Arabic	Krimchak	Romanian	Welsh
	Kurdish	Romansh	Yenish
Czech	Kven/Finnish	Russian	Yezidi
Danish	Ladino	Ruthenian	Yiddish

Amongst the major 20 languages in the participating cities, 10 languages are of European origin and 10 languages stem from abroad. These findings show that the traditional concept of language diversity in Europe should be reconsidered and extended. (Extra & Yagmur 2005)

But what is the "traditional concept" of language diversity?

2.1 The 24 official languages as a symbol of European linguistic diversity

The European Union considers its linguistic diversity a valuable asset. Article 22 of the Charter of Fundamental Rights of the European Union (The Member States, 2012) states that "[t]he Union shall respect cultural, religious and linguistic diversity." However, member states have the exclusive right to define and recognize national and regional minority languages, and language policies are highly controversial.

Meanwhile, the EU prides itself on standing up for language diversity through the use of the 24 official languages in the main EU institutions. From a practical point of view, this position involves a major challenge that deserves closer attention.

For instance, in the European Parliament, parliamentary documents are published in all the official languages "as EU citizens must be able to read legislation affecting them in the language of their own country" (European Parliament 2020) and members of the European Parliament have the right to speak and write in any of the official languages. Rule 167 of the Rules of Procedure of the European Parliament is related to languages, and specifies that: (i) all documents of Parliament shall be drawn up in the official languages; (ii) all members shall have the right to speak in Parliament in the official language of their choice; (iii) interpretation services shall be provided and (iv) the President of the Parliament shall rule on any alleged discrepancies between the different language versions (European Parliament 2021).

As for the citizens of the EU, according to the Treaty on the Functioning of the European Union (TFEU[1]), all European citizens have the right to address the official EU institutions in any of the EU's official languages and to receive an answer in that language. This is intended to make the EU institutions more democratic and accessible to EU citizens. Other provisions related to multilingualism in the TFEU are contained in articles 20, 24 and 342.

Some people think that 24 official languages is too many, and others that 24 official languages is not enough. Some countries try alternative approaches. For instance, Catalan, Euskara and Galician, all spoken in Spain, are considered "additional languages" by the EU (they are co-official languages together with Spanish in their respective territories). This status means that any communication from an EU citizen in these languages has to be translated in Spain into a "procedural language" of the EU, and the answer from the EU institution will be also translated from the procedural language into the additional language. The cost of these translations is borne by Spain.

The use of three procedural languages, English, French and German, is intended to simplify multilingual communication in the EU: given 24 official languages, the EU is faced with a total of 552 possible translation combinations, "since each language can be translated into 23 others" (European Parliament

---

[1]The most recent, consolidated version of the TFEU is available from https://eur-lex.europa.eu/ legal-content/EN/TXT/PDF/?uri=CELEX:12012E/TXT&from=EN. Unless otherwise indicated, all urls mentioned in this chapter were more recently accessed in January 2022.

2020) and this would be difficult to handle for all EU documentation. For this reason, there are norms to establish which documents are translated into the other 23 languages and which are translated just into the three procedural languages.

The European Commission's Directorate-General for Translation (DGT) translates texts for the institutions and the citizens of the EU. As of 2022 it produces more than 2.75 million translated pages per year, 91% of which are translations from English, 2% from French, just under 1% from Spanish, and slightly less again from German. Other source languages combined account for around 5% of translation activity. Of all translated documents, 63% are translated internally by the DGT and 37% are outsourced to external companies. Some 55% of translations involve EU law-making, 22% external communication and the web, 12% communication with other EU institutions and national parliaments, 5% correspondence with EU citizens, 4% other official documents, and 2% public consultation on EU policies. The translation budget for 2022 was 355 million euros, or 0.2% of the whole EU budget (European Commission, Directorate-General for Translation 2022).

2.2 Machine translation enters the fray

The DGT has an in-house staff of 2,000, between linguists and support staff, and works with several thousand selected external translators (European Commission, Directorate-General for Translation 2022). The translations they produce, in all language combinations, are stored in the Euramis system (the EURopean Advanced Multilingual Information System), which includes, for instance, the *Acquis Communautaire*, a corpus of the EU's legislative documents in all 24 of its official languages (European Commission, EU Science Hub 2022). In order to increase productivity and reduce costs, the DGT has incorporated machine translation into some of its workflows, most recently using a system called eTranslation.[2] The use of eTranslation is expected to save time and money for the EU, but not only that. Eventually, as machine translation develops further, it could contribute to an increase not only in the number of documents that are translated and that otherwise would not have been considered for translation, but also, at some time in the future, to an expansion of the set of languages for which translation is available, and hence to a better reflection of European language diversity; an ideal that, without machine translation, would have been inconceivable just a few years ago. This might be the only way that indigenous or regional minority languages, as well as "non-territorial" or even immigrant minority languages, will gain representation in the EU institutions alongside official, national languages.

---

[2]https://ec.europa.eu/info/resources-partners/machine-translation-public-administrations-etranslation_en

2.3 What does multilingualism mean to the EU?

Policies on multilingualism are a way of organizing the above-mentioned language diversity, and affirming its richness. In the EU, multilingualism is also seen as a means of social cohesion and worker mobility: "[l]anguage competences contribute to the mobility, employability and personal development of European citizens" (Council of the EU 2014).

A multilingual approach to linguistic policies aims at promoting languages not only in multilingual states but also within organizations. We may talk about multilingualism in many forms, including:

- A multilingual policy, which is the policy of an organization, company or institution to use more than two languages for its internal and external communication.

- A multilingual European Union, which means that different languages co-exist in the EU.

- A multilingual citizen, who has the capacity to use several languages.

- A multilingual health system, which is a health system which incorporates linguistic diversity to improve health delivery to newly arrived people, for instance.

The main EU policies on multilingualism are reflected in a series of documents (European Council 2002, European Commission 2008, Council of the EU 2008a,b, 2011, 2014, European Council 2017).

In these EU policies and pronouncements on multilingualism, constant reference is made to language learning and, specifically, the "mother tongue plus two" policy, according to which citizens would learn "at least two foreign languages from a very early age" (European Council 2002). But would implementation of this policy make European citizens multilingual enough? From my point of view, there is a need to incorporate further elements into European policies on multilingualism.

Multilingualism is related to language policies, but that is not the full story. Cenoz (2013), who provides a wide spectrum of definitions of multilingualism, reminds us that multilingualism is multidimensional, involving, for example, the individual versus the social dimension, the proficiency versus use dimension, bilingualism versus multilingualism, etc. It can also be applied to geographical areas or social spheres. Moreover, it can be studied from different perspectives, including those of cognition, social construction, identity, language practices, multimodalities and technologies, among others. From the simplest definition in Wikipedia ("the use of more than one language, either by an individual speaker or by a group of speakers") to the more complex multidimensional definitions provided by Cenoz (2013), in this chapter I will adopt the European Commission's definition of multilingualism as "the ability of societies, institutions, groups and individuals to engage, on a regular basis, with more than one language in their day-to-day lives" (European Commission 2007). The term *engage* allows us to incorporate a useful nuance for the purposes of this book. By writing this chapter, I wish to invite readers to consider whether multilingualism can be defined from a technological perspective, adapting the above-mentioned definition used by the European Commission.

Discussion topic

Is there a "technological multilingualism", understood as the ability of societies, institutions, groups and individuals to engage, on a regular basis, with more than one language in their day-to-day lives, through multilingual translation tools?

Interestingly, the above-mentioned report from the High Level Group on Multilingualism, which provided our definition of multilingualism, mentions "the potential of multilingual electronic tools as support for non-specialist users of second and third languages" (European Commission 2007) as a research area. Likewise, the European Commission's communication on "Multilingualism – an asset and a commitment" (European Commission 2014) claims that "the language gap in the EU can be narrowed through the media, new technologies and translation services". This book aims to make a contribution precisely to this field.

2.4 EU actions for linguistic diversity

The EU's webpage on linguistic diversity[3] mentions the following initiatives to promote linguistic diversity: the European Day of Languages, Erasmus+ Mobility programmes, the European Capitals of Culture and the Creative Europe programme:

---

[3]https://ec.europa.eu/education/policies/linguistic-diversity_en

- Established by the Council of Europe in 2001, European Day of Languages[4] takes place on September 26th each year. On this day EU countries organize activities to promote linguistic diversity and the ability to speak other languages.

- Erasmus + Mobility programmes. Between 2014 and 2020, €14.7 billion was assigned to more than 4 million mobility grants, 2 million of which were designated for university students.

- The European Capitals of Culture is an initiative to highlight the diversity of cultures in Europe, including linguistic diversity. For instance, in 2020, European Capitals of Culture (and corresponding languages) were Rijeka (Croatian) and Galway (Irish and English).

- Creative Europe.[5] This European Commission framework programme supports the culture and audiovisual sectors, including literary translation. Specifically, it funds the translation of literary work from one European language to another.

- Another interesting initiative to promote linguistic diversity is the "European Language Label"[6] attached to EU funded projects. Although most of these projects are oriented towards language learning, some specifically target language diversity.

Discussion topic

From the current perspective, machine translation is not present enough in the EU discourse of language diversity and multilingualism. How could machine translation be included in language learning projects?

Including machine translation in multilingualism initiatives would allow us to increase the number of languages European citizens could become familiar with. It would also allow citizens to approach unknown languages with curiosity and without fear, to access unfamiliar language environments more easily and to respect local languages. Moreover, MT could be used to support reading comprehension in any unlearned languages.

---

[4]https://edl.ecml.at
[5]http://www.creativeeuropeuk.eu/funding-opportunities/literary-translation-0
[6]https://ec.europa.eu/education/initiatives/label/label_public/index.cfm

2.5 Multilingualism and language learning in the EU

According to the Council of Europe's Language Policy Portal:[7]

> language learners/users lie at the heart of the work of the Language Policy Programme. Whatever their status, all languages are covered: foreign languages, major languages of schooling, languages spoken in the family and minority or regional languages, as well as a specific programme on the linguistic integration of migrants and refugees.

Initiatives to foster multilingualism are many and varied, but language learning deserves closer attention, especially given the EU's above-mentioned "mother tongue plus two" policy.

Some of the EU's recent initiatives to improve language skills include the European Centre for Modern Languages (www.ecml.at; the Eurydice Report (Eurydice 2019), which provides information on policy efforts in Europe that support the teaching of regional or minority languages in schools; the Online Linguistic Support (OLS) platform;[8] the Common European Framework of Reference for Languages (CEFR); and Erasmus+ mobility programmes.

European projects funded to improve language learning deserve special attention. Methodologies, languages and countries involved vary enormously from one project to another. Table 2 lists some interesting examples.

Eurostat, the website for European Statistics,[9] provides statistics on the second and foreign languages studied by pupils at different education levels in the EU. According to Eurostat data from 2019, English was by far the most popular language at lower secondary level, studied by nearly 86.8% of pupils, followed by French (19.4%), German (18.3%) and Spanish (17.5%) (Eurostat 2022).

Discussion topic

In second language learning in Europe, is "multilingual" a euphemism for "English-speaking"?

Another interesting question is how many students learn two or more foreign languages, as recommended by the European Council (2002): it is known that

---

[7]https://www.coe.int/en/web/language-policy/home
[8]https://erasmusplusols.eu/en/about-ols/
[9]https://appsso.eurostat.ec.europa.eu

Table 2: Examples of European projects focused on language learning

Project	Languages	Specific features
iTongue: Our Multilingual Future (2013)	Not specified	Paralinguistic digital tools for foreign language learning
Massive open online courses with videos for palliative clinical field and intercultural and multilingual medical communication (2014)	DT, EN, FR, IT, ES, RO	20 multilingual fundamental palliative medicine procedures
Crafting Employability Strategies for HE Students of Languages in Europe (2015).	Not specified	Embedding employability within language teaching
LMOOCs for university students on the move (2018)	FR, ES	Open educational resources for university students
Gamifiying Academic English Skills in Higher Education: Reading Academic English App (2016).	Not specified	Game-based application to improve English academic reading skills of university students
E-LENGUA: E-Learning Novelties towards the Goal of a Universal Acquisition of Foreign and Second Languages (2015).	EN, AR, ES, FR, DE, IT, PT	Best practices of the integration of digital competences into the teaching of languages
EULALIA: Enhancing University Language courses with an App powered by game-based Learning and tangible user Interfaces Activities (2019).	IT, PO, ES, MT	Inclusive learning tools based on the paradigm of Mobile Learning and Game-Based Learning methodology and the application of Tangible User Interfaces (TUIs)

89.9% (almost 14 million) of secondary level pupils studied more than one foreign language in 2019 (Eurostat 2022). Among them, more than 7 million (48.1%) studied two or more foreign languages.

In short, of the 600 languages spoken around Europe by more than 700 million speakers (EU and non-EU) (World Bank 2020), the majority of EU students are learning one or two out of the following four as their first or subsequent foreign language: English, French, German or Spanish.

2.6 Levels of attainment

The European Survey on Language Competences (European Commission 2019) tested 54,000 secondary pupils (aged 14-15) in 16 educational systems, and covered the two most widely taught foreign languages in all concerned education systems. The survey tested writing, reading and listening comprehension. It did not test oral expression. The key finding of the survey was that only 42% of tested students reached the level of independent user (B1 and B2 in the Common European Framework of Reference for Languages) in their first foreign language, and only 25% reached this level in their second foreign language. Moreover, a large number of pupils did not even achieve the level of a basic user: 14% failed to achieve this level for their first foreign language and 20% failed to achieve it for their second foreign language (European Commission 2019).

In the same report, there are data from a 2018 flash Eurobarometer survey among 15-30 year-olds, where 85% of respondents stated that they wished to improve their proficiency in a language they had already learned (mainly English):

> This indicates that the survey respondents were not satisfied with the level they achieved at the end of compulsory education or they did not have a chance to maintain their level. One third of surveyed young Europeans said they were unable to study in a language other than the one they used in school (i.e. often the mother tongue). (European Commission 2019: 102)

2.7 Is there a role for machine translation in language learning?

We have already seen that language-learning efforts in the EU tend to be concentrated on a small number of large languages, and that learners do not always reach desired levels of competence in their chosen foreign languages. These circumstances suggest that further support for language learning is needed, and it behoves us to investigate whether such support could come in the form of machine translation. As neural machine translation learns faster than any foreign language learner, it could, in theory, be used to help learners read complex texts and develop more advanced written skills in their second language. They could learn how to make the most of machine translation in the second language so that they could detect and edit machine translation mistakes based on their knowledge of the second language. And while empirical studies of the use of machine translation in language classes are still thin on the ground, a small number of sources suggest interesting avenues of research. Relevant studies are discussed in Carré et al. (2022 [this volume]), which includes further ideas and strategies that can be used in language learning classes. Yet others are included in the database of activities of the MultiTraiNMT project (MultiTraiNMT 2020). My view is that there are many ways of using machine translation in language learning classes and there is no need to forbid its use if it is used in a conscious and critical way.

On occasion, however, there is just no time to train second language students. Indeed, in the history of machine translation there have been many occasions on which research was partially triggered by a perceived lack of people learning a particular foreign language. Cold War research into Russian-English machine translation is one such case (Gordin 2016). More recently, the Japanese organizers of the Tokyo 2020 Olympic Games (actually held in 2021 due to COVID-19) realized that learning Japanese was out of the question for most foreigners and that they needed a faster approach to overcome language barriers during the Olympics. The Japanese internal affairs ministry thus allocated ¥1.38 billion to machine translation research to improve the quality of real-time speech translation technology, with the aim of covering 90% of the language needs of the Olympic teams and tourists who, it was hoped, would go to Japan (Murai 2015). The Japanese government funded the research for a specific machine translation system to be used during Tokyo Olympics and private companies were tasked with the development of devices and mobile apps to run the system. The plan was that companies would recover their investment by selling the devices and apps subscriptions to users. In this case, the introduction of machine translation was the chosen shortcut to bring multilingualism to Japan, instead of language learning.

3 Case study: Multilingual universities

3.1 Internationalization and multilingualism

The European Commission's communication on "European higher education in the world" establishes the key priorities for the internationalization of European universities focused on mobility, digital learning, and the strengthening of strategic cooperation. Regarding languages, the communication notes that:

> proficiency in English is de facto part of any internationalization strategy for learners, teachers and institutions and some Member States have introduced, or are introducing, targeted courses in English (especially at Masters level) as part of their strategy to attract talent which would otherwise not come to Europe. (European Commission 2013)

At the same time, multilingualism is a significant European asset: it is highly valued by international students and should be encouraged in teaching and research throughout the higher education curriculum (European Commission 2013).

Indeed, the EU remains committed to multilingualism on university campuses: firstly, because multilingual campuses reflect European linguistic diversity; secondly, because they provide students with more mobility and employment opportunities; and thirdly, because they promote contact with different cultures and learning approaches. In a similar vein, Gao (2019) lists different reasons for universities to engage in internationalization, including the fact that internationalization can help prepare students to interact with people from different cultures as a way to create cultural understanding and reduce mutual hostility between countries. Internationalization poses challenges for universities however (ibid.), not least those related to multilingualism. Firstly, a lack of translation resources (including human resources) can prevent a university from becoming fully English-speaking. Secondly, internationalization can involve the displacement of native languages and a loss of language diversity. I see a role, however, for machine translation in counteracting these dangers. And the technology seems particularly promising, given shifting understandings of internationalization: traditionally, universities have developed plans to do "internationalization at home" (to attract foreign students), and "internationalization abroad" (to send students abroad). Mittelmcier et al. (2020) incorporate the concept of "internationalization at a distance" to develop online international distance learning models for campus-based institutions. The COVID-19 pandemic has undoubtedly given extra impetus to this third way. Technologies may change the way internationalization is conceived and machine translation is a technology that has potential to contribute to the internationalization game.

3.2 English as Lingua Franca (ELF), Local Languages (LLs) and machine translation

Universities' internationalization strategies are numerous, but mobility and running English or bilingual programmes are possibly the most visible ones. The latter strategy goes under different names, for example English as Lingua Franca (ELF), Englishization, and English-medium instruction (EMI). It has been defined as the use of "English as medium of instruction in institutions of higher education in non-English speaking countries" (Multilingual Higher Education 2016).

The decision to use English allows for attendance by international students. However, local students who are not fluent in English may feel betrayed if their local university worries more about international students than about them, especially if it is for economic reasons (as international students' fees are higher than local students' fees). Some universities opt to deliver MOOCs in English as a strategy to attract international students, but recent research suggests that the impact of MOOCs on international student enrolment is still minimal (Zakharova 2019).

As a way to overcome the tensions between English as Lingua Franca and local languages, House (2003) distinguishes between "languages for communication" and "languages for identification". According to House (2003: 560), languages for communication are instrumental in enabling communication with others who do not speak one's own L1. Languages for identification, on the other hand, are

> normally local languages, and particularly an individual's L1(s), which are likely to be the main determinants of identity, which means holding a stake in the collective linguistic-cultural capital that defines the L1 group and its members ... and the type of affective-emotive quality involved in identification. (House 2003: 561)

Under this approach, English would be used for communication between speakers who do not share the same language and for "pockets of expertise" (House 2003: 561) and languages for identification would be used between same-language speakers.

House (2003) presents a case study involving the use of English as a medium of instruction at Hamburg University (Germany), in which she examines how English interacts with the local language, and how international students perceive, and react to this "diglossic situation" (House 2003: 570). Results showed that English was not seen as being in competition with German. English was described as being in "a class of its own", a supranational, auxiliary means of communication. In this project "there were no signs (yet) of a threat to a native language

(German) and to multilingualism" (House 2003: 574) and international students were invited to learn German during the academic year.

3.3 A truly multilingual university

Current multilingual universities are universities which include EMI for international students, and/or universities in borderlands and/or areas with more than two official languages. Such universities may be multilingual for historical, political, geographical, economic, or other reasons, and finding the balance in their language policy may be a challenge for them. Neither internationalization nor multilingual policies can be improvised. Knight (1994: 12) proposed a six-phase model of the process of institutional internationalization:

- Awareness of need, purpose, and benefits

- Commitment by all university actors

- Planning: Identify resources, purposes and objectives, priorities and strategies

- Operationalize: Develop academic activities and services

- Review: Assess and enhance the quality, impact, and progress and

- Reinforcement: Develop incentives, recognition, and rewards.

Related specifically to multilingualism, this plan would require us to answer questions like: will EMI be restricted to international students/courses? Can a university be considered multilingual if EMI is used only for international students? Will international students be considered "multilingual" if they use only English in the "multilingual" university? Is it enough for a university to have its website in its official languages and English but deliver courses in local languages? Are courses to be delivered using more than one language or will instruction take place in just one language? Could the native languages of students (which may not be the official languages of the university) be incorporated into the courses? Is the language of instruction the only parameter to identify a "multilingual university"? In which languages are training materials to be offered? Will language proficiency be assessed together with non-linguistic content? How can local students be prepared for EMI? Does being multilingual mean using EMI? Does being multilingual mean using local languages and English? If so, in what proportion? How many multilingual strategies are enough to become a multilingual university? Which languages are needed to guarantee further integration of the university student into the geographical region or local economy? Will international students live in English-only "bubbles"?

On a truly multilingual campus, universities could welcome languages from international students as well as languages from socially or culturally marginalized groups. Many local languages have been historically undervalued in academia, with doubts expressed, for example about the extent of their academic vocabulary. An extreme case in point is that of Quechua: the first doctoral thesis fully written in Quechua was defended in 2019, some 468 years after the first university was established in Peru.[10]

The e-course *Multilingualism and plurilingualism in education* developed as part of the Erasmus+ project Multilingual Higher Education (2016), describes the language policies for different multilingual universities. For instance, at the University of Fribourg (Switzerland), there are courses offered in French and German. At the University of Helsinki (Finland), there are courses offered in Finnish, Swedish and English. At the Free University of Bozen-Bolzano, subjects are taught in German, Italian and Ladin, and in English as a lingua franca. At the University of Luxembourg, at least 20% of all courses should be taught in the three languages of instruction – French, English and German.

Gao (2019: 89) proposes measurement dimensions and indicators to distinguish between strategic aspiration and reality when it comes to internationalization. Her proposals have been adapted below specifically to multilingualism, our field of interest.

Under the dimension of university governance, actions promoting multilingualism could include: (i) A supportive multilingual policy framework/organizational structure; (ii) A languages office/translation services; (iii) Machine translation infrastructure; (iv) Multilingual presence/signage at the university; (v) Development of multilingual awareness and skills among staff; (vi) Budget for multilingualism initiatives; and (vii) Monitoring/evaluation systems for multilingual performance.

From an academic perspective, actions promoting multilingualism could include: (i) Multilingual courses (why does a course have to be in one and only one language?); (ii) Multilingual teaching, normalizing multilingual classes; (iii) Multilingual research and multilingual conferences; (iv) Multilingual students in the class, involving interaction between international and local students; and

---

[10]https://www.theguardian.com/world/2019/oct/27/peru-student-roxana-quispe-collantes-thesis-inca-language-quechua

(v) Multilingual visiting scholars; (vi) Multilingual curricula; (vii) Multilingual research journals; (viii) Multilingual extracurricular activities and (ix) Cultural diversity visibility.

And last, but not least, the university could provide multilingual orientation programmes, multilingual support and multilingual libraries.

3.4 Ideas for using machine translation in teaching, research and administration in multilingual universities

Multilingual universities could employ machine translation systems capable of translating as much as possible between English and local languages. One strategy might be using free online machine translation services, but the users should be aware of machine translation mistakes and be able to handle them properly, either by correcting them themselves or asking for professional post-editing services. Further information on post-editing can be found in O'Brien (2022 [this volume]).

Another strategy would be to develop university-customized quality machine translation resources between local languages and English, as explained further in Ramírez-Sánchez (2022 [this volume]). If resources allowed, a customized machine translation system could be shared between universities in Europe and beyond.

In the truly multilingual campuses of the future:

- International students could mix with local students, and have machine translation resources available to follow the class in any local language as there would be: (i) teaching materials in different languages (assuming copyright issues have been resolved); (ii) access to multilingual glossaries and databases for specialized terminology; (iii) a recording of the class using available voice recognition, transcription and machine translation features, etc.

- Students would learn post-editing skills to review machine translation results, either in English and/or other languages, in order to be able to use machine translation output wisely.

- Universities would provide post-editing services for good-quality teaching guides and teaching materials.

- Multilingual research dissemination and multilingual publications would be encouraged, providing embedded machine translation features.

- Rather than struggling through talks and conference papers in faltering English, visiting professors who wish to would express themselves in their native languages and translation/interpreting services would be provided, either human (if there is funding), or machine.

- Multilingual activities would be organized on campus, in various fields such as music, theatre, cuisine, politics, literature, solidarity, social service, etc.

In a truly multilingual university, local languages, English, and other languages brought by mobility students should be able to coexist. This strategy would help international students integrate into a multilingual environment.

4 Conclusion

This chapter has championed the idea of machine translation as a tool to foster multilingualism in Europe. As seen in the chapter, the EU has published charters, treaties and parliamentary documents promoting multilingualism as a core value in Europe that has to be fostered and preserved. However, despite all efforts and resources put into language learning, the goal of learning one's "mother tongue plus two" is difficult to reach. On the one hand, in practice, most EU citizens are learning only English as a foreign language. On the other hand, the learning curve in language learning is long and slow. In this context, machine translation seems to offer some support to those who do not have the time or resources to keep learning more and more languages.

The chapter also explores the case of universities as small multilingual communities who can design language policies that promote multilingualism. Language policies may generate tensions on campuses for a number of reasons, but most campuses are multilingual in practice nowadays, either through the internationalization/Englishization of the university or due to the arrival of foreign students. In this context, the chapter explores the need to design language policies that acknowledge the potential of machine translation to facilitate multilingualism, without forgetting the challenges that machine translation presents, especially those related to quality and ethics. As we say in Spanish, my aim here is to *abrir el melón* (literally to 'open the melon') of machine translation in multilingualism and language learning. Opening the melon means tackling a question that needs to be dealt with sooner or later, although nobody wants to do it because the consequences are unknown. In other words, nobody knows if the melon will be sweet enough to eat, but there is only one way to find out. Even if existing machine translation systems do not communicate the non-literal meaning of *abrir el melón,* anyone reading a literal machine translation will still learn a useful Spanish metaphor. And who knows? This metaphor may even travel to new languages and cultures, as it allows a long and complex meaning to be conveyed in just three words. This is multilingualism in action.

References

Carré, Alice, Dorothy Kenny, Caroline Rossi, Pilar Sánchez-Gijón & Olga Torres-Hostench. 2022. Machine translation for language learners. In Dorothy Kenny (ed.), *Machine translation for everyone: Empowering users in the age of artificial intelligence,* 187–207. Berlin: Language Science Press. DOI: 10.5281/zenodo.6760024.

Cenoz, Jasone. 2013. Defining multilingualism. *Annual Review of Applied Linguistics* 33. 3–18. DOI: 10.1017/S026719051300007X.

Council of Europe. 2020. *Languages Covered by the European Charter for Regional or Minority Languages.* https://www.coe.int/en/web/european-charter-regional-or-minority-languages/languages-covered.

Council of the EU. 2008a. *Council conclusions of 22 May 2002 on multilingualism (2008/c140/10).*

Council of the EU. 2008b. Council resolution of 21 November 2008 on a European strategy for multilingualism. *OJ C 320* 16.12.2008. 1–3.

Council of the EU. 2011. *Council conclusions on language competences to enhance mobility 2011.* https://eur-lex.europa.eu/LexUriServ/LexUriServ.do?uri=OJ:C:2011:372:0027:0030:EN.

Council of the EU. 2014. *Conclusions on multilingualism and the development of language competences.* https://www.consilium.europa.eu/uedocs/cms_data/docs/pressdata/en/educ/142692.pdf.

European Commission. 2007. *Final report from high level group on multilingualism.* europa.eu/en/publication-detail/-/publication/b0a1339f-f181-4de5-abd3-130180f177c7. ISBN: 978-92-79-06902-4 https://op.

European Commission. 2008. *Multilingualism: an asset for Europe and a shared commitment.* Communication from the Commission to the European Parliament, the Council, the European Economic and Social Committee and the Committee of the Regions. https://eur-lex.europa.eu/legal-content/EN/TXT/PDF/?uri=CELEX.

European Commission. 2013. *European higher education in the world.* Communication from the Commission to the European Parliament, the Council, the European Economic and Social Committee and the Committee of the Regions. COM (2013) 499. https://ec.europa.eu/transparency/regdoc/rep/1/2013/EN/1-2013-499-EN-F1-1.pdf.

European Commission. 2014. *Multilingualism – an asset and a commitment.* https://eur-lex.europa.eu/legal-content/EN/TXT/?uri=LEGISSUM:ef0003.

European Commission. 2019. *Education and training monitor.* https://op.europa.eu/webpub/eac/education-and-training-monitor-2019/en/.

European Commission. 2021. *Why is multilingualism important?* https://eceuropa.eu/education/policies/multilingualism/about-multilingualism-policy_en.

European Commission, Directorate-General for Translation. 2022. *Translation in figures 2022.* https://data.europa.eu/doi/10.2782/253419.

European Commission, EU Science Hub. 2022. *Dgt-Translation Memory.* https://joint-research-centre.ec.europa.eu/language-technology-resources/dgt-translation-memory_en.

European Council. 2002. *Presidency conclusions of the Barcelona European Council meeting 15 and 16 March 2002.* https://ec.europa.eu/commission/presscorner/detail/en/PRES_02_930.

European Council. 2017. *European council conclusions on security and defence, social dimension, education and culture, and climate change.* 14 December. https://www.consilium.europa.eu/en/press/press-releases/2017/12/14/european-council-conclusions/.

European Parliament. 2020. *Multilingualism in the European Parliament.* https://www.europarl.europa.eu/about-parliament/en/organisation-and-rules/multilingualism.

European Parliament. 2021. *Rules of Procedure of the European Parliament.* https://www.europarl.europa.eu/doceo/document/RULES-9-2021-01-18-RULE-167_EN.html.

Eurostat. 2022. *Pupils by education level and number of modern foreign languages studied - absolute numbers and % of pupils by number of languages studied.* Online data code: EDUC_UOE_LANG02. https://ec.europa.eu/eurostat/databrowser/view/educ_uoe_lang02/default/table?lang=en.

Eurydice. 2019. *The teaching of regional and minority languages in schools in Europe.* https://op.europa.eu/s/n8TH. Luxembourg: Publications Office of the European Union. DOI: 10.2797/472090.

Extra, Guus & Kutlay Yagmur. 2005. Multilingual cities project: Crossnational perspectives on immigrant minority languages in Europe. *Noves SL. Revista de Sociolingüística* 1. 1–9.

Gao, Catherine Yuan. 2019. *Measuring university internationalization.* Cham: Palgrave Macmillan. DOI: 10.1007/978-3-030-21465-4.

Gordin, Michael. D. 2016. The Dostoevsky machine in Georgetown: Scientific translation in the Cold War. *Annals of Science* 73(2). 208–223.

House, Juliane. 2003. English as a lingua franca: A threat to multilingualism? *Journal of Sociolinguistics* 7(4). 556–578.

Knight, Jane. 1994. *Internationalization: Elements and checkpoints.* CBIE Research No. 7. Ottawa: Canadian Bureau for International Education (CBIE)/Bureau canadien de l'éducation internationale (BCEI).

Mittelmeier, Jenna, Bart Rienties, Ashley Gunter & Parvati Raghuram. 2020. Conceptualizing internationalization at a distance: A "third category" of university internationalization. *Journal of Studies in International Education* 25(3). 266–282.

Multilingual Higher Education. 2016. *Cooperation for innovation and exchange of good practices.* Erasmus+ Programme of the European Union. https://sisu.ut.ee/multilingual/book/6_2_Internationalization-domination-of-English.

MultiTraiNMT. 2020. *Machine translation training for multilingual citizens.* Erasmus+ Project. www.multitrainmt.eu.

Murai, Shusuke. 2015. *Translation tech gets Olympic push.* The Japan Times [Mar 31 2015]. https://www.japantimes.co.jp/news/2015/03/31/reference/translation-tech-gets-olympic-push/.

O'Brien, Sharon. 2022. How to deal with errors in machine translation: Post-editing. In Dorothy Kenny (ed.), *Machine translation for everyone: Empowering users in the age of artificial intelligence*, 105–120. Berlin: Language Science Press. DOI: 10.5281/zenodo.6759982.

Ramírez-Sánchez, Gema. 2022. Custom machine translation. In Dorothy Kenny (ed.), *Machine translation for everyone: Empowering users in the age of artificial intelligence*, 165–186. Berlin: Language Science Press. DOI: 10.5281/zenodo.6760022.

Wikizero. 2020. *ISO-639-3.* https://www.wikizero.com/en/ISO_639-3.

World Bank. 2020. *Total population – European union.* https://data.worldbank.org/indicator/SP.POP.TOTL?locations=EU..

Zakharova, Ulyana S. 2019. Online course production and university internationalization: Correlation analysis. In Mauro Calise, Carlos Delgado Kloos, Justin Reich, Jose A. Ruiperez-Valiente & Martin Wirsing (eds.), *Digital education at the MOOC crossroads. Where the interests of academia and business converge*, 102–107. Cham: Springer.

Chapter 2

Human and machine translation

Dorothy Kenny
Dublin City University

> This chapter introduces the reader to translation and machine translation. It attempts to dispel some myths about translation, and stresses the importance of translators in creating equivalence between source and target texts. Ultimately, the chapter aims to help readers construe human-produced translations as training data for machine translation. The chapter goes on to present some of the most useful distinctions made in machine translation: between types of machine translation systems and different uses of machine translation output. In particular, it attempts to explain contemporary machine translation as an application of the branch of artificial intelligence known as machine learning, and, more specifically, of deep learning.

1 What is translation?

This is a book about machine translation, which can be succinctly defined as translation performed by a computer program. This definition still leaves open the question, however, of what *translation* is. The reader should be made aware, at this point, that there is a vast amount of scholarship in the area known as *translation studies* that asks precisely this question, and that tracks the role of translation in diverse cultural, scientific and political arenas, to name just a few. It would be impossible to do justice to this rich field here, and the reader is referred instead to sources such as Baker & Saldanha (2020) for further information. We will content ourselves here by saying that most commentators would agree that translation is the production of a text in one language, the target language, on the basis of a text in another language, the source language. The notion of text is important. It refers to instances of real language use, whether spoken or written. In general, we expect texts to meet certain criteria: they should be coherent and

Dorothy Kenny. 2022. Human and machine translation. In Dorothy Kenny (ed.), *Machine translation for everyone: Empowering users in the age of artificial intelligence*, 23–49. Berlin: Language Science Press. DOI: 10.5281/zenodo. 6759976 "hang together" properly; they should serve some kind of purpose, even if it is just to say "hello" to someone. We also usually have particular expectations regarding what texts will or should be like, given the particular language and context. This chapter, for example, hopefully meets the reader's expectations of a chapter in a collected English-language volume that is designed to be used as a textbook. It addresses a particular subject field or *domain*, namely machine translation, and adopts the conventions of a particular *genre*, that of a textbook.

The idea that translation involves texts is old hat to anyone who works in the area; it is so obvious that is doesn't need to be said. But in a world where most people don't think too much about translation, it is worth reminding ourselves that we translate texts and not languages. Languages are vast, complicated, abstract systems that are put to use in potentially infinite examples of human communication and expression. Texts are concrete instances of language in use. They normally have recognizable beginnings and endings, and even if individual languages seem to offer endless potential for creating sometimes unpredictable meanings and high levels of ambiguity, in any given text much of that potential simply falls away. It does not matter, for example, that *shower* in English can mean (1) a brief period of rain, (2) a device used for personal washing, or (3) a gift-giving party, all of which would be translated differently into a language like French, if what we are doing is translating a shower installation guide for a manufacturer of bathroom fittings. Unless the author is engaging in some witty wordplay, which is unlikely given the genre, we are dealing with the second meaning of *shower*. Focusing on texts rather than languages keeps things real, and manageable.

A second element of the definition of translation given above is the contention that translation involves the production of a text on the basis of another, pre-existing text. This clearly establishes translation as involving *a relationship between two texts*, commonly known as the *source text* and the *target text*.[1] Some commentators would go further than this and say that the relationship in question is one of having the "same meaning", but many philosophers and linguists – who understand meaning admittedly in quite sophisticated, technical ways – tend to shy away from claims of "same meaning" in translation. One reason for doing so is that it can be difficult to isolate the meaning of a text from the situations in which it is created and used. We might consider the meaning of a text

---

[1] A third element of our definition, of course, relates to the fact that source and target texts are in two different languages. We are thus concerned with *interlingual translation*. Some commentators, most notably Jakobson (1959), have recognized other types of translation, such as intralingual and intersemiotic, but a discussion of these categories is beyond the scope of this chapter.

to be what its writer or speaker wanted to say, but often we cannot be sure what they intended. Or we can associate meaning with our own interpretation of a text, but then we have to concede that other people might interpret the same text in a different way. A further issue that arises in the context of translation is that a perfectly valid target text may say more or less than its source text, simply because the language it is written in requires it to do so.

An example might help here. The opening line of a fairly recent memoir (Tammet 2006) is reproduced in example (1):

(1)   I was born on 31 January 1979 – a Wednesday.

Its translation into French (Tammet 2009) appears in example (2):

(2)   Je suis né le 31 janvier 1979. Un Mercredi.

Despite almost total word-for-word alignment between the two sentences, the French sentence actually says more than the English. It tells the reader that the writer, the *I* in English, is male, because if the writer was female, then the correct form in example (2) would be *née* and not *né*. Given certain tense forms, involving certain verbs, written French is obliged to signal the sex of the person in question.

But how does the translator into French know that the person saying "I" is male? This is, after all, the opening line of the book. Well, the book is a memoir, and the conventions of the genre require the enunciating subject to be the author of the memoir, and the translator knows whose book he is translating. It says it in the contract and on the cover of the book. The fact that French needs to specify the sex of a person in certain situations where this can be left vague in English does not cause the translator any headaches. It is a non-problem; but this very simple example shows two important things: the first – already mentioned – is that sometimes translations can mean more than their source texts. The second is that sometimes information that is required to translate a sentence cannot be found in that sentence. Rather one has to look into (1) the wider text – the front cover, for example – which is sometimes also called the *co-text*, the text that goes with a given fragment of text, or (2) the *context*, understood here as the wider situation that is relevant to the text, to find out how to proceed.

In other cases, a translation might say more than its source text not because the target language requires it, but because the genre does. In a study involving user interfaces for computer-aided design tools, Moorkens (2012) found that the single-word heading *Selecting* in English was commonly translated in a way that made explicit what was to be selected, yielding a variety of different translations, a sample of which is presented below, back-translated into English:

(3) selection of polygon

(4) selection of line

(5) selection of ellipse

(6) selection of rectangle

and so on.

   This kind of explicitation, which results in translations saying more than their source texts, is not uncommon. The converse can also happen of course; in cases where it would be impossible or unusual for a target text to be as explicit as its source text, the translator can choose to leave out information. This can some-times happen for language-typological reasons. For example, English belongs to a group of languages that frequently use verbs to describe the *manner* in which something or someone moves. Spanish, on the other hand, tends to use verbs to describe the *path* that is followed; it can encode the manner of motion in an adverbial phrase, but sometimes translators into Spanish will choose not to refer to manner of motion at all, as to do so would give it undue prominence, from the Spanish point of view. Slobin (2003) gives examples (7) and (8), by way of illus-tration. While the verb "stomped" in the English describes a way of walking in which the feet strike the ground heavily and noisily, the verb in Spanish "salió" simply captures the fact that the character in question has left the house.

(7) He stomped from the trim house

(8) Salió de la pulcra casa
     'exited from the trim house.'

   There is a second way in which the Spanish sentence in (8) says less than its English counterpart in (7): the Spanish does not contain a subject pronoun equivalent to "he". This is because Spanish is predominantly a pro-drop language, meaning it can happily omit subject pronouns as most of the information they contain is available anyway from the ending on the verb in question, in this case, "salió", which indicates third-person singular, past tense. What's missing in Spanish but present in English is, of course, the gender of the subject. A reader of the Spanish text will, however, carry over knowledge of the (male) subject from the earlier co-text, and so they are not left in the dark. So by omitting the pronoun in Spanish, the translator has followed the norms of the target language and done no harm to the reader's ability to know what is going on in the novel.

   The arguments and examples given above are intended to explain why so many scholars are reluctant to say that a source and target text have the same meaning. What we are more likely to agree on is the idea that translations approximate their source texts. For all sorts of reasons, translators have to make decisions about what to prioritize when translating, what they need to say and what they should leave up to readers to work out for themselves.[2] The meanings that they help target-text readers to construct for themselves are likely to be compatible to a very large extent with the meanings that source-text readers construct, but in many cases they will not be identical. And that is generally not a problem.

But if we cannot call the relationship between a source text and a target text – or more probably snippets of such texts – one of "same meaning", then what can we call it? One answer is to call this relationship one of *equivalence*. Equivalence as a term has a chequered history in translation studies, but if it is understood as a relationship that emerges from the decision-making of a translator, a relationship that arises between two text snippets because the translator has deemed them to be of equal value in their respective co-texts and contexts, then equivalence can be a perfectly serviceable term. It allows us to say things like "salió" in example (7) is equivalent to "he stomped" in example (8). This equivalence is clearly not fixed for all eternity, and it certainly cannot be generalized to all other contexts in which the word "stomped" might appear, but this does not matter, if we concede that "salió" was a fair exchange for "he stomped" in this particular case.[3]

2 What makes translation difficult?

Books about machine translation frequently start with discussions of why translation is difficult, homing in on the kind of monolingual ambiguity and the systematic differences between languages alluded to above. Inter-linguistic differences might also be exemplified using cases where two languages are said to distribute meaning differently across the words in equivalent sentences. In examples (9) and (10), taken from the proceedings of the European Parliament, for example, the fact of liking something is expressed in the verb "like" in English, and what is liked is expressed in a complement to that verb "working with you". In German, what is liked is expressed in the verb "kooperiere", while the fact of liking is expressed in an adverb "gern".

---

[2]The examples we have given here are primarily caused by mismatches between linguistic systems, but a translator might chose to omit or change a detail in a source text for cultural reasons, to avoid confusing readers with unfamiliar references, or even to avoid offending readers or a censor. Or they may be constrained by space, as often happens in the production of subtitles.
[3]The idea of equivalence being based on exchange value is developed in the work of the translation scholar Anthony Pym. See, for example, Pym (2010).

(9)   I like working with you.

(10)   Ich kooperiere gern mit Ihnen.
        'I cooperate happily with you.'

While such examples tell us something interesting about how psychological states are expressed in English and German, they don't really constitute a translation problem – for a human being, at least. A speaker of German with basic competence in English will be able to translate sentence (9) with little difficulty. Non-isomorphism between languages, the idea that languages are structured differently, does not in itself cause problems for translators.

Another linguistic phenomenon that is said to be tricky involves discontinuous dependencies, where two words that belong together are separated by one or more intervening words. "Send" and "back" in example (11), for instance, should be understood as a single lexical item meaning 'return'. Again, readers with a basic grasp of English generally have no problem working this out.

(11)   Send your certificate of motor insurance back.[4]

Another frequently posited difficulty in translation is presented by idioms. Idioms are understood here as phrases whose meaning cannot be inferred on the basis of their constituent parts. Idioms, in other words, are non-compositional. A good example is "old hat", as used in 1 of this chapter. If you describe something as "old hat" you mean that it is so familiar that it has become tedious even to speak of it. The expression has nothing to do with head wear. Idioms, like other types of figurative language, where a word or expression should not be interpreted literally, can sometimes cause confusion for readers who have not encountered them before, but even if you did not understand "old hat" at first glance in this chapter, you are likely to have reasoned that the discussion had not moved on to millinery, and that a non-literal interpretation was in order. When this happens to a translator, she is likely to simply look the idiom up in an online dictionary, on the well-founded assumption that the expression is common enough to be included in such a dictionary. In other words, although the expression is non-compositional and figurative, it is still conventional. Despite the fact that the translator has hit a problem, in the sense that her flow has been broken, the problem is easily resolved and finding the solution will probably bring the translator considerable pleasure. (Translators, like all linguists, generally like learning new things about their working languages.)

---

[4]There are five intervening words in this case, making it one of the longest instances of a discontinuous phrasal verb in the sample of English known as the British National Corpus.

But even experienced translators will sometimes admit to difficulty in translating texts that are highly technical and for which they lack sufficient training. Whereas a translator with an educational or professional background in legal studies or practice might relish working on the translation of legislation, a specialist in automotive engineering will run (or drive) a mile from such work. It can also happen that, even within their own domain, translators can come across source texts that are badly written, or incomplete, or written in a way that makes them extremely difficult to understand. Or they may have no problem understanding the original, but face serious challenges in tracking down suitable terminology in the target language to label specialized concepts encountered in the source text. An unreasonable deadline, or a malfunctioning software program, are other factors likely to cause professional translators headaches. But you rarely hear a professional translator complain about linguistic ambiguity, non-isomorphism, discontinuous dependencies or non-compositionality.

The reason these phenomena appear so frequently in discussions of machine translation is, of course, that – in certain circumstances – they can cause problems for machines.

3 How do translators normally solve translation problems?

The above discussion mentioned a few real-world problems professional translators sometimes face. Here we look at a sample of problems that are related to the words on the page or, more probably, the screen. When a professional translator does not understand something in the source text, or cannot recall a specialized term in the target language, or is struggling to come up with a way of formulating an idea in the target language, she will usually divert her attention from the text at hand, and do some research. A translator grappling with the niceties of wastewater treatment, for example, may go to the website of various local authorities to see how they explain the technology involved. She might access one of the many publicly available termbanks to find an equivalent for a given term. She might consult other documentation produced by her client's company or speak to engineers at the company. She could consult with her colleagues, if she has any, or post a query to a translator's forum. The main thing is that most professional translators will realise when they have a gap in their knowledge, or need inspiration, and they will conduct conscientious research to address that gap, solve the translation problem and move on.

Dorothy Kenny

You might ask why it is so important to sketch how human translators work in a book about machine translation. The answer is twofold: firstly, in a very real way (elaborated upon by Rossi & Carré 2022 [this volume]) human translation sets the standard by which machine translation is judged, and anything that contributes to the maintenance of high quality in human translation is ultimately of relevance to machine translation. Likewise, human translation processes can help to put into sharp relief occasional deficits in machine translation. Human translation has a role to play, in other words, in both the evaluation of machine translation output and in the diagnosis of problems in that output. Secondly, and even more crucially, most contemporary machine translation relies on translations completed by humans to learn how to translate in the first place. This point is expanded upon below.

Before we close off our discussion of how human translators work however, we need to introduce a technology that has become indispensable for many translators: translation memory.

4 Translation memory

In the 1990s translators working in the burgeoning software localization industry found themselves translating texts that were either extremely repetitive in themselves or that repeated verbatim whole sections of earlier versions of a document. This was the case, for example, with software manuals that had to be updated any time there was a new release of the software. Rather than translate each sentence from scratch, as if it had never been translated before, they invented a tool that would store previous translations in a so-called *translation memory*, so that they could be reused. The tool, known as a *translation memory tool*, would take in a new source text, divide it into segments – sentences or other sensible units like headings or cells in tables – and then compare each of these segments with the source-language segments already stored in memory. If an exact match or a very similar segment was found, then the corresponding target-language segment would be offered to the translator for re-use, with or without editing. As translators worked their way through a new translation assignment, they would get hits from the translation memory, accept, reject or edit the existing translation and update the memory as they went along, adding their own translations for the source-language segments for which no matches existed. Over time, the translation memories grew extremely large. Some companies who were early adopters of the technology built up translation memories containing hundreds of thousands and then millions of *translation units*, that is source-language segments aligned with their target-language segments. Example (12) shows a simple translation unit based on a headline (in English and German) taken from a translation memory consisting of data from the website of the European Parliament. It is presented in a format known as tmx (for "translation memory exchange"). The tags <tu> and </tu> open and close the translation unit, the tags <tuv> and </tuv> open and close each *variant* within the translation unit,[5] and the tags <seg> and </seg> open and close the *segment* or text string in that language.

(12)
```
<tu>
  <tuv xml:lang="EN">
  <seg>A common blacklist for unsafe airlines</seg>
  </tuv>
  <tuv xml:lang="DE">
  <seg>Unsichere Luftfahrtunternehmen kommen auf eine schwarze
  Liste</seg>
  </tuv>
</tu>
```

Private translation enterprises also accumulated large translation memories, which came to be regarded as valuable linguistic assets that could help control translation costs and enhance competitiveness. International organizations such as the Institutions of the European Union adopted the technology and built up huge multilingual translation memories, which they in turn made freely available to computer scientists in the knowledge that they could support research agendas in natural language processing.

While translation memory was originally conceived as a way of improving, among other things, the productivity of human translators, it also eventually supported efforts to increase automation in the translation industry: on the one hand, translation memory tools enabled translation data to be created in great quantities and in a format that could be easily used in machine translation development (see below); on the other hand, the tools used to manage them provided an editing environment in which machine translation outputs could later be presented to human translators for editing alongside human translations retrieved from conventional translation memory.

Translation memories can be seen as a special type of *parallel corpus*, that is a collection of source texts aligned at sentence level with their target texts. In cases where translations were created without the use of a translation memory tool, translated texts could still be aligned with their source texts after the fact. So, for example, the translated proceedings of the multilingual European Parliament

---

[5]The first variant in this case is in English ("EN"), and the second in German ("DE").

were extracted from the web and aligned with each other to create the multilingual Europarl Corpus (Koehn 2005), which in turn gave a significant boost to machine translation research. Aligned parallel corpora do not have to be in tmx format. Often they take the form of files with thousands (or even millions) of lines, each line occupied by a single sentence, whose position in the file matches exactly that of its translation in another file in a given target language, so line x in the target language file contains the translation of line x in the source language file.

5 What is machine translation?

Based on the definitions given at the start of this chapter, we can say that machine translation involves the automatic production of a target-language text on the basis of a source-language text. As with other types of translation, we can expect the target text to allow an interpretation that is in most ways compatible with that of the source text. Although if we have already conceded that human translations can result in slightly different meanings to their source texts, then maybe we should allow machine translations to do the same. The important thing is that obvious divergences between source and target text, for example, where Japanese gives more information than English, should be motivated by the language pair, the genre or some other reasonable cause.

Machine translation was one of the first non-numerical applications of the digital computers that emerged in the aftermath of the Second World War. Early efforts to automate translation seem primitive by today's standards, although it has to be acknowledged that the protagonists were working with extremely limited resources in the 1950s and 1960s (Hutchins 2000). Nevertheless, automatic translation systems were in operation primarily in defence, government and international organisations by the late 1960s and 1970s, and by the end of the century their use was expanding in commercial settings. The technology became available to millions of internet users in 1997, when the American search engine AltaVista starting giving access to free, online machine translation under the Babel Fish name. In the decades since then, the internet has expanded rapidly, and now boasts some 4.66 billion users (Johnson 2021). By 2016, perhaps the best-known free, online machine translation system, Google Translate, was reported to have over half a billion users, translating over 100 billion words per day and supporting 103 languages (Turovsky 2016).[6] In combination with search

---

[6]As of May 2022, Google Translate supports 133 different languages, although to varying degrees (Caswell 2022).

engines like Google Search or Microsoft Bing, for example, machine translation can be used to expand a search and then to translate relevant foreign-language web pages back into the user's language.

But it's not all about web pages. Machine translation is also used in combination with technologies like automatic speech recognition and speech synthesis, or optical character recognition and digital image processing, allowing users to have spoken conversations in two or more languages, or read road signs written in unfamiliar writing systems, often using an app installed on their mobile phones. In some cases, these apps now even work offline and users can justifiably claim to be carrying a machine translation system in their pocket. Machine translation is also increasingly used in areas previously considered beyond the capacity of the technology, for example in audio-visual translation, to translate the subtitles of foreign-language movies and TV series into the language of a new market. Indeed, subscription video streaming services thrive on a model that brings the so-called long tail of lesser-known titles to a new audience, and many of these titles are lesser-known partly because they were originally made in a foreign language. Audio-visual content is thus becoming just the latest in a long line of commercial products whose markets can be expanded through machine translation. In the seventy or so years since its inception, machine translation has thus moved from being the preserve of governments and international organizations to being a mass consumer good.

Despite the undoubted usefulness of machine translation in the kind of scenarios addressed above and its capacity to do good in other, for example, humanitarian settings (Nurminen & Koponen 2020), it comes with some health warnings. First, just like human translators, machine translation systems can make mistakes. Errors might range from the amusing but trivial to the extremely serious (for example in healthcare, news translation or international diplomacy). Whole branches of research are thus devoted to *estimating* the quality that given machine translation systems are likely to produce, *evaluating* particular outputs, designing ways to correct errors by *post-editing* machine translation output or helping the machine produce better output in the first place, usually by *pre-editing* source texts to make them easier to translate. These areas are discussed in detail in Chapters 3 to 5 of this book. Machine translation also raises a surprising number of moral and legal issues, as addressed by Moorkens (2022 [this volume]) on ethics, and to a lesser extent by Carré et al. (2022 [this volume]) on machine translation for language learners.

Many casual users of machine translation may feel that they do not need to know much about any of these areas to get what they need from the technology: if you are simply using machine translation to get the gist of a text, to understand the basic contents of a web page, for example, then this might be true. Such uses, which often fall under the heading of machine translation for *assimilation*, generally involve low-stakes, private use of the translated text in question, with little risk of reputational or other damage. If, however, you want to use machine translation for *dissemination*, for example to publish your blog in a second language, or to advertise your business, then it is wise to understand the risks involved and even to take measures to mitigate them. The ability to do so is a component of what is now known as *machine translation literacy* (Bowker & Ciro 2019). Other components include having a basic understanding of how machine translation actually works, and of the wider societal, economic and environmental implications of its use. While this might seem like esoteric knowledge, it turns out to be highly transferable, as contemporary machine translation is based on the same principles as a whole host of other technologies that are contributing to profound changes in many aspects of contemporary life, and especially how we work. In short, machine translation is now, for the most part, an application of machine learning, and more specifically of deep learning. These concepts are explained briefly below, and treated in greater depth by Pérez-Ortiz et al. (2022 [this volume]) on how neural machine translation works. If you are a translation student, a professional translator, or are employed in some other capacity in the translation industry, then you are probably strongly motivated to learn about what happens "under the hood" in machine translation systems. You are probably also interested in how you can get the best out of the technology, by customizing it for your needs. This is addressed in Ramírez-Sánchez (2022 [this volume]). The following paragraphs, on the other hand, should be read by anyone who is curious about how machine translation can be said to be the linguist's entrée into the wonderful world of machine learning.

6 Artificial intelligence, machine learning and machine translation

Contemporary machine translation is frequently mentioned alongside a number of other related concepts, including artificial intelligence, machine learning, artificial neural networks and deep learning, some of which can be difficult to differentiate for the uninitiated. Sources like Goodfellow et al. 2016 use a Venn diagram to explain how they relate to each other. Artificial intelligence (AI) is the most general category, represented by the biggest circle. It is often defined as the branch of computer science that aims to create machines – or more specifically computer programs – that can solve problems of the kind that would normally require human intelligence. The machines in question don't necessarily have to *think* like humans, rather they need to *act* like an intelligent human would. They might be designed to solve fairly narrowly defined problems, like recognizing faces. Such goals are the stuff of *narrow AI*, also known, somewhat unkindly, as *weak AI*. So-called *strong AI* is a more aspirational undertaking. It would involve either *general AI* – in which machines would have human-like intelligence, be self-aware, able to learn and plan for the future – or *superintelligence*, which would involve intelligence that exceeds the abilities of any human. It is fair to say that translation, as practised by professional, human translators, requires the kind of intelligence that strong AI aspires to, but that such intelligence still remains beyond the capacity of machine translation systems.

6.1 Rule-based machine translation

One way to tackle the challenges of AI is to attempt to give a computer program all the knowledge it would need to solve a particular problem, and rules that specify how it can manipulate this knowledge. In the case of machine translation, for example, you can give the program a list of all the words in each of the source and the target languages, along with rules on how they can combine to create well-formed structures. You can then specify how the words and structures of one language can map onto the words and structures of the other language, and give the machine some step-by-step instructions (an *algorithm*) on how to use all this information to create translated sentences. This approach, known as *rule-based machine translation* (RBMT), dominated machine translation up until the early part of this century. When free online machine translation first became available in 1997, for example, it was based on RBMT (Joscelyne 1998). RBMT was beset by a number of problems, however. It was very expensive to develop, requiring highly skilled linguists to write the rules for each language pair and, like other knowledge-based approaches to AI (Goodfellow et al. 2016), it suffered from knowledge bottlenecks: it was simply impossible in many cases to anticipate all the knowledge necessary to make RBMT systems work as desired. This applies both to knowledge about language and knowledge about the wider world, so-called *real-world knowledge*.[7]

---

[7] Although RBMT has fallen out of favour generally, at the time of writing, it is still used in a small number of systems, especially for translation between very closely-related languages. See, for example, Apertium (Forcada et al. 2011).

6.2 Data-driven machine translation

This is where machine learning comes in. Machine learning is based on the premise that rather than telling a machine – or, more precisely, a computer program – everything it needs to know from the outset, it is better to let the machine acquire its own knowledge. The machine does so by observing how the problem it is intended to solve has been solved in the past. We have already seen how translation problems and their solutions can be captured at segment level in the translation units stored in translation memories and other parallel corpora. These translation units constitute the *training data* from which contemporary machine translation systems learn. This is why such systems are usually categorized as *data-driven*. And learning from data is what distinguishes machine learning from other types of AI.

Data-driven machine translation is divided into two types: *statistical machine translation* and *neural machine translation*, each of which is addressed below.

6.3 Statistical Machine Translation

Statistical Machine Translation (SMT) systems basically build two types of statistical models based on the training data:[8] the first model, known as the *translation model*, is a bilingual one in which words and so-called *phrases* found in the source-language side of the training data appear in a table alongside their translations as identified in the target-language side of the training data, and each source-target pairing is given a probability score. The ensuing structure is known as a *phrase table*. Table 1 contains an example of an excerpt from such a phrase table.[9]

Table 1: Excerpt from a Phrase Table showing *a me piace*, observed translations in Europarl and their probabilities

	English	Probability
a me piace	I like	0.78
a me piace	I should like to	0.11
a me piace	I admire	0.11

---

[8]A statistical model is a mathematical representation of observed data.

[9]The example is greatly simplified, as it shows only sensible Italian-English pairings. In reality, an SMT system would learn a translation model that contains lots of nonsensical pairings, most of which would, however, be assigned very low probabilities. It would also reserve some probability mass for previously unseen pairings.

The term "phrase" is something of a misnomer here however, as the strings in question don't necessarily correspond to phrases as commonly understood in linguistics. Rather they are *n*-grams, that is, strings of one, two, three or *n* words that appear contiguously in the training data. In the previous sentence, "appear contiguously" is a bigram, for example, and "appear contiguously in" is a trigram.

The second model, known as the *language model* is a monolingual model (or combination of models) of the target language. Again, it is based on *n*-grams. A trigram target language model, for example, would give the probability of seeing a particular word in the target language, given that you had already seen the two words in front of it. A trigram model could tell you the probability of seeing the word "gorgonzola" if you have already seen "I like" in the Europarl corpus, for example. It turns out to be 0.024, which means that while "I like gorgonzola" does occur in the training data (it actually occurs four times) there are many words other than "gorgonzola" that are much more likely to follow "I like".[10]

In SMT systems, the translation model is supposed to capture knowledge about how individual words and *n*-grams are likely to be translated into the target language, while the language model tells you what is likely to occur in the target language in the first place. What is really important from the current perspective, is that linguists don't have to hand-craft these models. Rather they are learned directly from the data by the machine in a *training* phase. In a second phase, called *tuning*, system developers work out the weight that should be assigned to each model to get the best output. Once the system is trained and tuned, it is ready to translate previously unseen source sentences. Translation (as opposed to training) is called *decoding* in SMT. It generally involves generating many thousands of hypothetical translations for the input sentence, and calculating which one is the most probable, given the particular source sentence, the models the system has learned, and the weights assigned to them.

SMT was state-of-the-art in machine translation for at least a decade up to 2015. It represented a huge advance compared to the RBMT systems that preceded it, but suffered from a number of deficiencies, most of them due to the fact that relatively short *n*-grams were used to build models and that *n*-grams in the same sentence were translated almost as if they were independent of each other. SMT performed particularly poorly on agglutinative and highly inflected languages. Other problems included word drop, where a system simply failed to translate a word, and inconsistency, where the same source-language word was translated two different ways, sometimes in the same sentence. By 2015, SMT was already

---

[10]The version of Europarl used here and in Table 1 is accessible through the Sketch Engine interface at sketchengine.eu.

being displaced by a competing approach to data-driven machine translation, the above-mentioned neural approach. Within a matter of two years the transition to neural machine translation was complete.

But if SMT is becoming obsolete, you might wonder why it is mentioned here at all. SMT is introduced here for the purpose of opening up the area of machine learning to the reader. SMT showed that machine translation systems that learned from data worked better than those that didn't. It thus paved the way for machine learning approaches in machine translation. SMT developers also made remarkable contributions to machine translation research, by promoting new methods and sharing their programs, but also by collecting translation data, from bilingual and multilingual parliaments, international organizations, the world wide web and so on, and sharing these data with the global research community. It should also be noted that SMT is still used in the translation industry, albeit in limited contexts: a supplier of machine translation services might, for example, first create an SMT system to see how viable the project is and whether or not it is worthwhile investing time and effort in subsequently developing a neural system.

Our main interest in discussing SMT is, however, to show that there is more than one way of learning from data[11] and, more importantly for our purposes, of representing those data. As we have seen, SMT represents translation knowledge in phrase tables, and target language knowledge in separate n-gram models. In such models, words (and strings of words) are still recognizable as themselves but, crucially, they are related to each other using probability scores. And it is these scores that allow the systems to work. The probability of any given target sentence being the translation of a given source sentence can be computed simply by multiplying the translation probabilities of its component n-grams as found in the phrase table, and the probability of any given target-language sentence occurring can be computed by multiplying the probabilities of its component n-grams, as indicated by the language model. A single equation can then be used to bring the different models together to compute the most likely translation.[12]

Another reason to address SMT is that doing so gives us a convenient excuse for introducing concepts such as n-grams, which turn out be to extremely important in other areas in natural language processing in general, and in machine translation evaluation in particular, as addressed by Rossi & Carré (2022 [this volume]).

---

[11]In fact, we have said very little about the specific algorithms used by SMT systems to learn. The interested reader is referred to Koehn (2010).

[12]The equation in question is based on Bayes Theorem, and SMT offers the translation scholar an entrée into the machine learning approach known as Bayesian optimization.

6.4 Neural Machine Translation

SMT had its heyday between 2004 and 2014. Most major users and suppliers of machine translation, including Google Translate (from 2007) and the European Commission (from 2010) were using the technology and in so-called *shared task evaluations*[13] SMT constantly came up trumps. Until 2015, that is. That year a neural machine translation (NMT) system developed at Stanford University beat a number of SMT systems – by a wide margin and on what was considered a difficult language pair, namely English-German (Bentivogli et al. 2016). The Stanford success heralded the beginning of what Bentivogli et al. (2016) call "the new NMT era." The excitement was palpable among researchers and especially in the press. Grand claims were made about the new technology, for example, that it was as good as professional, human translation and had thus reached *human parity.*[14] It was also claimed, with some justification, that NMT could learn "idiomatic expressions and metaphors", and "rather than do a literal translation, find the cultural equivalent in another language" (Marking 2016).[15] But while there is some truth in such claims, they should not be over-interpreted. An NMT system might indeed produce an idiomatic translation, but this is generally because the data it has learned from contain hundreds or maybe thousands of examples of that very translation. An NMT system (in this case Google Translate) does not *know* it is being idiomatic, or using a cultural equivalent, when it correctly translates the German idiom:

(13)   Ich habe die Nase voll.

   'I have the nose full.'

as

(14)   I'm sick of it.

Rather it is outputting what it has learned from data.[16]

But why is NMT so much better that SMT, if it is simply learning from data? Is that not what SMT was already doing? The answer lies in the kind of representations that NMT systems use and in the kind of models they learn.

---

[13] In shared task evaluations, computer scientists pit their systems against each other to see which performs best for a given language-pair and with different types of training data.

[14] This claim was famously made by researchers at Microsoft who had been working on Chinese-to-English translation (Marking 2016). It was contested by many commentators, including Toral et al. (2018).

[15] These comments were made by Alan Packer of Facebook in 2016 (Marking 2016).

[16] This particular translation has also been verified by Google Translate's user community.

6.4.1 Models in NMT

Let's start with models. A computer *model* is an abstract, mathematical representation of some real-life event, system or phenomenon. One use of such a model is to predict an answer to a previously unseen problem. A computational model of translation, for example, should be able to predict a target-language sentence given a previously unseen source-language sentence.[17]

We have already seen that SMT systems use probabilistic models of translation and the target language that are encapsulated in phrase tables and *n*-gram probabilities. NMT systems, in contrast, use models that are inspired, even if only loosely, by the human brain. They use artificial neural networks, in which thousands of individual units, or *artificial neurons*, are linked to thousands of other artificial neurons (let's just call them *neurons* from now on). In such a network, each neuron is activated depending on the stimuli received from other neurons, and the strength or *weight* of the connections between neurons. As Forcada (2017) explains, the activation states of individual neurons do not make much sense by themselves. It is, instead, the activation states of large sets of connected neurons that can be understood as representing individual words and their relationships with other words. The trick in training an NMT system is to learn precisely those weights that will result in the best performing model of translation, that is, the model whose activation states allow it to predict the best translations.

So how is this done? Like in all machine learning, the system learns from data. A neural model of translation is built step by step by exposing a learning algorithm to vast quantities of parallel data. In successive passes, the algorithm learns weights and keeps adjusting those weights, so that the predictions of the model it builds get closer and closer to a desired "correct" answer. More precise details of how this feat is accomplished are given by Pérez-Ortiz et al. (2022 [this volume]), and readers looking for a comprehensive technical discussion of NMT can also refer to Koehn (2020). It suffices to say here that data-driven machine translation is typical of machine learning in that it involves technologies that are developed to solve problems to which humans already know the answer and to which, in fact, humans have already supplied at least one, if not several correct answers. Such correct answers may be present in the training data or they may be arrived at through generalization from the training data. When a machine translation system is tested to see whether it is improving during training or to compare it to another system once training has finished, we also test by giving it

---

[17]When speaking of mathematical models, it is common to speak of *predicting* answers. For our purposes, however, there is little practical difference between *predicting* and *outputting* an answer, which is what machine translation systems do when they are actually being used.

a problem to which we already know the answer. Typically, we ask it to predict the translation of several sentences it has never seen before but for which we already have good (human) translations that we set aside specifically for this purpose.

When an NMT system has been trained to our satisfaction, it can be put into use in a real translation scenario. We no longer talk about "testing" the system, and instead talk about "using" it. When an NMT system is in actual use, most people say that the system is "translating". As with SMT, computer scientists also use the term *decoding* for the moment when an NMT system produces an output in the target language.

6.4.2 Representing words in NMT

We have already said that a mathematical model is a representation of some system, event or phenomenon. There is much debate over the status of mathematical and other scientific models, but that need not detain us here. We will take the view that a model represents something quite complex, with many interconnected parts, and that if we want to talk about a simpler or more granular entity – a number like 5, for example, or an object like an apple – we can simply use the generic term *representation* to refer to ways in which that entity is depicted.

Representations are important, because, as Goodfellow et al. (2016) point out, how ideas are represented affects what we can do with them, in computer science and in daily life. A good example of how representation affects human beings' performance is given by the difference between Arabic and Roman numerals. Most people would find it much easier to divide 125 by 5, for example, than to divide CXXV by V, even though CXXV and 125 (and V and 5) represent exactly the same quantity.

Words can also be seen as representing ideas. So the word *apple*, for example, might be understood as representing a particular type of fruit. Another way of representing the same fruit would be to draw a picture of it. The word and the picture would have different properties, of course, which allow you to do different things with them. You can spellcheck a (written) word, for example, but not a drawing.

In NMT yet another type of representation is used: the vector, which is a fixed-sized list of numbers. The word *apple* could be represented by a vector like [1.20, 2.80, 6.10] for example. To many people this seems incredible. It is difficult to see how a list of numbers can represent a word.[18] Things start to make slightly

---

[18] Note how we have shifted here from talking about the representation of ideas to the representations of words. What we have in training corpora are millions of identifiable words. They are what we try to represent in NMT.

more sense if we say that vectors are quite good at representing relationships between words. The vector [1.20, 2.80, 5.50], for example, could be the vector for *pear*. It differs from the vector for *apple* in just the last number. If we see the numbers in the vector as representing dimensions in an imaginary three dimensional space, this would make the words *apple* and *pear* very close to each other. And presumably they would both be far from less related words, like *helicopter* or *very*. Vectors have other interesting properties that make them particularly attractive to computer scientists. You can add a vector to another vector, for example, or multiply them and so on. Try doing that with the words themselves, or with drawings of apples and pears!

So how did our vectors for *apple* and *pear* end up so suspiciously similar in the above example? The truth is, we just made them up. In a real NMT scenario, we would get a computer program to *learn* suitable vectors for all instances of all words in our corpus directly from that corpus. (Remember, in machine learning, the computer program has to work these things out for itself, with or without human supervision.) The vector-based representations of words that the machine learns are called *word embeddings*. The reason why embeddings for related words end up looking similar to each other is that they are built up on the basis of where particular words are found in the training data. If it turns out that two words tend to keep turning up in the same or similar co-texts – both *apple* and *pear* occur very regularly before the word *tree* for example; both appear regularly after *peel*, *slice* and *dice* – then they will end up with similar embeddings.

Word embeddings are not built in one go, but rather in successive *layers*, as described in Pérez-Ortiz et al. (2022 [this volume]). An artificial neural network that has multiple layers sandwiched between its external layers is known as a *deep neural network*.

Deep learning, in turn, is simply the branch of machine learning that uses multiple layers to build representations. In a deep neural network, the external layers correspond to inputs and outputs of the network and are visible to the human analyst. The intermediary, or *hidden*, layers have traditionally been less open to scrutiny, however, giving deep learning a reputation for opacity, and encouraging some commentators to misleadingly use the word "magic" to describe the internal workings of deep neural networks. The mystique of NMT is added to when big tech companies report on their successes in building multilingual translation models, sometimes involving hundreds of languages, and which can cope with translation between languages for which there was no "direct" bilingual training data.[19] Researchers in AI have not been oblivious to problems caused by

---

[19] See https://ai.googleblog.com/2016/11/zero-shot-translation-with-googles.html and https://about.fb.com/news/2020/10/first-multilingual-machine-translation-model.

perceived opacity, however, and in the areas known as *explainable AI* (XAI) and *interpretable AI*, efforts are now being made to open up the "black box" of deep learning, so that its inner workings can be more easily understood by users, explanations can be provided for particular outputs and systems can be improved (see, for example, Vashishth et al. (2019)).

7 The advantages and disadvantages of neural machine translation

NMT is generally considered the best performing type of machine translation invented so far. It performs better than SMT, for example, because it can build up very rich representations of words as they appear in a given source text, taking the full source sentence into account, rather than mere *n*-grams. When it produces translations, an NMT system considers both these rich representations and the emerging target sentence at the same time. Because NMT handles full sentences, it is better at dealing with tricky linguistic features like discontinuous dependencies and it handles all sorts of agreement phenomena better than SMT.

But while contemporary NMT systems certainly handle full sentences, until recently, they did not look beyond the current sentence. This meant that they could not use information from a previous sentence to work out what a pronoun like "it" refers to in the current sentence, or that the understood subject of a Spanish verb is feminine (in cases of pro-drop in Spanish). This restriction to sentence-level processing can cause lots of other problems that only become apparent when users translate full texts rather than isolated sentences. The problem is currently being tackled by researchers working in the area of *document-level machine translation*, however (see, for example, Bao et al. (2021)). NMT can also output words that don't actually exist in the target language. Far more seriously, NMT output can be fluent but inaccurate. And when a translation looks and sounds good, one might neglect to check that it is compatible with the source text. Like other technologies trained on large quantities of existing text, it can also amplify biases encountered in the training data. A well documented form of the amplification of bias is the way in which many systems over-use male forms. Given a Spanish sentence that does not have a subject pronoun, like in example (8) above, many NMT systems will output a male subject pronoun in English by default. NMT developers are seeking solutions to this problem. Some systems now output both male and female pronouns and let users choose the one they prefer. Other steps that users can take to get the best out of a given NMT system are addressed in Chapters 4 and 5 of this book.

Other problems have less to do with the translations that NMT systems output and more to do with wider environmental and societal concerns: NMT systems take much longer and much more computing power to train than their predecessors and use up vast quantities of energy in the process. They usually require dedicated, expensive hardware in the form of graphical processing units. They also need massive quantities of training data, which are not available for every language pair.

Improvements in the technology have also led some people to question the wisdom of learning foreign languages: if a machine can translate anything anyone else says or writes in a foreign language into your language, why go to all the trouble of learning their language? Such arguments are based on a very limited understanding of the benefits of second or foreign language learning, however, and ignore the fact that machine translation is viable for only a small number of the world's languages. They also tend to see machine translation as being in competition with language learning, rather than possibly being an aid in the process. Chapters 1, 6 and 9 of this book have more to say on the broader ethical and societal issues raised by the use of machine translation in language learning and other aspects of our lives.

8 Systems, engines and custom NMT

In this chapter so far, we have attempted to explain in a very general way what translation is, what machine translation is and how different types of machine translation work. We draw the chapter to a close with some brief comments on particular machine translation systems and the related concept of a machine translation engine.

In common usage, a machine translation *system* often refers to a machine translation product or service made available by a single supplier or developer. Google Translate is thus understood as Google's machine translation system; while Microsoft has a system called Microsoft Translator. These systems are accessible as services across various platforms. A user might install Google Translate as an app on their mobile phone, for example, or simply use Google Translate on the web, having accessed it using their web browser. They might also access it through an *API* (for "application programming interface") in a third party's software.[20]

---

[20]We use Google Translate here simply because it is probably the most familiar machine translation service. All Big Tech companies offer machine translation "solutions" of one kind or another, as do a whole host of specialist machine translation providers.

In relatively specialized contexts, for example in research papers or profes-sional translation environments, people often talk about machine translation "en-gines". An *engine* in such contexts is basically a machine translation program (or even a "model") that has been trained to deal with a particular language pair and, often, domain or genre. A commercial machine translation company may, for example, offer its customers access to an English-French engine that was trained on a parallel corpus of financial statements; or a Chinese-German engine that has been trained using only medical texts. Customers might even be able to build or customize their own machine translation engines, using their own data. This kind of service was pioneered by companies like KantanAI.[21] Custom ma-chine translation is discussed in greater depth by Ramírez-Sánchez (2022 [this volume]), and the MultiTraiNMT project has developed a bespoke pedagogical interface that allows students to train their own NMT engines.[22]

9 Four last things you need to know about machine translation

Many readers are likely to use only free, online machine translation and so will encounter only generic engines built for the language pair that interests them. But even these readers should be interested to learn that:

- different systems may output different translations;

- different engines in the same system may output different translations;

- a single system may output different translations for the same input de-pending on the co-text;

- a single system's outputs may change over time.

For example, at the time of writing, DeepL's French-to-British English engine outputs (16) for the sentence in (15), where the French expression *mon petit doigt me dit* (literally 'my little finger tells me') is used to mean something like 'I have a hunch' or 'someone I won't name has told me'. As the reader will note, the British English translation in (16) uses an entirely appropriate figurative expression with a similar meaning.

(15)   Mon petit doigt me dit que tu es marié.

---

[21]https://www.kantanai.io
[22]http://www.multitrainmt.eu

(16)   A little birdie tells me that you are married. (DeepL UK)

Google Translate, on the other hand, outputs the inappropriately literal translation in (17).

(17)   My little finger tells me you're married. (Google Translate)

Also at the time of writing, DeepL's French-to-American English engine outputs (18) but if the sentence is changed by a single word as in (19), then DeepL's French-to-American English engine performs much better, as seen in (20).

(18)   My little finger tells me that you are married. (DeepL US)

(19)   Mon petit doigt me dit que tu es parti.

(20)   A little birdie tells me that you've left. (DeepL US)

By the time the reader reads this, however, the outputs of both systems may have changed completely, as models are retrained and users correct faulty outputs.

10 Conclusions

In one way, NMT is just the latest in a line of technologies designed to automate translation, albeit one that has risen to prominence remarkably quickly. Its success could lead to policy makers and ordinary citizens questioning the value of learning foreign languages or training human translators. But such positions would ignore the fact that NMT still relies on human translations or at least translations validated by humans as training data. And because NMT, like other types of machine translation, is not invincible, its outputs still need to be evaluated and sometimes improved by people who can understand both source and target texts. There is also a pressing need for machine translation literacy among even casual users of the technology, so that they do not suffer unnecessarily because of ignorance of how the technology works. Given the right conditions, NMT can be a vital pillar in the promotion and maintenance of multilingualism, alongside language learning and continued translation done or overseen by humans. The rest of this book is dedicated to creating those conditions.

References

Baker, Mona & Gabriela Saldanha (eds.). 2020. *The Routledge encyclopedia of translation studies*. 3rd edition. London/New York: Routledge.

Bao, Guangsheng, Yue Zhang, Zhiyang Teng, Boxing Chen & Weihua Luo. 2021. G-transformer for document-level machine translation. In *Proceedings of the 59th annual meeting of the Association for Computational Linguistics and the 11th international joint conference on Natural Language Processing (volume 1: long papers)*, 3442–3455. Association for Computational Linguistics. https:// aclanthology.org/2021.acl-long.267.

Bentivogli, Luisa, Arianna Bisazza, Mauro Cettolo & Marcello Federico. 2016. Neural versus Phrase-Based Machine Translation quality: A case study. In *EMNLP 2016*. arXiv:1608.04631v1.

Bowker, Lynne & Jairo Buitrago Ciro. 2019. *Machine translation and global research*. Bingley: Emerald Publishing.

Carré, Alice, Dorothy Kenny, Caroline Rossi, Pilar Sánchez-Gijón & Olga Torres-Hostench. 2022. Machine translation for language learners. In Dorothy Kenny (ed.), *Machine translation for everyone: Empowering users in the age of artificial intelligence*, 187–207. Berlin: Language Science Press. DOI: 10.5281/zenodo.6760024.

Caswell, Isaac. 2022. *Google Translate learns 24 new languages.* https://blog.google/products/translate/24-new-languages/.

Forcada, M. L., M. Ginestí-Rosell, J. Nordfalk, J. O'Regan, S. Ortiz-Rojas, J. A. Pérez-Ortiz, F. Sánchez-Martínez, G. Ramírez-Sánchez & F. M. Tyers. 2011. Apertium: A free/open-source platform for rule-based machine translation. *Machine Translation* 24(1). 1–18.

Forcada, Mikel. 2017. Making sense of neural translation. *Translation Spaces* 6(2). 291–309.

Goodfellow, Ian, Yoshua Bengio & Aaron Courville. 2016. *Deep learning*. Cambridge, MA: MIT Press.

Hutchins, John (ed.). 2000. *Early Years in Machine Translation. Memoirs and Biographies of Pioneers*. Amsterdam/Philadephia: John Benjamins.

Jakobson, Roman. 1959. On linguistic aspects of translation. In Reuben A. Brower (ed.), *On Translation*, 232–239. Cambridge, MA: Harvard University Press.

Johnson, Joseph. 2021. *Worldwide digital population as of January 2021.* statista.com/statistics/617136/digital-population-worldwide/.

Joscelyne, A. 1998. AltaVista translates in real time. *Language International* 10(1). 6–7.

Koehn, Philipp. 2005. Europarl: A parallel corpus for Statistical Machine Translation. In *Proceedings of Machine Translation Summit X*, 79–86. https://aclanthology.org/2005.mtsummit-papers.11.

Koehn, Philipp. 2010. *Statistical Machine Translation.* Cambridge: Cambridge University Press.

Koehn, Philipp. 2020. *Neural Machine Translation.* Cambridge: Cambridge University Press.

Marking, Marion. 2016. *Facebook says Statistical Machine Translation has reached end of life.* https://slator.com/facebook-says-statistical-machine-translation-has-reached-end-of-life.

Moorkens, Joss. 2012. *Measuring consistency in translation memories: A mixed-methods case study.* Unpublished PhD thesis. Dublin: Dublin City University. https://doras.dcu.ie/17332/.

Moorkens, Joss. 2022. Ethics and machine translation. In Dorothy Kenny (ed.), *Machine translation for everyone: Empowering users in the age of artificial intelligence,* 121–140. Berlin: Language Science Press. DOI: 10.5281/zenodo.6759984.

Nurminen, Mary & Maarit Koponen. 2020. Machine translation and fair access to information. *Translation Spaces* 9(1). 150–169.

Pérez-Ortiz, Juan Antonio, Mikel L. Forcada & Felipe Sánchez-Martínez. 2022. How neural machine translation works. In Dorothy Kenny (ed.), *Machine translation for everyone: Empowering users in the age of artificial intelligence,* 141–164. Berlin: Language Science Press. DOI: 10.5281/zenodo.6760020.

Pym, Anthony. 2010. *Translation and text transfer.* Tarragona: Intercultural Studies Group.

Ramírez-Sánchez, Gema. 2022. Custom machine translation. In Dorothy Kenny (ed.), *Machine translation for everyone: Empowering users in the age of artificial intelligence,* 165–186. Berlin: Language Science Press. DOI: 10.5281/zenodo.6760022.

Rossi, Caroline & Alice Carré. 2022. How to choose a suitable neural machine translation solution: Evaluation of MT quality. In Dorothy Kenny (ed.), *Machine translation for everyone: Empowering users in the age of artificial intelligence,* 51–79. Berlin: Language Science Press. DOI: 10.5281/zenodo.6759978.

Slobin, Dan. 2003. Language and thought online: Cognitive consequences of linguistic relativity. In Dedre Gentner & Susan Goldin-Meadow (eds.), *Language in mind: Advances in the investigation of language and thought,* 157–191. Cambridge, MA: MIT Press.

Tammet, Daniel. 2006. *Born on a Blue Day.* London: Hodder & Stoughton.

Tammet, Daniel. 2009. *Je suis né un jour bleu.* Paris: J'ai Lu.

Toral, Antonio, Sheila Castilho, Ke Hu & Andy Way. 2018. Attaining the unattainable? Reassessing claims of human parity in neural machine translation. In *Proceedings of the third conference on machine translation: Research papers,* 113–123. Brussels: Association for Computational Linguistics. DOI: 10.18653/v1/W18-6312. https://aclanthology.org/W18-6312.

Turovsky, Barak. 2016. *Ten years of Google Translate.* https://www.blog.google/products/translate/ten-years-of-google-translate/.

Vashishth, Shikhar, Shyam Upadhyay, Gaurav Singh Tomar & Manaal Faruqui. 2019. Attention interpretability across NLP tasks. *CoRR* abs/1909.11218. http://arxiv.org/abs/1909.11218.

Chapter 3

How to choose a suitable neural machine translation solution: Evaluation of MT quality

Caroline Rossi

Université Grenoble-Alpes

Alice Carré

Université Grenoble-Alpes

Machine translation (MT) is evolving fast, and there is no one-size-fits-all solution. In order to choose the right solution for a given project, users need to compare and assess different possibilities. This is never easy, especially with MT outputs that look increasingly good, thus making mistakes harder to spot. How can we best define and assess the quality of a neural MT solution, so as to make the right choices? The first step is certainly to define needs as precisely as possible. Having defined a pragmatic view of quality, we introduce the key notions in human and automatic evaluation of MT quality and outline how they can be applied by translators.

1 Introduction

Beyond the hype about neural machine translation (NMT), users do notice that machine-translated texts have been getting better. The main point of this chapter is to show that even though machine translation (MT) outputs may appear to be more fluent than before, they are not necessarily easier to deal with. Besides, NMT outputs are likely to vary, and should be considered in context and according to the needs of end-users. In what follows, we suggest definitions of quality

Caroline Rossi & Alice Carré. 2022. How to choose a suitable neural machine translation solution: Evaluation of MT quality. In Dorothy Kenny (ed.), *Machine translation for everyone: Empowering users in the age of artificial intelligence*, 51–79. Berlin: Language Science Press. DOI: 10.5281/zenodo.6759978 and measures that can be used to reach beyond the apparent ease and fluency of NMT outputs.

The overarching question that this chapter seeks to answer is: how can NMT solutions be assessed in a trustworthy and useful way? The answer may vary, for example, according to use cases and text types. In what follows, we explain the key issues with MT evaluation, with a view to helping users to choose an MT engine that suits their specific needs.

1.1 Assessing Machine Translation quality: What are we talking about?

Starting from a broad definition of quality in translation, we see that it covers both product and process: "Quality in translation is both the quality of an end-product (the translated material) and the quality of the transaction (the service provided)" (Gouadec 2010: 270). Besides, translation quality assessment will very much depend on the context in which the translation is done, and the expectations of translator trainers will certainly differ from those of a client who needs a translation for specific purposes. In other words, "the notion of quality is relative" (Grbić 2008: 232). In translation studies, quality has been notoriously difficult to define and inevitably variable: a number of review studies thus relate changes in translation theories to changing views of quality (see e.g. Drugan 2013; House 2015). And when it comes to assessing the quality of MT outputs, different definitions of quality are again used. "The evolution and widespread adoption of translation technologies, especially machine translation (MT), have resulted in a plethora of typically implicit and differently operationalized definitions of quality and respective measures thereof" (Doherty 2017: 131). As far as MT is concerned, quality has been seen more as a means to an end (namely improving systems), and so a pragmatic approach has prevailed, often involving a combination of human and automatic evaluation (Doherty 2017: 133). Before moving on to present existing means of evaluation and how they might be combined, let us explain why a pragmatic approach is needed.

From the point of view of MT users, the quality of an MT output is a complex thing to assess. Indeed, if quality crucially depends upon the system used, the context of the translation and the needs of end-users are also key factors to take into account. Consider a fairly simple example: you have probably found it easy to adjust to poorly translated instructions in a user manual, because you already had quite a clear idea of how to use the product you had bought, or because the pictures were enough to guide you. In such circumstances, we are likely to find relatively high tolerance for MT errors (Castilho & O'Brien 2016). Now consider a completely different setting that also involves technical texts, but with an added legal dimension: users of translated patents need precise and relevant information, so tolerance for MT errors will be much lower. Looking at NMT for the patent domain, Castilho et al. (2017: 113) have, for instance, evidenced a tendency of NMT to omit elements from the source text, in a context where a piece of information missing from the machine-translated text may have serious consequences. In both cases, a pragmatic approach to quality assessment would imply using measurable indicators of usefulness, such as user satisfaction ratings, productivity increases in post-editing, or increased sales based on machine-translated descriptions of products.

Overall, assessing translation quality is far from trivial, and several factors come into play when evaluating a translation, whether it is done by humans or machines. For a start, there is usually more than one valid solution in translation: the same source text can have several translations, all equally acceptable. What is more, if the evaluation of a translation is entrusted to human evaluators, the evaluation process will often be subjective: indeed, it is not uncommon for evaluators to disagree on the level of quality of a given translation. Evaluations based on what humans *do* with translations can be objective, however, when they use productivity measures. Overall, in order to compensate for subjectivity, it is essential to clearly define the objectives and indicators of each evaluation. Another disadvantage of human evaluation is that it is also a time-consuming and resource-intensive process. As an alternative to human evaluation, it is possible to use algorithms to carry out an automatic evaluation, which is certainly cheaper and faster than human evaluation, but also sometimes less relevant, because it may not track usefulness in a particular application. Both types of evaluation thus have advantages and disadvantages; and your choice should depend above all on your translation project and needs.

1.2 Good-enough quality: Think twice!

Using a pragmatic approach to MT assessment, as proposed above, it becomes clear that not all MT errors or approximations have the same impact. Cooking recipes often provide us with a good testing ground, because the results of the translation are easy to see (and taste), and as a matter of fact they have been used for some time now to produce jokes about MT errors. Here is an example of a lasagne recipe, machine translated from French into English, together with a question: would you be able to make the lasagne if you could use only this MT output?

Table 1: Examples of NMT errors (underlined) found in a translated recipe (FR>EN)

French source text[a]	English NMT output
Préchauffez votre four à 180°C. Dans un plat à gratin beurré, versez un peu de béchamel. Déposez une couche de pâte et poser une couche de farce a la viande. Déposez à nouveau des pâtes, béchamel et viande.	Preheat your oven to 180°C. In a buttered gratin dish, pour a little béchamel. Put a layer of dough and a layer of meat stuffing. Put a layer of pasta, béchamel and meat filling on top.
Terminer par une couche de pâte avec de la béchamel et saupoudrez de fromage râpé. Laissez cuire 35 à 40 minutes.	Finish with a layer of dough with béchamel and sprinkle with grated cheese. Leave to cook for 35 to 40 minutes.

[a]Lasagnes de grand-mère (French recipe): https://www.750g.com/lasagnes-r66998.htm

You would certainly be surprised at the result, since variation in the French source text between the singular and plural of "pâte(s)" results in the appearance of dough in a recipe that really only includes pasta. You might be cautious and cunning enough to guess, but trusting the rather fluent MT output would have resulted in baking a different dish, and the mistake was induced by just one letter (a plural ending). Even though the machine-translated text is very fluent and reasonably accurate on the whole, and would require only small changes to improve it, we see that one serious issue is enough to make the translation dysfunctional. The recipe's relative simplicity, together with knowledge about a common dish, could help readers work their way around this problem, but with many other text types and specialized domains these elements won't apply. What is more, the evaluation method proposed here involves humans, ingredients and a kitchen: it would be a very expensive test, and one that is hardly ever used.

Besides such misfires, most MT users are likely to encounter problems with abstract notions and metaphorical expressions. In the example in Table 2, which shows part of the blurb for a book published in French alongside its translation into English by an NMT system, would an English-speaking reader be able to guess that "a veritable pie in the sky" (English MT output for the French "véritable tarte à la crème") meant a well-trodden path or prefabricated subject?

If you're already used to dealing with MT, you probably recognise these mistakes, and a number of others. Experience makes a difference! And the more

Table 2: Example of mistranslation of an idiomatic expression (underlined)

French source text[a]	English NMT output
L'indépendance du parquet, véritable tarte à la crème remise sur le plateau à chaque campagne présidentielle, était aussi une proposition du candidat Macron. Il ne l'a pas tenue.	The independence of the public prosecutor's office, a veritable pie in the sky put forward in every presidential campaign, was also a proposal by candidate Macron. He did not keep it.

[a]French source text: https://www.grasset.fr/livres/ministere-de-linjustice-9782246827504

fluent the MT output, the more caution is needed: recent studies have shown that students' correction rates were lower with NMT than other less fluent types of MT (Yamada 2019). Getting used to the recurrent problems found in NMT outputs for a given language pair (and domain) will help you detect them and fix them more efficiently.

To conclude, even though NMT quality has undeniably been getting better, it is probably not easier to deal with than other types of MT, and MT is never a simple recipe for success. Instead, you will need to pay attention to small mistakes hidden in a fluent MT output, and to carefully consider your needs before deciding whether an MT solution is appropriate.

2 Choosing a suitable MT engine for specialized translation purposes

While the previous section has been mostly concerned with general aspects of NMT use and assessment, choosing a suitable MT engine for professional translation purposes means taking into account a variety of other aspects. Crucially, an MT engine that suits your professional purposes has to respect the privacy requirements of your client, be seamlessly buildable into your workflow, offer your language pairs and provide you with an output that you can post-edit with minimal effort to meet your client's needs. The quality of the output will depend on the specialized domain and text type, the trainability of the engine, and the pre-editing and post-editing effort you are willing to put in.

2.1 Privacy and confidentiality

How does an MT system handle your data? Even though this question is a vital one for you and your commissioner or client, most MT solutions do not provide you with a clear answer or any kind of warning at first sight. Instead, you will have to read privacy statements carefully and make sure you have made the right choice before you start.

For instance, this warning is found in the privacy statement of eTranslation, the EU's NMT system: "Users should exercise their judgement when submitting potentially sensitive documents to any online service, including eTranslation". Such warnings are valid even for solutions in which the data is not kept on the provider's servers, and privacy issues may indeed arise from simple situations in which data has been transferred only to be deleted a few moments later. Concerns about confidentiality mean that the use of even internal MT systems like eTranslation has been forbidden in hearings at the Court of Justice of the European Union. This is because no MT system could possibly conform to the strict confidentiality requirements for such hearings[1] (C. Lenglet, personal communication).

Of course, the risk that privacy issues will arise with free online MT is considerably higher, because data is kept and reused constantly. Thus, some of the confidential segments of a text inadvertently fed to a free MT system could be leaked in unexpected ways (for more information on how to handle your data ethically and safely, see Moorkens 2022 [this volume]).

2.2 Comparing MT outputs

You may wish to test several MT tools with the same source text and compare the outputs in order to identify the best tool for your needs.

There are several ways to compare outputs depending on the question you seek to answer. The scores used for comparison may, for example, be based on human assessment, automatic evaluation and or the measurement of post-editing (hereafter PE) effort. The measurement of PE effort is covered in more detail in O'Brien (2022 [this volume]). It suffices to say here that an MT output that requires little or no PE is considered "better" than one that requires a lot of PE, and that PE effort is used to measure quality in cases where there is a realistic assumption that machine translated texts will be used for dissemination purposes. (See Kenny (2022 [this volume]) on the distinction between MT for assimilation and MT for dissemination.) In the rest of this chapter, we focus on human assessment and automatic evaluation of MT outputs.

---

[1] As described and explained here: https://eur-lex.europa.eu/legal-content/en/TXT/PDF/?uri=CELEX:32013D0488

2.3 Human evaluation

Human assessment relies on human evaluators assessing the output of one or more systems. This is usually done sentence by sentence (or "segment" by "segment"), but document-level evaluations have also been carried out (see, for example, Castilho 2020). Human evaluators are usually asked to score each segment using two different criteria. The first, known as *adequacy*, measures the amount of meaning in the source segment that is rendered in the machine translated segment. Adequacy is usually measured on an ordinal scale: a typical scale ranges from 1 (understood as indicating that none of the meaning expressed in the source segment is expressed in the machine translated segment) to 4 (understood as meaning that all the meaning expressed in the source segment is expressed in the machine translated segment). Sometimes five-point scales are used, but with an uneven number of points in the scale, there is always a risk that evaluators will overuse the middle point. The second criterion, known as *fluency*, measures "the extent to which the translation follows the rules and norms of the target language" (Castilho et al. 2018: 18). In principle, fluency judgements can be made without the evaluator even looking at the source segment. They also usually rely on four-point ordinal scales, with 1 indicating that there is "no fluency" in the machine translated segment, while 4 denotes a native-like segment (Castilho 2020: 1152-1153). Adequacy and fluency evaluations are generally considered to be extremely time-consuming and, therefore, expensive to conduct.

A more straightforward — and thus faster — comparison of outputs from two different MT systems can be conducted by simply asking evaluators to rank the outputs, that is, to say which one is "better" without specifying why. This approach has been used by many MT providers to get fast feedback from online users. A good example was Microsoft's use of this approach to get user evaluations of outputs from its statistical and neural MT systems in 2017, as reported in Moorkens (2018).

Other MT providers have developed more elaborate interfaces to assist in human evaluations of MT outputs. Kantan AI, for example, offers a tool call KantanLQR (for "Language Quality Review") which allows users to specify which quality criteria (for example, adequacy, fluency, terminology use, etc.) are most important for their purposes and then to compare up to four different MT outputs, based these quality indicators.[2] Tools like this are particularly useful, as they provide visualizations, often in the form of pie charts and bar charts, of human evaluators' scores for individual segments, and they can compute overall

---

[2] For more information, see: https://kantanmt.zendesk.com/hc/en-us/articles/115003644483-What-is-KantanLQR- and https://twitter.com/i/status/1466392446552657927.

scores for different MT engines or systems. They also typically have functions designed for use by project managers in translation companies, as well as the actual evaluators. Non-commercial tools such as PET (Aziz et al. 2012) are also available to help in human evaluations of MT outputs, and are frequently used by academic researchers.

Other familiar tools that can be used to support human evaluations include spreadsheet programs. These allow manual input of scores into tables like that suggested in Table 3. In-built functions can then be used to compute average scores for the quality indicators you have used. A variety of free-to-use online forms can also be used to conduct human evaluations.[3] These are particularly useful for conducting surveys, and can often automatically compute summary and other statistics in the same way that spreadsheets do.

Table 3: Suggested spreadsheet for comparing MT solutions

Source text	NMT1	NMT2	NMT3	Preferred output	Comments
Segment 1					
Segment 2					

2.4 Error typologies

Sometimes human evaluators are asked not just to score a machine translated segment or document using one of the metrics described above, but to say precisely what is wrong with the particular output, by assigning each error in the segment to a category specified in an *error typology*. Categorizing errors is an important step in diagnosing problems in MT output, often in an effort to provide feedback to system developers.

Error typologies tend to be rather complex, however. The Multidimensional Quality Metrics (MQM) framework, for instance, includes an extensive list of error categories (Mariana et al. 2015: 140). For the sake of simplicity and ease, a limited set of common errors could be used in an evaluation, such as the one selected by Moorkens for a practical in-class translation evaluation exercise (Moorkens 2018: 380). It includes:

- Word order errors (incorrect word order at phrase or word level)

---

[3]Perhaps the best known example is Google Forms. See https://support.google.com/docs/answer/6281888?hl=en&co=GENIE.Platform%3DDesktop

- Mistranslations (incorrectly translated word, wrong gender, number, or case)

- Omissions (words from the source text have been omitted from the target text)

- Additions (words not in the source text have been added in the target text)

It might turn out that the small sample of MT output selected for evaluation is not representative enough of each engine's performance, and, ideally, the comparison should be repeated on different samples before choosing the best engine or system. However, while large institutions may have the means of conducting large-scale evaluation campaigns, smaller translation services and freelancers may do better to turn to automatic metrics and measuring post-editing effort.

2.5 Using automatic evaluation metrics

Being much faster and cheaper than human assessment, automatic evaluation metrics (AEMs) allow MT users to assess the quality of MT outputs as frequently as required. For example, if you are training your engine, running tests after each change allows you to check whether your engine has improved for your purposes. If you are not training an engine yourself, but are able to choose one from among several for a given project, AEMs allow you to evaluate multiple MT outputs for the same source text sample.

Human translators often produce widely different translations for the same source text. MT systems therefore cannot be expected to match a human translation exactly. But because a machine translation that is very similar to a human translation might be better than one that differs greatly from it, many AEMs are based on the principle of similarity: the evaluation tool is fed both a human-generated "gold standard" or *reference translation*, and the system output, known as the *candidate translation* (sometimes called *hypothesis*). It then compares the candidate against the reference translation and computes the similarity or dissimilarity. To take variation across reference translations into account, some evaluation tools can be fed multiple reference translations.[4]

A large number of AEMs, or variations of existing AEMs, have been proposed over the last two decades. In this section we concentrate on just a handful of AEMs however, basing our selection on what readers are likely to encounter in

---

[4]In such cases, a decision needs to be made on how to compute the length of the reference translation. Multi-reference BLEU, for example, uses the length of the reference "closest in size to the candidate translation" (Qin & Specia 2015: 114)

the evaluation interfaces mentioned elsewhere in this chapter, namely KantanMT and MutNMT. Readers interested in expanding their knowledge of AEMs beyond those covered here are referred to Koehn (2010) and Koehn (2010). In the interests of consistency, we follow the terminology and notation used by Koehn and apply his explanations, where applicable, in the evaluation of NMT outputs in a worked example below.

The example is based on an excerpt from a user manual for a transceiver,[5] and is reproduced in Figure 1.

Source text:	Battery pack is attached to the transceiver.

Figure 1: source text of the main example for this section

The sentence appears in a bulleted list of conditions under which the transceiver is guaranteed to be water-resistant (see Figure 2).

Important note
Water resistance of the transceiver (IP57: 1 meter / 30 minutes) is assured only when the following conditions (*sic*):

- Battery pack is attached to the transceiver;

- Antenna is connected to the antenna jack;

- and MIC/SP cap is installed in the MIC/SP jack.

Figure 2: excerpt from a transceiver user manual

While it is written for the general public, the source text is a technical text and its translation would thus constitute a specialized translation task. It addresses the domain of radio communication, and therefore has to respect the terminology and phraseology of that domain, and its genre is that of a user manual, which means in turn that it should follow the conventions of such documents. For example, each concept should be referred to using one term only (i.e., synonyms are not permitted), and each term should correspond to one concept only (a property known as *monosemy*), instructions should be kept short and simple, and instructions should all be written following the same pattern. (For more on domains and genres, see Kenny 2022 [this volume].) In our proposed translation project, the

---

[5]The VX-450 series of Vertex Standard, now discontinued.

target text will have to be translated into French and will have the same function as the source text: it will be provided to customers along with the transceiver.

In what follows, we will consider this excerpt and the way it was translated by three different MT tools. The first one (hereafter *system A*, the output of which is called *candidate A*) is eTranslation, the EU's MT tool.[6] The second one (hereafter *system B*, which outputs *candidate B*) is Google Translate.[7] The third one (hereafter *system D*, which outputs *candidate D*) is DeepL Translator.[8] At the time of writing, these systems are freely accessible to the general public, with one proviso: eTranslation requires would-be users to register and to belong to one of three categories of users: SMEs, Public Service Officials and Public Sector Service Providers.

Some of the more basic AEMs that we will present in this section can be computed by hand. However, for the more complex metrics we will use MutNMT to compute scores.[9] While we are presenting an example to give readers an idea of how these metrics work, we would like to make it clear here that the exact computation of an AEM score varies depending on the particular implementation details of each metric: if you use different tools to compute what seems to be the same AEM (say, BLEU, for instance), you may well get different results.[10] The discrepancy in results may have its origins in the way the tool deals with quotation marks, hyphens, breaking and non-breaking spaces, etc., before computation, in the way it defines tokens (does it take into account apostrophes, hyphens, punctuation or linguistic information such as lemmas or multiple-word units?), in its sensitiveness to case, or in metric parametrization specifics (e.g., what order of *n*-grams is used for the exact implementation?).[11] In our example, we changed the apostrophes in candidate D to those used in the reference translation. This way, the different coding of smart and straight quotes will not interfere with the AEM results, and we can focus on the translation output *per se*. Furthermore, when we compute AEMs by hand for the purposes of explanation, we consider hyphens and apostrophes as word "breaks". This means that the total word count of our reference translation (see Figure 3) is eight.

---

[6] https://webgate.ec.europa.eu/etranslation/translateTextSnippet.html

[7] https://translate.google.com/?hl=en

[8] https://www.deepl.com/en/translator. Note that we are referring to DeepL as "system D" and not "system C" in order to avoid confusion in cases where we use *C* to refer to a candidate translation.

[9] https://mutnmt.prompsit.com/index

[10] Note, however, that there has recently been an effort to normalize and group reference implementations of AEMs in software such as Matt Post's sacrebleu (Post, 2018).

[11] The authors would like to thank Gema Ramírez-Sánchez for her explanations.

| Reference translation: | La batterie est installée sur l'émetteur-récepteur. |

Figure 3: reference translation for example

Figure 4 shows the source text, candidate translations and reference translation that we will consider in what follows.

Source text:	Battery pack is attached to the transceiver.
Reference:	La batterie est installée sur l'émetteur-récepteur.
Candidate A (eTranslation):	Le bloc-batterie est fixé à l'émetteur-récepteur.
Candidate B (Google Translate):	La batterie est fixée à l'émetteur-récepteur.
Candidate D (DeepL) :	Le bloc-piles est fixé à l'émetteur-récepteur.

Figure 4: Main example for this section – source text, reference translation and candidate translations

What can a human evaluator say about these examples? Firstly, the term "battery pack" should be translated by "batterie", unless the customer has specified otherwise. The translation "bloc-piles" (candidate D) is plainly wrong: this transceiver does not function on "piles", which are electrochemical cells designed to be used once and then discarded, but rather on a "batterie", that is a rechargeable pack of cells. In this case, the transceiver operates on a lithium-ion battery. Talking of "bloc-batterie" (candidate A) is not intrinsically incorrect. Rather, it is not idiomatic; it is a calque, i.e. an overly word-for-word translation, of the English sentence. Secondly, the verbal form "is attached to" can just as well be rendered by "est installée sur" or by "est fixée à": this is a matter of personal preference. Thirdly, "transceiver", which is a contraction of "transmitter-receiver" should ideally be translated by "émetteur-récepteur", as is the case in all translations shown in Figure 4. However, "radio" or even "appareil" ("device") would have worked just as well for the purposes of this translation project (for more on translation and equivalence, see Kenny 2022 [this volume]). Now, let us take an in-depth look at how AEMs would assess these candidate translations.

2.5.1 Core concepts: *n*-grams, precision, recall and F-measure

In this section, we present four concepts that constitute the building blocks of the more elaborate AEMs we present in subsequent sections: *n-grams, precision, recall* and *F-measure.*

2.5.1.1 *n*-grams

n-grams (see Kenny 2022 [this volume]) are normally understood in translation as *n*-word sequences. In our example sentence, "battery" is a 1-gram or *unigram*, "battery pack" is a 2-gram or *bigram* and "battery pack is" is a 3-gram or *trigram*. Other orders of *n*-gram are simply called 4-gram, 5-gram, etc., making "battery pack is attached" a 4-gram.

n-grams are commonly used in language modelling, where, for example, a trigram probability states the probability of seeing a word given that you have already seen the two words before it.

When we discuss AEMs, *n*-grams are merely *n*-word sequences in the candidate translation that also occur in the reference translation. More recently, AEMs have been proposed which consider sequences of characters instead of words. *N*-grams are then understood as sequences of *n* characters, rather than sequences of *n* words.

We will be using the notion of *n*-grams as *n-word sequences* when discussing BLEU (see 2.5.4.), and of *n*-grams as *n-character sequences* when discussing ChrF3 (see 2.5.5).

2.5.1.2 Precision and recall

Precision is a very basic concept used in various branches of natural language processing. It can be explained using a very simple example. If a teacher asked a student to name the days of the week in English, and the student replied "Monday, Tuesday", then the student would have given two correct answers and no incorrect answers. Because precision is understood as the ratio of correct answers given to the total number of answers given, the student would score two out of two, which is equal to an impressive precision score of 100%.

But the teacher would see the student's answer as very problematic, because the teacher knows what the answer *should have been*, and that the student has neglected to mention five of the seven days of the week. The teacher could therefore object that the student's *recall* is bad, where recall is understood as the ratio of correct answers given to the total number of correct answers (in the ideal reply). In this case, the student's recall score would be two out of seven, or just under 29%.

In the context of the automatic evaluation of MT, precision computes the ratio of correct words in the candidate translation, i.e., those that also occur in the reference translation, to the total number of words in the candidate:

$$\text{precision of } C = \frac{\text{no. of correct words in } C}{\text{no. of words in } C} \tag{1}$$

where C is the candidate translation.

Let us consider our example. In Figure 5, the candidates are compared against the reference, and "correct" words, i.e. words that also occur in the reference, are underlined, while "incorrect" words, i.e. words that do not occur in the reference, are crossed out.

Source text:	Battery pack is attached to the transceiver.
Candidate A (eTranslation):	~~Le bloc~~-batterie est ~~fixé à~~ l'émetteur-récepteur.
Candidate B (Google Translate):	La batterie est ~~fixée à~~ l'émetteur-récepteur.
Candidate D (DeepL):	~~Le bloc-piles~~ est ~~fixé à~~ l'émetteur-récepteur.
Reference:	La batterie est installée sur l'émetteur-récepteur.

Figure 5: source text, reference translation, candidate translation

Let us now work out the precision of each candidate. System A's output has five correct words out of a total of nine, which gives a precision of 0.56, or 56%.[12] System B's output has six correct words out of eight, so its precision score is 0.75, or 75%. Finally, system D's output has four correct words out of nine, which gives a precision of 0.44, or 44%. According to this metric, system B's output is better than that of system A or system D.

Recall, in the same context, computes the ratio of correct words in the candidate to the total number of words in the *reference*:

$$\text{recall of } C = \frac{\text{no. of correct words in } C}{\text{no. of words in } R} \tag{2}$$

where C is the candidate translation, and R the reference translation.

In other words, recall takes into account not just what the candidate translation said, but what it should have said.

Let us go back to our example (Figure 6).

The reference translation comprises eight words. System A's output has five correct words out of a total of eight in the reference translation, and thus a recall ratio of 0.63, or 63%. System B's output has a total of six correct words, which makes for a recall of 0.75, or 75%, while system D's output has a total of four correct words, which makes for a recall of 0.5, or 50%. According to this metric, system B's output is again better than system A's or D's.

---

[12]In this section, all results will be rounded to the nearest hundredth when dealing with score ranges comprised between 0 and 1, and to the nearest unit when dealing with percentages.

Source text:	Battery pack is attached to the transceiver.
Candidate A (eTranslation):	~~Le bloc~~-batterie est ~~fixé à~~ l'émetteur-récepteur.
Candidate B (Google Translate):	La batterie est ~~fixée à~~ l'émetteur-récepteur.
Candidate D (DeepL):	~~Le bloc-piles~~ est ~~fixé à~~ l'émetteur-récepteur.
Reference:	La batterie est installée sur l'émetteur-récepteur.

Figure 6: Source text, reference translation, candidate translation

2.5.1.3 *F-measure*

The student in our example above could choose to prioritize precision over recall and thus refuse to give any more answers after "Monday, Tuesday", because they do not want to risk giving a wrong answer. Alternatively, they might choose to prioritize recall by blurting out tens of answers in the hope that enough of them are actually correct. They thus might reply "Monday, Tuesday, Wednesday, Thursday, Friday, Saturday, Sunday, January, February, March, April, May, June, July, August, September, October, November, December". Their recall would now shoot up to 100% as they would have given seven out of seven correct answers (for the days of the week), but their precision will plummet to under 37% as only seven out of the nineteen answers in their reply are correct. From the teacher's point of view, neither strategy is ideal. What the teacher wants is for the student to optimize both precision and recall as the same time. They need a score that combines both. This is where the F-measure comes in.

In mathematical terms, the *F-measure* is the harmonic mean of precision and recall. It is computed as follows:

$$F = 2 \cdot \frac{\text{precision} \cdot \text{recall}}{\text{precision} + \text{recall}} \tag{3}$$

which can also be reformulated as:

$$F = 2 \cdot \frac{\text{no. of correct words in } C}{\text{no. of words in } C + \text{no. of words in } R} \tag{4}$$

where C is the candidate translation, and R the reference translation.

Let us compute the F-measure of our three candidate translations in Table 4.

System A's output gets an F-measure of 59%, while system B's output gets an F-measure of 75% and system D's output an F-measure of 47%. According to this metric, system B's output is still better than system A's or D's.

Caroline Rossi & Alice Carré

Table 4: Precision, recall and F-measure of candidates A, B and C

Metric	Candidate A	Candidate B	Candidate D
precision	56%	75%	44%
recall	63%	75%	50%
F	$2 \cdot \frac{56 \cdot 63}{56+63} = 59$	$2 \cdot \frac{75 \cdot 75}{75+75} = 75$	$2 \cdot \frac{44 \cdot 50}{44+50} = 47$

With the three metrics *precision, recall* and *F*, the higher the score, the better the MT output is deemed to be. However, these metrics work at the word level and do not take word order into account.

2.5.2 Translation error rate (TER)

The *translation error rate* (also called translation *edit* rate, or TER) takes word order into account.

It is based on the *word error rate* (WER), which uses the Levenshtein distance. The Levenshtein distance computes the difference between sequences (in the present case, sequences of words); it is defined as "the minimum number of editing steps – insertions, deletions, and substitutions – needed to match two sequences" (Koehn 2010: 224). WER then normalizes that distance by the length of the reference (Koehn 2010: 225):

$$\text{WER} = \frac{\text{no. of substitutions} + \text{no. of insertions} + \text{no. of deletions}}{\text{no. of words in } R} \quad (5)$$

where R is the reference translation.

However, when sequences of words or indeed whole clauses are moved elsewhere in a sentence, each word move counts as two errors (one deletion and one insertion), which can result in a very poor WER.

TER solves this by adding a shift operation, which means that moving any sequence of words counts only as one error:

$$\text{TER} = \frac{\text{no. of shifts} + \text{no. of substitutions} + \text{no. of insertions} + \text{no. of deletions}}{\text{no. of words in } R}$$

$$(6)$$

where R is the reference translation.

Let us go back to our example. Compare candidate translations A, B and D with the reference translation (Figure 7). What is the minimum number of steps required to go from candidates A, B and D to the reference translation?

111111111
1111111111111111111111111

Caroline Rossi & Alice Carré

Table 4: Precision, recall and F-measure of candidates A, B and C

Metric	Candidate A	Candidate B	Candidate D
precision	56%	75%	44%
recall	63%	75%	50%
F	$2 \cdot \frac{56 \cdot 63}{56+63} = 59$	$2 \cdot \frac{75 \cdot 75}{75+75} = 75$	$2 \cdot \frac{44 \cdot 50}{44+50} = 47$

With the three metrics *precision, recall* and *F*, the higher the score, the better the MT output is deemed to be. However, these metrics work at the word level and do not take word order into account.

2.5.2 Translation error rate (TER)

The *translation error rate* (also called translation *edit* rate, or TER) takes word order into account.

It is based on the *word error rate* (WER), which uses the Levenshtein distance. The Levenshtein distance computes the difference between sequences (in the present case, sequences of words); it is defined as "the minimum number of editing steps – insertions, deletions, and substitutions – needed to match two sequences" (Koehn 2010: 224). WER then normalizes that distance by the length of the reference (Koehn 2010: 225):

$$\text{WER} = \frac{\text{no. of substitutions} + \text{no. of insertions} + \text{no. of deletions}}{\text{no. of words in } R} \quad (5)$$

where R is the reference translation.

However, when sequences of words or indeed whole clauses are moved elsewhere in a sentence, each word move counts as two errors (one deletion and one insertion), which can result in a very poor WER.

TER solves this by adding a shift operation, which means that moving any sequence of words counts only as one error:

$$\text{TER} = \frac{\text{no. of shifts} + \text{no. of substitutions} + \text{no. of insertions} + \text{no. of deletions}}{\text{no. of words in } R}$$

$$(6)$$

where R is the reference translation.

Let us go back to our example. Compare candidate translations A, B and D with the reference translation (Figure 7). What is the minimum number of steps required to go from candidates A, B and D to the reference translation?

66

Source text:	Battery pack is attached to the transceiver.
Candidate A (eTranslation):	Le bloc-batterie est fixé à l'émetteur-récepteur.
Candidate B (Google Translate):	La batterie est fixée à l'émetteur-récepteur.
Candidate D (DeepL):	Le bloc-piles est fixé à l'émetteur-récepteur.
Reference:	La batterie est installée sur l'émetteur-récepteur.

Figure 7: Source text, candidate translations A, B and C, and reference translation

TER is a heuristic process, i.e. an iterative process, where the algorithm tries to find the best solution (the minimal number of steps required to go from one sequence to another) by testing successive hypotheses. To calculate the TER manually, one can use a matrix. However, we are going to propose a shorter, if imperfect way,[13] for the sake of explanation: let us compare each candidate translation, and count the number of matches, shifts, substitutions, additions and deletions. Remember, the number of matches will not go into the final calculus. As we mentioned before, we consider hyphens and apostrophes as word "breaks". A tool that does not consider them as breaks would treat "l'émetteur-récepteur" as one word rather than three and get a different result.

2.5.2.1 Candidate A

Table 5: Operations needed to transform candidate A into reference.

Operation	Edited words	Number of editing steps
Matches	batterie, est, l', émetteur, récepteur	5
Shifts		0
Substitutions	le/la, fixé/installée, à/sur	3
Insertions		0
Deletions	bloc	1

Let us now compute the TER for candidate translation A:

$$\text{TER}_A = \frac{0 + 3 + 0 + 1}{8} = 0.5 = 50\%$$ (7)

---

[13]Note that our examples contain no shifts, so that TER equals WER here.

Caroline Rossi & Alice Carré

2.5.2.2 Candidate B

Table 6: operations needed to transform candidate B into reference.

Operation	Edited words	Number of editing steps
Matches	la, batterie, est, l', émetteur, récepteur	6
Shifts		0
Substitutions	fixée/installée, à/sur	2
Insertions		0
Deletions		0

Let us now compute the TER for candidate translation B:

$$\text{TER}_B = \frac{0 + 2 + 0 + 0}{8} = 0.75 = 75\% \tag{8}$$

2.5.2.3 Candidate D

Table 7: operations needed to transform candidate D into reference.

Operation	Edited words	Number of editing steps
Matches	est, l', émetteur, récepteur	3
Shifts		0
Substitutions	le/la, bloc/batterie, fixé/installée, à/sur	4
Insertions		0
Deletions	piles	1

Let us now compute the TER for candidate translation D:

$$\text{TER}_D = \frac{0 + 4 + 0 + 1}{8} = 0.63 = 63\% \tag{9}$$

Systems A's output gets a TER score of 50%, system B's a TER score of 75% and system D's a TER score of 63%. Because WER and TER are error rates, these metrics take mismatches, and not matches, into account. This means that contrarily to the precision, recall and F-measure scores, the lower the value, the better the MT output is deemed to be. Thus, according to this metric, the best output would be candidate A.

2.5.3 Human translation edit rate (HTER)

Because the candidate translation could be acceptable while still being quite different from the reference translation, a metric that assesses the former against the latter could be unfairly harsh on the MT system. Alternatively, we can compute the *human translation edit rate* (HTER): in this variant, we ask a human evaluator to post-edit a candidate MT output, and we count the number of editing steps needed to transform that candidate output (and possibly other candidates) into the post-edited version (Snover et al. 2006).

Let us go back to our example. Compare candidate translations A, B and D with a post-edited segment, which could be any of the candidate translations, edited by a human reviser (Figure 8): what is the minimum number of steps required to go from candidates A, B and D to the post-edited segment?

Source text: Battery pack is attached to the transceiver.

Candidate A (eTranslation): Le bloc-batterie est fixé à l'émetteur-récepteur.

Candidate B (Google Translate): La batterie est fixée à l'émetteur-récepteur.

Candidate D (DeepL): Le bloc-piles est fixé à l'émetteur-récepteur.

Post-edited segment: La batterie est fixée à l'émetteur-récepteur.

Figure 8: Source text, candidate translations A, B and D, and post-edited segment

Again, remember the number of matches will not go into the final calculus.

2.5.3.1 Candidate A

Table 8: operations needed to transform candidate A into post-edited segment.

Operation	Edited words	Number of editing steps
Matches	batterie, est, à, l', émetteur, récepteur	6
Shifts		0
Substitutions	le/la, fixé/fixée	2
Insertions		0
Deletions	bloc	1

Let us now compute the HTER for candidate translation A:

$$\text{HTER}_A = \frac{0 + 2 + 0 + 1}{8} = 0.38 = 38\% \tag{10}$$

2.5.3.2 Candidate B

Table 9: operations needed to transform candidate B into post-edited segment.

Operation	Edited words	Number of editing steps
Matches	la, batterie, est, fixée, à, l', émetteur, récepteur	8
Shifts		0
Substitutions		0
Insertions		0
Deletions		0

Let us now compute the HTER for candidate translation B:

$$\text{HTER}_B = \frac{0 + 0 + 0 + 0}{8} = 0 = 0\% \tag{11}$$

2.5.3.3 Candidate D

Table 10: operations needed to transform candidate D into post-edited segment.

Operation	Edited words	Number of editing steps
Matches	est, à, l', émetteur, récepteur	4
Shifts		0
Substitutions	le/la, bloc/batterie, fixé/fixée	3
Insertions		0
Deletions	piles	1

Let us now compute the HTER for candidate translation D:

$$\text{HTER}_D = \frac{0 + 3 + 0 + 1}{8} = 0.5 = 50\% \tag{12}$$

Systems A's output gets an HTER score of 38%, system B's an HTER score of 0% and system D's an HTER score of 50%. Remember, because TER and HTER are error rates: the lower the value, the better the MT output is deemed to be. Thus, according to this metric, the best output would be candidate B.

Table 11: TER and HTER scores for each candidate translation

Metric	Candidate A	Candidate B	Candidate D
TER	50%	25%	63%
HTER	38%	0%	50%

Now, compare the TER and HTER scores for each candidate translation in our example (Table 11): they all get a lower, i.e. better, HTER than TER. Our example confirms that "the edit rate between a machine translation and its postedited version is dramatically lower than between the machine translation and an independently produced human reference translation" (Koehn 2020: 52). This difference could be taken as a reminder of the dangers of under-post-editing, which can happen when post-editors work under too much time pressure.[14]

2.5.4 Bilingual evaluation understudy (BLEU)

The *bilingual evaluation understudy* (BLEU) metric represents the *n*-grams shared between a candidate machine translation and a reference translation.[15] Therefore, it takes both the number of matching words and word order into account. It is usually set to consider *n*-grams from unigrams to 4-grams and can allow for different *n*-grams to be weighted differently.

Figure 9 presents a candidate and a reference translation for the sentence made famous by René Magritte's painting *The Treachery of Images*. The candidate translation shares five out of a possible six 1-grams with the reference, if we count the punctuation mark at the end of the sentence as a 1-gram. The candidate also contains four out of the five 2-grams in the reference ([is not], [not a], [a pipe], [pipe .]), and three out of the four 3-grams in the reference ([is not a], [not a pipe], [a pipe .]). Finally, it contains two of the three 4-grams in the reference. Here, the overlapping 4-grams are [is not a pipe] and [not a pipe.], the first of which is illustrated in Figure 9.

---

[14]The authors would like to thank Mikel Forcada for this comment.
[15]As mentioned above, note that BLEU can also allow for the use of multiple reference translations.

Source text:	Ceci n'est pas une pipe.
Candidate Translation (fictional):	That is not a pipe .
Reference:	This is not a pipe .

Figure 9: candidate and reference translation for the sentence Ceci n'est pas une pipe, showing one 4-gram overlap.

Because the BLEU score computes the ratio of n-grams in the candidate translation that also occur in the reference translation, it is a precision metric. Table 12 thus presents the precision scores (expressed as a ratio and a decimal fraction) for each order of n-gram in our candidate translation.[16]

Table 12: Precision (from 1-grams to 4-grams) for the candidate translation 'That is not a pipe'.

Metric		
Precision (1-gram)	5/6	0.83
Precision (2-gram)	4/5	0.80
Precision (3-gram)	3/4	0.75
Precision (4-gram)	2/3	0.66

To compute an overall BLEU score for a candidate translation, we compute the geometric mean (a special type of "average") of these individual precision scores. It turns out to be just under 0.76 or 76%.[17] (This is actually a very high BLEU score, but then the example was a very simple one.)

It should be noted, however, that BLEU scores are usually computed over entire corpora, not individual sentences. And because precision metrics can be tricked by systems that produce translations only for words the system is sure of (think of the student who refuses to name more days of the week, in case they get any wrong), BLEU uses a *brevity penalty*. The brevity penalty is the ratio between the number of words in the candidate translation and in the reference translation (for more on this, see Koehn 2020: 227). It kicks in when the candidate translation is shorter than the reference translation. No brevity penalty is imposed in the case

---

[16]The presentation used in Table 12 is borrowed from (Koehn 2010: 227).

[17]Readers can use familiar spreadsheet software to calculate geometric means. A specifically-designed *BLEU score calculator* may also need to take into account any extra weight for, e.g., longer n-grams, and should have a way of *smoothing* out any zeros that appear in the n-gram precision scores. For details, see Post (2018).

of the sentence in Figure 9, however, as the candidate is the exact same length as the reference.

Although this metric is often referred to as "the BLEU score", there are so many different parameters that go into computing BLEU scores (Post 2018) that it can be very difficult for non-specialists to find out and understand how exactly a given AEM tool computes it. What is important for translators who wish to use this AEM to assess MT outputs is that the scores they get for different candidate translations are consistently calculated: put simply, make sure you use the same MT evaluation tool, that you understand the settings it uses, and, if some of them are user-definable, that you use the same settings when comparing candidate translations using that AEM. This way, you will get comparable scores.

By way of illustration, Table 13 shows the BLEU scores computed by two different calculators, those provided by MutNMT and Tilde, for the candidate translations in Figure 4.[18]

Table 13: Sentence-level BLEU scores for candidate translations A, B and D using MutNMT and Tilde

BLEU Calculator	Candidate A	Candidate B	Candidate D
MutNMT	15%	31%	15%
Tilde	50%	61%	47%

According to these scores, system B's output is better than system A's. This is consistent with our findings so far. But the actual values vary dramatically and the user would need to investigate why this might be the case.

2.5.5 ChrF3

The CHRF score is an F-measure based on character n-grams. Therefore, it is based both on precision and recall. Remember the formula for the F-measure:

$$F = 2 \cdot \frac{\text{precision} \cdot \text{recall}}{\text{precision} + \text{recall}} \tag{13}$$

The formula for the CHRF score is:

$$\text{ChrF}\beta = (1 + \beta^2) \cdot \frac{\text{ChrP} \cdot \text{ChrR}}{\beta^2 \cdot \text{ChrP} + \text{ChrR}} \tag{14}$$

---

[18]https://mutnmt.prompsit.com/index; MutNMT uses the SACREBLEU algorithm (Post 2018). Tilde's "interactive bleu score evaluator" is available at https://www.letsmt.eu/Bleu.aspx.

where

- CHRP is the character n-gram precision, i.e. the number of correct character n-grams in the candidate translation divided by the total number of n-grams in the candidate translation,

- CHRR is the character n-gram recall, i.e. the number of correct character n-grams in the candidate translation divided by the total number of character n-grams in the reference translation, and

- β is a parameter which assigns β times more importance to recall than to precision. If $\beta = 1$, then they are equally important; CHRF1 is the harmonic mean of character n-gram precision and recall (Popović 2015).[19]

The CHRF3 score, then, is a variant of CHRF where $\beta = 3$, i.e. recall has three times more weight than precision. According to Popović (2015), experiments have shown that CHRF, and especially CHRF3, represent promising metrics for automatic evaluation of MT output.

As with BLEU, we will not calculate ChrF3 scores here. However, it is interesting to compare the scores given by an AEM tool.

Table 14 shows the ChrF3 scores of candidates A, B and D, as computed by MutNMT.

Table 14: ChrF3 score for candidate translations A, B and D

Metric	Candidate A	Candidate B	Candidate D
ChrF3	64%	69%	49%

According to these scores, system B's output is once again rated better than system A's and system C's.

2.5.6 A word of caution: AEM scales

To end this section on AEMs, we would like to sound a note of caution: when dealing with AEM scores, make sure you know what the numbers mean. Some scores can be reported as decimals or as percentages (e.g. 0.8 or 80%). And on a scale from 0 to 1 (or 0% to 100%), 0 could be the best score and 1 the worst for one

---

[19]Note that this also applies to F: thus far, all F-measures were F_1 measures where $\beta = 1$. The value of β may be changed.

metric (e.g. TER) while 1 could be the best score and 0 the worst for another (e.g. BLEU).

We have also seen that caution should be exercised when comparing metrics computed with different tools: indeed, the algorithms behind apparently similar AEMs might differ in ways the non-specialist user is unaware of.

Finally, it should be said that to make the most of these different metrics, users will need to reflect on what the scores mean for their purposes and get used to them. Comparing different AEMs and combining them with human evaluation will help, even though you might be faced with differences (Doherty 2017: 134). Human evaluation can take into account context in a better way, provided that it is not done with segments presented in a random order: evaluators can then look for errors in pronouns, for instance, while AEMs mostly operate at word and sentence level. One interesting way to combine measures is to use both HTER, which gives you a measure of technical post-editing effort, and a temporal measure, which tells you how long post-editing took.[20] O'Brien (2022 [this volume]) gives an overview of measures of post-editing effort.

2.6 Type-token ratios

The *type-token ratio* (TTR) is not quality metric as such. Rather, it provides a global insight on the lexical variety of a text. It is mentioned here because it has become one of the metrics used to comment on ways in which machine translated text can differ from other texts in the same language (see Toral 2019), and some evaluation interfaces, including that of MutNMT, are now reporting this metric.

TTR basically measures vocabulary variation (or *lexical variety*, Williamson 2009) within a text or corpus. The number of running words in a text is referred to as the number of *tokens*. But words can be repeated in a text; if the same word occurs three times in a text, for example, it counts as three tokens, but only as one *type*. The relationship between number of tokens and number of types is called type-token ratio and is computed as follows:

$$\text{type token ratio} = \frac{\text{no. of types}}{\text{no. of tokens}} \quad (15)$$

or

$$\text{type token ratio} = \frac{\text{no. of types}}{\text{no. of tokens}} \cdot 100 \quad (16)$$

---

[20]While averaging them into a single score might not be very telling, looking for correlations could help to identify the most serious problems.

The first method gives results ranging from 0 to 1, while the second gives percentages, ranging from 0% to 100%. The higher the type-token ratio, the more varied the vocabulary in the text under scrutiny.

However, several warnings have to be issued regarding this metric. Firstly, TTR is highly sensitive to text-length. Indeed, the longer a text is, the more often such words as determiners and articles will be repeated. Moreover, because texts, especially specialized texts, have a thematic unity, terms are repeated. Therefore, the longer the text segment under consideration, the lower the TTR. Because of this sensitivity of TTR to text length, TTR may have to be standardized across blocks of a given number of tokens (e.g. 1,000 tokens) depending on the task at hand. Standardizing in this way would allow you to compare the TTR of your machine translated corpus with that of a corpus of different length in the same (target) language.

Secondly, while lemmatization does not matter when comparing texts in the same language, TTR has to be lemmatized when comparing two or more languages as some languages have richer inflectional morphology than others and thus would be expected to have more lexical variety, simply because they have, for example, more forms for any given verb. If you are simply using standardized TTRs to compare the lexical variety of machine translated texts with that of other texts in the same language however, then lemmatization will not be necessary.

Lastly, bear in mind that a higher TTR, that is, one that indicates more lexical variety, does not necessarily equate with higher complexity. For example, consider the sentences "The girl saw a fire." and "The lexicographer observed the conflagration." Both sentences are made up of five words (tokens), but while the former has five types, the latter has only four (because the token "the" occurs twice). The first sentence thus has a TTR of 1 or 100%, while the second has a TTR of 0.8 or 80%. But in spite of being less varied than the first sentence, the second sentence is more complex.[21]

As already indicated, segment-level comparisons of TTRs might not make much sense, but at text or corpus level, same-language comparisons of standardized TTRs could give us valuable information, depending on the kind of text we are dealing with. This chapter has focused on specialized translation. But there are different kinds of specialized translation, which follow different conventions. Contrary to literary or marketing translation, where higher lexical variety (and thus a higher TTR) could be associated with higher quality and make the reading all the more pleasant for the user of the target text, technical translation often has to comply with certain conventions that tend to decrease the lexical variety of

---

[21]The authors would like to thank Dorothy Kenny for this comment.

texts while making them easier to use for the end user. The main example used in this chapter comes from a user manual, which means in turn that it should follow such conventions as using a single term for a single concept, with no variation, and that instructions should as far as possible be written following the same pattern. For example, if "transceiver" was translated at times by "émetteur-récepteur", and at others by "radio" and by "appareil", it would lead to a higher TTR, while introducing uncertainty for the end user.

This leads us to conclude this section with a second word of caution.

3 Conclusion

In this chapter we have sought to illustrate what a pragmatic approach to MT evaluation implies for specialized translators or trainees. This approach has been called pragmatic because it considers evaluation as a means to an end, and implies choosing among different methods depending on the situation, often using a combination of human and automatic evaluation.

While the comparison of MT outputs has been used as a method throughout this chapter, it is worth noting that specialized translators are rarely given a choice about what evaluation metric to use in current translation scenarios. Rather, they often need to make a quick judgement on whether a given MT solution is fit for purpose, or provide a general assessment of its quality.

We have thus explained how evaluations of MT outputs might be conducted, using a combination of human and automatic evaluation metrics. We have explained the latter in great detail because we believe that, for all their limitations, they can be put to good use if understood properly, and combined with human evaluation.

References

Aziz, Wilker, Sheila Castilho & Lucia Specia. 2012. PET: a tool for post-editing and assessing machine translation. In *Proceedings of the eight international conference on language resources and evaluation (LREC'12)*, 3982–3987.

Castilho, Sheila. 2020. On the same page? Comparing inter-annotator agreement in sentence and document level human machine translation evaluation. In *Proceedings of the 5th conference on machine translation (WMT)*, 1150–1159. https://aclanthology.org/2020.wmt-1.137.pdf.

Castilho, Sheila, Stephen Doherty, Federico Gaspari & Joss Moorkens. 2018. Approaches to human and machine translation quality assessment. In Federico Gaspari Joss Moorkens Sheila Castilho & Stephen Doherty (eds.), *Translation quality assessment: From principles to practice*, 9–38. Cham: Springer.

Castilho, Sheila, Joss Moorkens, Federico Gaspari, Iacer Calixto, John Tinsley & Andy Way. 2017. Is neural machine translation the new state of the art? *The Prague Bulletin of Mathematical Linguistics* 108. 109–120. DOI: 10.1515/pralin-2017-0013.

Castilho, Sheila & Sharon O'Brien. 2016. Evaluating the impact of light post-editing on usability. In *10th international conference on language resources and evaluation (LREC)*, 310–316. May 2016, Portorož, Slovenia. ELRA.

Doherty, Stephen. 2017. Issues in human and automatic translation quality assessment. In Dorothy Kenny (ed.), *Human issues in translation technology*, 131–148. London: Routledge.

Drugan, Joanna. 2013. *Quality in professional translation: Assessment and improvement*. London: Bloomsbury.

Gouadec, Daniel. 2010. Quality in translation. In *Handbook of translation studies. Volume 1*, 270–275. John Benjamins Publishing Company.

Grbić, Nadja. 2008. Constructing interpreting quality. *Interpreting* 10(2). 232–257.

House, Juliane. 2015. *Translation quality assessment: Past and present*. London: Routledge.

Kenny, Dorothy. 2022. Human and machine translation. In Dorothy Kenny (ed.), *Machine translation for everyone: Empowering users in the age of artificial intelligence*, 23–49. Berlin: Language Science Press. DOI: 10.5281/zenodo.6759976.

Koehn, Philipp. 2010. *Statistical Machine Translation*. Cambridge: Cambridge University Press.

Koehn, Philipp. 2020. *Neural Machine Translation*. Cambridge: Cambridge University Press.

Mariana, Valerie, Troy Cox & Alan Melby. 2015. The multidimensional quality metric (MQM) framework: A new framework for translation quality assessment. *The Journal of Specialised Translation* 23. 137–161.

Moorkens, Joss. 2018. What to expect from neural machine translation: a practical in-class translation evaluation exercise. *The Interpreter and Translator Trainer* 12(4). 375–387.

Moorkens, Joss. 2022. Ethics and machine translation. In Dorothy Kenny (ed.), *Machine translation for everyone: Empowering users in the age of artificial intelligence*, 121–140. Berlin: Language Science Press. DOI: 10.5281/zenodo.6759984.

O'Brien, Sharon. 2022. How to deal with errors in machine translation: Post-editing. In Dorothy Kenny (ed.), *Machine translation for everyone: Empowering users in the age of artificial intelligence*, 105–120. Berlin: Language Science Press. DOI: 10.5281/zenodo.6759982.

Popović, Maja. 2015. Chrf: Character n-gram f-score for automatic MT evaluation. In *Proceedings of the tenth workshop on statistical machine translation*, 392–395. Association for Computational Linguistics. 10.18653/v1/W15-3049.

Post, Matt. 2018. A call for clarity in reporting BLEU scores. In *Proceedings of the third conference on machine translation (WMT), Volume 1: research papers*, 186–191. Association for Computational Linguistics. DOI: 10.18653/v1/W18-6319.

Qin, Ying & Lucia Specia. 2015. Truly exploring multiple references for machine translation evaluation. In *Proceedings of the 18th annual conference of the European Association for Machine Translation*, 113–120. https://aclanthology.org/W15-4915/.

Snover, Matthew, Bonnie Dorr, Rich Schwartz, Linnea Micciulla & John Makhoul. 2006. A study of translation edit rate with targeted human annotation. In *Proceedings of the 7th conference of the Association for Machine Translation in the Americas: Technical papers*, 223–231. Cambridge, Massachusetts: Association for Machine Translation in the Americas. https://aclanthology.org/2006.amta-papers.25/.

Toral, Antonio. 2019. Post-editese: An exacerbated translationese. In *Proceedings of machine translation summit XVII*, 273–281. EAMT. https://www.aclweb.org/anthology/W19-6627/.

Williamson, Graham. 2009. *Type-token ratio*. Last retrieved 5 Dec. 2020. https://www.sltinfo.com/wp-content/uploads/2014/01/type-token-ratio.pdf.

Yamada, Masaru. 2019. The impact of Google neural machine translation on post-editing by student translators. *The Journal of Specialised Translation* 31(2019). 87–106.

Chapter 4

Selecting and preparing texts for machine translation: Pre-editing and writing for a global audience

Pilar Sánchez-Gijón
Universitat Autònoma de Barcelona

Dorothy Kenny
Dublin City University

Neural machine translation (NMT) is providing more and more fluent translations with fewer errors than previous technologies. Consequently, NMT is becoming a real tool for speeding up translation in many language pairs. However, obtaining the best raw MT output possible in each of the target languages and making texts suitable for each of the target audiences depends not only on the quality of the MT system but also on the appropriateness of the source text. This chapter deals with the concept of pre-editing, the editing of source texts to make them more suitable for both machine translation and a global target audience.

1 Introduction

Put simply, *pre-editing* involves rewriting parts of source texts in a way that is supposed to ensure better quality outputs when those texts are translated by machine.[1] It may involve applying a formal set of rules, sometimes called *controlled*

---

[1] As discussed in Rossi & Carré (2022 [this volume]), quality is not a fixed concept; rather, judgments about quality depend on a whole host of factors, including the intended purpose of a translation. For a detailed discussion of this highly mutable concept, see Drugan (2013) and Castilho et al. (2018).

Pilar Sánchez-Gijón & Dorothy Kenny. 2022. Selecting and preparing texts for machine translation: Pre-editing and writing for a global audience. In Dorothy Kenny (ed.), *Machine translation for everyone: Empowering users in the age of artificial intelligence*, 81–103. Berlin: Language Science Press. DOI: 10.5281/zenodo.6759980 *language* rules, which stipulate the specific words or structures that are allowed in a text, and prohibit others (see, for example, O'Brien 2003). Alternatively, it can involve applying a short list of simple "fixes" to a text, to correct wrong spellings, or impose standard punctuation, for example. Depending on the context, it might involve both of the above. Whatever the case, its main purpose, as understood here, is to improve the chances of getting a better quality target text once the source text has been machine translated. In cases where a source text is to be translated into multiple target languages, the benefits of pre-editing should, in theory, be observed over and over again in each of the target language texts. It is thus traditionally recommended in multilingual translation workflows.

Another way to ensure that a text is translatable is to write it that way in the first place. Writers whose work will ultimately be translated into multiple languages are thus often asked to write with a global audience in mind. As well as applying principles of "clear writing", they are asked, for example, to avoid references that may not be easily understood in cultures other than their own. This applies also to writers whose work will be read in the original language by international readers who are not native speakers of that language.

Given their similar aims, it is not surprising that there is often overlap between pre-editing rules, controlled languages and guidelines for clear writing or writing for global audiences. In this chapter, we give an overview of the kind of guidance commonly encountered in such sources, without attempting to be exhaustive. The reader must also remember that such guidance is always language specific: advice about the use of tense forms, for example, applies only to languages that have grammatical tense. Many do not. Guidance can also be language-*pair* specific or specific to a particular machine translation (MT) type or engine. A construction that caused problems in rule-based MT (RBMT) may no longer be an issue in neural MT (NMT), or it might be associated with errors in a neural engine trained on legal texts but not one trained on medical texts. In the case of writing with MT in mind, what turns out to be useful advice thus depends heavily on the context.

The advent of NMT, in particular, has made us rethink the usefulness of advice on pre-editing and controlled writing (see Marzouk & Hansen-Schirra 2019 and §2 below), but for much of the history of MT, pre-editing helped ensure the success of the technology. A good knowledge of MT made it possible to predict those aspects of the source language or the source text that would likely generate errors in translations produced by a given MT system, whether rule-based or statistical. However, one of the aspects that characterize NMT is precisely its lack of systematic error: it can be difficult to predict with any certainty what type of error will occur, and so attempting to pre-empt particular errors may seem ill-advised. The substantial improvement in the fluency and adequacy of translations obtained through NMT might also suggest that steps taken to improve output are an unnecessary luxury. In the context of NMT, it might seem, in other words, that pre-editing is, a priori, redundant. Improvements in MT do not diminish the benefits of all types of pre-editing, however. While some traditional pre-editing approaches may no longer be relevant, as will be discussed below, others become essential, especially if pre-editing is included in a translation pipeline in which there is no post-editing or in which "good enough" post-editing (see O'Brien 2022: §2 [this volume]) is performed. What is more, while improvements in quality certainly mean that the translation problems which used to characterize MT have been reduced to a great extent, errors have not been completely eliminated, as we will see below, and new errors are emerging for which MT has not been evaluated so far. These are linked to the nature of the translation commission (see below), the function of the source text and the assumed intention of its author, and it is in these cases that pre-editing continues to play a role in optimizing the use and increasing the effectiveness of MT.

The rest of this chapter starts out by discussing the background and uses of pre-editing in the more recent past and in current uses of NMT. The chapter goes on to describe the strategies involved in selecting texts for use with MT, and with the influence of English as a source language on machine translated texts. It then presents the case for writing for a global audience to start with. The chapter concludes by presenting common pre-editing guidelines, as well as the resources and tools used in this task.

2 Pre-editing and NMT

In the past, when rule-based systems produced obvious, and often systematic, errors in adequacy and fluency (see Rossi & Carré 2022 [this volume]), pre-editing was often necessary to get the best out of MT. Even after the transition to statistical MT (SMT), researchers still found pre-editing to be useful. Seretan et al. (2014), for example, working with the language pairs English-French, English-German and French-English, found that appropriate pre-editing led to quality improvements in the MT of user-generated content in both the technical and health domains. In a related study, also using SMT, Gerlach (2015) found that pre-editing English source texts resulted in faster post-editing of machine translations into French, although the overall impact on productivity in the extended workflow was less clear. Likewise, Miyata & Fujita (2017) found that pre-editing Japanese texts resulted in better translations into English, Chinese and Korean, confirming, in their view, the particular usefulness of pre-editing in multilingual SMT settings (ibid.: 54). The same researchers subsequently studied the influence of pre-editing on the output of two NMT systems, but this time found that there was very little correlation between the amount of pre-editing done and the amount of post-editing that was needed after pre-edited texts were machine translated from Japanese into English, Chinese or Korean (Miyata & Fujita 2021). Miyata and Fujita (ibid.) also looked at the effect of different types of pre-edits, and found that the edits that had been traditionally recommended in the context of MT were less frequently encountered in NMT workflows:

> Contrary to the acknowledged practices of pre-editing, the operation of making source sentences shorter and simpler was not frequently observed. Rather, it is more important to make the content, syntactic relations, and word senses clearer and more explicit, even if the ST becomes longer. (Miyata & Fujita 2021: 1547).

Other studies suggest that pre-editing is simply not an effective strategy with NMT systems. Marzouk & Hansen-Schirra (2019), for example, found that pre-edits improved the performance of an RBMT, an SMT, and a hybrid MT system, in the context of German-to-English technical translation, but they did not improve the performance of the NMT system they tested.[2] Among the few studies that are enthusiastic about pre-editing in the context of NMT is that by Hiraoka & Yamada (2019). They applied just three pre-editing rules to Japanese TED Talk subtitles, namely:

- fill in missing punctuation,

- fill in missing grammatical subjects and/or objects,[3] and

- write out proper nouns in the target language.

According to Hiraoka and Yamada (ibid.), the implementation of these three edits improved the translation into English of the subtitles using an off-the-shelf NMT system. In some rare cases, however, it resulted in dis-improvements in the MT output.

---

[2]Like other authors, Marzouk & Hansen-Schirra (2019) are careful to point out that their research is based on so-called *black-box* systems, that is, off-the-shelf systems whose internal workings cannot be scrutinized by the analyst.

[3]Japanese, like Spanish, is a "pro-drop" language (see Kenny 2022: §1 [this volume]), meaning that certain pronouns can be omitted without impeding comprehension. In Japanese, these can be either subject or object pronouns.

Given the lack of clear research evidence to support the use of pre-editing in NMT workflows, industrial users of NMT are best advised to test the effects of pre-edits carefully before promoting their use in production environments. As indicated in the Introduction to this chapter, they may find that certain edits are useful only for particular language pairs, given particular genres and particular NMT engines and the training data they are based on.

3 Genre and domain-based advice

From the point of view of professional translators (and the translation industry), the use of MT on a regular and integrated basis within translation projects is associated with specific text *genres* and *domains* (see Kenny 2022: §1 [this volume]). In the past, the focus on genres and domains that used predictable, and sometimes repetitive or restricted words and structures, meant that controlled language approaches made sense: in contexts where a quick and cost-effective translation was needed (for example, in the case of in-house technical documentation that was not available to the general public), the words and structures used in source texts were controlled to ensure the success of the MT. In the era of data-driven translation, a focus on genre and domain continues to make sense, as the training data used by the SMT and NMT engines in operation in industry are also genre- and domain-specific, or such engines can at least be customized for these genres and domains (see Ramírez-Sánchez 2022 [this volume]).

Based on their own experience with MT, many language service providers thus recommend restricting the use of MT, and by extension, NMT, to the translation of:

Certain types of technical documentation: These usually involve already standardized texts, in which terminology use is already strict in itself, the style is direct and simple, and the use of linguistic resources closely resembles the application of controlled language rules. The conceptual framework that underpins such technical documentation may also be identical in both the source and target "locales". The technical specifications for a personal computer that is marketed in Ireland and France remain substantially the same, for example, and so there is vast common ground when it comes to translating a text listing those specifications from English into French; extensive adaptation to take the French target user or a new conceptual framework into account is not necessary. In cases where NMT is used to translate such texts, controlled-language rules governing lexical selection or the use of pronouns like *it* probably still have some potential for application, while rules of a syntactic nature may be unnecessary.

The straightforward nature of technical specifications contrasts with marketing and legal materials associated with the same product, which might need adaptation to make them more acceptable to potential buyers, or compliant with the target legal framework. Indeed, legal translation provides one of the best examples of a domain where it is sometimes necessary to "rethink" a text completely in translation, so that it can be accommodated by a new conceptual system.

For more on the domain- and genre-specific nature of translation, see Olohan (2015) and Šarcevic (1997).

Low-risk internal documentation: These are texts which have very low visibility and where the consequences of less-than-optimal translation are not serious (see Canfora & Ottmann 2020 and Moorkens (2022 [this volume])) for more detailed discussions of risk in MT use.) They may even be limited to use within the user's or client's company. A priori, considerations such as naturalness or fluency in the target language are less relevant than would otherwise be the case (although NMT generally produces quite fluent output anyway), but companies may still wish to control lexical selection and lexical variability.

Low-risk external documentation: This refers to texts that are consulted only occasionally or sporadically, or texts that are used as a help database or similar, and that are often not produced by the client, but by the community of users of its service or product. In many such cases, the MT provider may explicitly deny liability for any losses caused by faulty translations.

MT is not usually recommended for texts of a more visible nature whose purpose is not just to inform or give instructions but also to be "appellative", that is, to arouse a particular interest in the reader, for example, in a certain brand, or to elicit a certain behaviour. In other words, the more informative a text is, the more it limits itself to the literalness of its message, the less implicit information it contains and the less it appeals to references linked to the reader's culture or social reality, the greater the expected success of MT.

4 The influence of English in controlled domains

RBMT, and later SMT, worked particularly well in environments where both language use and the nature of text genres were not figurative or creative but literal and with clear genre conventions. The source language in many cases was, without a doubt, English. The other major languages became target languages, which means that translations in certain contexts have been highly conditioned by English, giving rise to texts in which linguistic aspects have been homogenized with a view to simplifying the text to facilitate comprehension by the end reader. This is the case of genres such as user manuals for consumer goods, which, in languages such as Spanish, have—in our experience, but see also Navarro (2008) and Aixelá (2011), among others—been heavily influenced by the English source texts, both from a macro-textual point of view (in their text structure and the development of textual argumentation) and a micro-textual one (as seen in lexical, morphological and syntactic borrowings).

The objective of communication in controlled domains is to facilitate the reading and understanding of the text based on an unambiguous and precise wording, so that the original text is as easy to read as it is to translate quickly. In some industries a further step is taken and controlled languages are used to ensure that texts are free of ambiguity. In these cases, the influence of English as a source language on the other languages is much more evident.[4] The aircraft industry is an example of a context in which the rules of a controlled language are established in English and then applied in the target languages (Ghiara 2018).

These examples demonstrate the need in certain domains to control the linguistic resources used in the source text to ensure a quick and accurate translation. In these cases, the aspect of correctness of the translated text in general, and when using MT in particular, takes precedence over any other communicative aspect of the target text. Nevertheless, the arrival of NMT means that MT is now used beyond domains that are limited to specific audiences, as is described in the following section.

5 Writing for a global audience

Sometimes the objective of pre-editing is not a matter of avoiding errors in the translated text, but rather of ensuring that the translation, beyond conveying a meaning consistent with that of the source text, also achieves the same or a

---

[4]Seoane Vicente (2015) provides an exhaustive review of the use of English as a controlled language in different domains.

similar effect on the reader of the target text as the source text did on its reader, to the extent that this is possible. It is a question of making a text available to a global audience and attempting to have the same effect on readers in each target language.

Whether the text is to be translated with an MT system or not, from a communication perspective, for years it has been considered advisable to have the translation already in mind during the drafting phase of the source text. In fact, the preparation of documentation for translation forms part of their training for technical writers (Maylath 1997).

Over the last 50 years, the translation industry, and all related interested parties from translators to major technology developers and distributors, have learned that the best translation strategy requires appropriate internationalization of the product (Fry 2003: 14). The best way to adapt a product to any other region is to exclude those aspects which are unique to the source text region where it is being designed and developed. In this way, any digital product can be localized and used in the target language and on any device or platform, without its original design having to be modified. Something similar also appears to have happened with texts designed to be published in different languages.

Both language service providers and developers of localized digital products have found that pre-editing source texts is the key to their global communication strategy. Many language service companies advertise on their websites that good multilingual communication strategies begin with developing an appropriate source text. Digital product developers have likewise discovered that the best strategy for communication with their users and potential customers is based on keeping a global user in mind. This strategy is embodied in a set of guidelines that should be taken into account when drawing up the contents of any text. Google's documentation style guide, for example, features a basic "writing for a global audience" principle, and sets out a series of guidelines in English that facilitate the translation of documentation into any target language. These include, among others, general dos and don'ts, such as use present tense, provide context, avoid negative constructions when possible, write short sentences, use clear, precise, and unambiguous language, be consistent and inclusive (Google 2020).

Today's translation technologies make it possible to combine the use of computer-aided translation tools like translation memory tools (see Kenny 2022: §4 [this volume]) and MT systems. So, the limitations of MT in this sense are not technological, but rather determined by the quality of the raw MT output (is it error-free?) and appropriateness for the target communicative context (register, tone, genre conventions, and any other issues relevant for the translation to fulfil its communicative function).

In the case of textual genres that formally follow very rigorous conventions and essentially have an informative or instructive communicative function (for example, technical documentation, or similar), MT produced by a quality translation engine can give good or very good results, depending on the language pair and other factors. In these cases, "pre-editing" can be limited to spellchecking the source text, since these genres do not usually involve stylistic or referential features (see below) that take them outside the realm of standard and non-complex source text use.

However, genres which have a mixture of more than one communicative function, for example the recently popular "unboxing" videos for technical gadgets, which are often both instructive (informative) and entertaining (appellative and expressive), are not so simple to deal with using MT.

Texts belonging to yet other genres may contain references to the social, economic or cultural life of their source communities that allow source text readers to identify with the text, but may not have the same effect on the target text language reader (see §6.4 on referential elements). Other possible obstacles for some MT engines include rhetorical and stylistic devices (contractions, abbreviations, neologisms, incomplete sentences, etc.), that shape the source text, and with which the source text readers can identify.

NMT allows users to obtain translations with fewer and fewer errors of fluency or adequacy. It enables translations to be completed very quickly. Moreover, it seems to achieve excellent results when translating many different text genres. But a text written grammatically in the target language and without translation errors may still not be an *appropriate* translation. Pre-editing makes it possible to ensure the appropriateness of the translation with a global audience in mind. Currently, this phase is seldom used in the translation industry. In the past, some global companies using SMT or RBMT pre-edited their original texts to avoid recurring translation errors using their own systems. With NMT, pre-editing may become widespread in the industry as part of a strategy that not only avoids translation errors but also contributes to making the raw MT output appropriate to the contexts of use of the target translation.

6 Pre-editing guidelines

6.1 Opening remarks

Pre-editing is based on applying a series of specific strategies to improve MT results when preparing content for a global audience or in controlled domains. Pre-editing helps to ensure clear communication in controlled domains targeting global audiences. In this context, the predominant textual type is informational, where there is no creative or aesthetic use of language but a literal and unambiguous use with the intention of either informing or instructing the text's recipient. The following are the most common guidelines used in communication for a global audience, and are the basis for pre-editing strategies. The aim of most of these guidelines is to increase MT effectiveness in producing grammatically correct translations that reproduce the source text "message" and also to obtain translations that are appropriate to the communicative situation of the receiver according to the text function and the context in which it is used. These guidelines can be grouped into three different categories:

1. Lexical choice

2. Structure and style

3. Referential elements

Whatever the case, the success of pre-editing will be determined by two considerations. First, the function of the (source and target) text: the greater the predominance of the informative or instructive function over the phatic or aesthetic functions, the more sense it makes to pre-edit the original text. Second, the kind of errors in the raw MT output that the chosen MT system provides and that should be avoided or minimized by pre-editing the source text.

Pre-editing has two objectives: to prepare the original text so that the most error-free possible raw MT output can be obtained, and also to prepare the original text so that its translation through MT is suitable for a global audience. The pre-editing guidelines presented in this section respond to these two objectives.

6.2 Lexical guidelines

As will be seen in Pérez-Ortiz et al. (2022 [this volume]), the way each word or unit of meaning is processed in NMT is determined by its context and vice versa. A lexical choice in a text is linked to the range of texts and contexts in which the same choice is used. Let's take the case of a source text to be translated by MT and, consequently, to be published in several target languages in the shortest time possible. An appropriate choice of words in the source text can contribute not only to avoiding translation errors, but also to complying more effectively with the linguistic uses in accordance with the function of the text and the reason for its publication. Table 1 contains typical guidelines related to the lexicon.

Table 1: Typical lexical pre-editing guidelines

Guideline	Explanation
Avoid lexical shifts in register	Avoid words that can change the style of the text or the way it addresses the receiver. This facilitates understanding the text and normalizes the way the receiver is addressed.
Avoid uncommon abbreviations	Only use commonly-found abbreviations. Avoid abbreviated or reduced forms that cannot be easily translated from their immediate context.
Avoid unnecessary words	Avoid unnecessary words for transmitting the information required. Using more words than needed means that the NMT system handles more word combinations and has more opportunities to propose an inappropriate or erroneous translation.
Be consistent	Use terminology in a consistent and coherent way. Avoid introducing unnecessary word variation (that is, avoid synonymy).

6.3 Structure and style

The way a text is formulated in general, and its individual sentences in particular, are as important in terms of comprehensibility as the lexicon used. The order in which ideas are interrelated, at the sentence level, throughout a text, or even intertextually, contributes to the reader's comprehension and interpretation. In the case of NMT, the options adopted in the source text activate or inhibit translation options. An unnecessarily complex and ambiguous text structure that allows objectively different interpretations increases the possibility of the NMT system proposing correct translations of microstructural elements (terminology, phrases or syntactic units) which, when joined together in the same text, generate texts that are internally incoherent, suggest a different meaning to the source text, or are simply incomprehensible.

Table 2 gives pre-editing guidelines regarding the style and structure of the text. Most of them are not only aimed at optimizing the use of NMT systems, but also at the success of the translated text in terms of comprehensibility and meaning.

Most of the guidelines listed in Table 2 are aimed at producing a simple text that can be easily assimilated by the reader of the source text. In the case of NMT engines trained with data sets already translated under these criteria, source text pre-editing helps to obtain the best raw MT output possible. Note, however, that if an engine is trained on "in-domain" data, that is, using a specialized and homogeneous dataset, based on texts of a particular genre and related to a particular field of activity (see Ramírez-Sánchez 2022: §2.1 [this volume]), then the best possible pre-editing, if needed, will involve introducing edits that match the characteristics of that genre and domain. In addition to this general advice, in many cases it is also necessary to take into account guidelines that are specific to the source or target language. This might mean avoiding formulations that are particularly ambiguous, not only for the MT system, but also for the reader.

If we take English for instance, avoiding ambiguous expressions means, for example, avoiding invisible plurals. A noun phrase such as "the file structure" could refer to both "the structure of files" and "the structure of a particular file". Although this ambiguity is resolved as the reader moves through the text, the wording of the noun phrase itself is not clear enough to provide an unambiguous translation. Another example of ambiguous structures in many languages, not only in English, is often the way in which negation is expressed. Sentences such as "No smoking seats are available." are notorious for giving rise to different interpretations and, consequently, incorrect translations.

Verb tense forms are another aspect that may be simplified for the sake of intelligibility for the reader and error-free translations. Although the translation of the different verb tense forms and modes does not necessarily pose a problem for MT, an inappropriate use of verb tenses in the target language, despite resulting in well-formed sentences, can lead to target translation text comprehension errors. Typical guidance related to verb forms is given in Table 3.

Table 2: Aspects related to structure and style in pre-editing

Guideline	Explanation
Short and simple sentences	Avoid unnecessarily complex sentences that introduce ambiguity. This makes it easier to understand the text, both the source and translation. Syntactic structures based, for example, on anaphoric or cataphoric references may not be correctly handled by the NMT system and may lead to omissions or mistranslations. Avoid syntactic ambiguities subject to interpretation.
Complete sentences	Avoid eliding or splitting information. The compensation mechanisms for the not explicitly mentioned information typical of the source language do not necessarily work in the target language. For instance, a sentence with a verb in passive form which does not make the agent explicit can lead to misunderstanding in target texts. The same can happen when one of the sentence complements is presented as a list of options (in a bulleted list, for example). In such cases, the sentence complement is broken down into separate phrases which the NMT system may process incorrectly. Remember that MT systems normally use the sentence as a translation unit (see Kenny 2022: §7 [this volume]), i.e., the text between punctuation marks such as full stops, or paragraph breaks.
Use parallel structures in related sentences	Use the same syntactic structure in sentences in a list or that appear in the same context (e.g., section headings, direct instructions). This kind of *iconic linkage* (see Byrne 2006) usually makes it easier to understand the text, both the source and translation. In addition, it allows for the systematic identification of errors during a post-publishing phase.
Active voice	Where appropriate, use mainly the active voice or other structures that make "participants" in an action explicit (taking into account the conventions of the text genre and the languages involved).
Homogenous style	Maintain a homogeneous style. This facilitates understanding the text, both the source and translation. This is particularly related to preparing texts for a global audience.

Table 3: Aspects related to pre-editing verb forms

Guideline	Explanation
Use the active voice.	Where possible and appropriate, use the active voice.
Use simple verb tense forms; preferably the present or past simple.	Depending on your language pair and the MT engine, you may wish to avoid using compound verb forms. Although the same compound form may exist in both languages, it may not be used in the same way and may lead to different interpretations.
Avoid concatenated verbs.	Avoid unnecessary concatenations of verbs that make it difficult to understand and translate the text.

6.4 Referential elements

Referential elements are all those which substitute for or make reference to another element, whether in the same text, in the case of *intratextual* references, or outside of the text, in the case of *extratextual* references. The most illustrative example of this is pronouns, like *I, he, she, him, her,* etc., and the related category of possessive determiners, such as *my, his, her,* etc.

Pronouns with the referent in the same sentence are not usually problematic from an NMT point of view. When they are within the same sentence, there are usually no gender or number agreement problems between possessive determiners and nouns (see Bentivogli et al. (2016) for an early discussion of how the treatment of agreement phenomena in MT improved with the advent of NMT.) This is also the usually case when successive pronouns throughout the text maintain the same referent (e.g., in the case of the same subject in consecutive sentences). In other cases, however, pronouns may be translated according to the way in which the training corpus treats them most frequently. This issue is particularly sensitive when the text alternates between different referents. In these cases, even though the human reading of the text leaves no doubt as to who or what is the referent of each pronominal form, MT systems are usually unable to maintain this consistency and tend to homogenize the pronominal forms, using those that are most common.

Consequently, in the case of languages that reflect relationships between referent and pronominal forms through mechanisms such as gender and number agreement, the agreement may be lost. This particular kind of problem can usually be minimized by the use of simple sentences.

An example may help here. Example (1) contains an instance of a possessive determiner *su*, which, taken out of context, can mean either 'his' or 'her'. In example (1), the only possible interpretation is 'her', as indicated in the gloss translation provided. DeepL,[5], however, translates the instance of *su* in question as 'his', as it cannot establish the referential link between *su* and *María*.

(1) María llamó, pero Pepe no llamó. El sonido de *su* llamada me despertó.

'Maria called, but Pepe didn't call. The sound of *her* call woke me up.'

DeepL: 'Maria called, but Pepe didn't call. The sound of *his* call woke me up.'

As regards extratextual references, in addition to all the references inherent to the nature of the documentation being translated – for example, specific legislation in documents of a legal nature – there are two types of references that need to be taken into account during the pre-editing phase: 1) those that address the reader, and 2) any cultural references the reader identifies with.

As argued in the previous section, from a stylistic point of view it is best to compose simple, short sentences and use a direct style with the active voice or passive sentences that include the agent and patient. This style is especially appropriate for instructive texts. In the case of instructive texts, the direct style and active voice mean that the text always addresses a reader directly. In this type of sentence, MT tends to reflect the most frequent use found in the corpus, so if the target language allows the reader to be addressed in more than one way, it could alternate between the different options – more or less formal or explicit – and cause cohesion problems throughout the text that could be avoided by pre-editing.

Extratextual references to cultural aspects with which the reader of the source text particularly identifies are difficult to deal with generically. In many cases, pre-editing the text consists of making all the implicit information related to these cultural references as explicit as possible, keeping the global audience in mind.

In both cases (references to the reader and cultural references), MT pre-editing should take into account the target reader's language and profile.

---

[5]https://www.deepl.com/en/translator accessed January 2022

7 Pre-editing tools and resources

As can be seen from the previous subsections, pre-editing has to be carried out within the framework of a translation (or multilingual publication) project, so the same conditioning factors that guide a translation project need to be taken into consideration in pre-editing. A *style guide* is used to detail how to pre-edit the original texts properly. It sets out how each of the aspects should be edited in a structured manner, with examples of sentences with and without pre-editing. It is comparable to a post-editing guide, with the difference that examples are usually given in the source-text language only.

The purpose of pre-editing guides is to provide orientation about language use when preparing the text contents. These writing guidelines aim to avoid MT errors when translating the source text to different languages and to ensure that the best possible text is produced for a global audience. For this reason, they give both micro-structural (recommended or required words or recommended syntactic structures) as well as macro-structural indications on writing. The latter are aimed at providing the source text, and its subsequent translations, with the necessary mechanisms to guarantee intratextual and extratextual cohesion. When the text is embedded in a digital product or is part of the documentation linked to a consumer good, consistent use of language and referential elements (such as terminology) in all texts related to that consumer good contributes to extratextual cohesion.

A guide oriented to the preparation of contents to be published and translated also includes instructions about actions to be taken and tools that facilitate them. Comparable to the quality assurance (QA) phase in translation, preparing the text content also has to follow standards that guarantee its quality and, consequently, the success of its translation. In this case, it is not only a question of producing a grammatically correct translation, but also maintaining the client's language standard.

The actions required to control the quality of the source language content are usually as listed in Table 4.

It is important to pay attention to aspects of the text that are designed to meet with the approval of particular readerships. Inclusive language, for example, can help to avoid reader rejection of both the source and translated texts. As is the case with post-editing (see O'Brien 2022: §2 [this volume]), pre-editing attempts to avoid expressions which could be interpreted as offensive or rude. Guidelines for text content are set out by the author or publisher of the text, so for example, the pre-editing guidelines of a given company may touch upon or mandate

Table 4: QA in pre-editing

Pre-editing quality assurance (QA)	Explanation
Proofing for spelling and grammar	Guarantee that the source text is free of spelling errors which could generate comprehension difficulties by readers, or MT errors.
Using established lexicon	Check the glossary has been applied appropriately, without introducing unnecessary variation in the use of undesired synonyms. The aim here is to guarantee systematic use of terminology set out in the glossary (including trade names or proper nouns of any kind). Also, use the specialized and non-specialized lexicon as unambiguously as possible.
References to the reader	If the text is expressly addressed to the reader, then check the same style of reference is used throughout.
Style	Check that the language style is maintained consistently throughout the text. Avoid shifts in style within the same text.

gender, racial, cultural, and all kinds of inclusivity in language use. This point is particularly relevant in gender-inflected languages.

Preparing a source text for a global audience, or pre-editing, is carried out with tools that assist the writer. Most text editing programs include the most basic functions necessary to carry out pre-editing as well as QA. Other functions are available only through dedicated authoring tools. Table 5 summarizes the main functions of controlled language checkers that assist source text pre-editing.

Most editing programmes include functions that allow this type of action to be performed to one degree or another. However, when pre-editing is part of a

Table 5: Functions of controlled language checkers

Computer assisted pre-editing	Explanation
Proofing for spelling and grammar	Use the grammar and spell checker.
Using established lexicon	Use dictionaries and glossaries that establish recommended and prohibited lexical items.
References to the reader	Use the grammar checker adapted to appropriate expressions according to the pre-editing guide.
Style / register	Use the grammar checker adapted to the level of formality for the commission through suggestions concerning modifying the text.

multilingual content publishing strategy, these programmes often prove wanting. A multilingual content publishing strategy based on pre-editing and using a specific language, means homogenizing all the company or institution's communication: the content published on the web, social networks, FAQ sections, etc. In these cases, it is necessary to resort to controlled language checkers with pre-editing functions that can be integrated into the flow of content publication and, by extension, the production of translations.[6] These kinds of authoring tools usually go far beyond simply checking spelling and lexical aspects; in fact, in some cases they even provide revision proposals depending on the degree of formality of the text at any given time. In most cases, these tools are included as an additional menu in programs that are usually used to produce content, from web content managers to e-mail or social network managers. In this way, both the content author and the pre-editor can use these tools directly in the flow of creating and publishing each piece of content without the need to resort to external tools.

---

[6]Various controlled language checkers and other writing aids are available. Commercial tools include acrolinx (https://www.acrolinx.com/) and ProWritingAid (https://prowritingaid.com/).

8 Who should pre-edit? And when?

Texts to be translated by MT have traditionally been pre-edited in-house in large corporations as part of the technical writing phase, which requires a high level of proficiency in the source language, while knowledge of the target language(s) is not essential.

Today, the accessibility of NMT and the quality of its results allow translators in many major languages to consider including MT in their own workflows. "MT-literate" translators (Bowker & Ciro 2019) can determine whether they can benefit from incorporating NMT based on their own experience, or even by translating small samples of the source text. The typical way to assess the use of NMT is usually by analysing the resulting translated text. If the text requires limited post-editing, it is considered suitable for NMT. However, the wording of the *source text* is rarely questioned. There are texts that, due to their function and visibility, should be translatable through NMT without any major difficulties. However, if the text is unnecessarily complex, incoherent, or does not meet the established editorial standard, translating it via NMT may only accentuate these problems. In these cases, pre-editing could prove useful so that the source text has the necessary cohesion, style and use of rhetorical devices to respect the author's intention, the function of the text and, at the same time, guarantee its comprehensibility and translatability. This is not a task which is commonly practised in the translation industry, but it is one that may become more common in the near future as a response to the need to publish content in several languages.

When the client has no previous language strategy for producing linguistic content, the skills translators have acquired make them best suited to take on the task of pre-editing texts in their mother tongue or the first foreign language into which they usually translate. Their knowledge of contrastive grammar and lexical nuances in the language combination allows them to perform the necessary edits to produce a text in the source language that is functional and understandable by the reader, and which in turn generates as few errors as possible in the text translated via NMT. In addition, their knowledge of the corresponding societies and cultures allows them to assess which referential aspects can be successful in both texts, source and target, and how to make them explicit. Their skills in both languages as well as their knowledge of both cultures and societies, mean translators are the experts best suited to prepare monolingual content intended for bilingual or multilingual publication. Their main working language will still be their mother tongue, but in this case, they do not produce a final text, but rather a machine translated text that can be understood by the end reader in another language. Thus, the post-editing phase can be minimized, although in no case should it be omitted.

Pre-editing as part of the provision of translation services makes sense whether the content is written solely to generate a translation or if it is also to be published in the source language. In both cases, pre-editing makes it possible to guarantee the quality of the original and to optimize the use of NMT.

9 Concluding remarks

The main objective of MT as a resource in translation projects is to increase productivity and, consequently, reduce the time needed to generate a good quality translation. In this sense, pre-editing manages to optimize the source text content so as to minimize errors in the translated text (when MT is used for assimilation) and the editing needed to guarantee the expected quality (when MT is followed by post-editing or used as a resource for human translation).

When NMT is capable of producing translations with virtually no fluency or adequacy errors in informative or instructive texts, then the challenges for MT go beyond these text types. However, translating texts with different communicative functions, such as for games or texts of a more appellative nature, is not only a matter of avoiding errors. It is necessary to produce a translation that is in line with the intention of the source text and with which the target reader can identify in the same way as the source text reader. In this case, pre-editing takes on an added value: the preparation of a text suitable for publishing multilingual content.

As a strategy, pre-editing may play a certain role in foreign language learning. But its main environment is in multilingual content publishing. Although it was originally part of translation workflows for technical documentation and the like, the expansion of NMT could lead to pre-editing being applied to texts of a more complex nature, or even to translators eventually putting their skills at the service of the source text, instead of focusing on the target text, as has happened throughout centuries of translation history.

References

Aixelá, Franco. 2011. An overview of interference in scientific and technical translation. *The Journal of Specialised Translation* 11. 75–88. https://www.jostrans. org/issue11/art_aixela.pdf.

Bentivogli, Luisa, Arianna Bisazza, Mauro Cettolo & Marcello Federico. 2016. Neural versus Phrase-Based Machine Translation quality: A case study. In *EMNLP 2016*. arXiv:1608.04631v1.

Bowker, Lynne & Jairo Buitrago Ciro. 2019. *Machine translation and global research*. Bingley: Emerald Publishing.

Byrne, Jody. 2006. *Technical translation. Usability strategies for translating technical documentation*. Dordrecht: Springer.

Canfora, Carmen & Angelika Ottmann. 2020. Risks in neural machine translation. *Translation Spaces* 9(1). 58–77.

Castilho, Sheila, Stephen Doherty, Federico Gaspari & Joss Moorkens. 2018. Approaches to human and machine translation quality assessment. In Federico Gaspari Joss Moorkens Sheila Castilho & Stephen Doherty (eds.), *Translation quality assessment: From principles to practice*, 9–38. Cham: Springer.

Drugan, Joanna. 2013. *Quality in professional translation: Assessment and improvement*. London: Bloomsbury.

Fry, Deborah. 2003. *The localization industry primer*. 2nd edition. Updated by Arle Lommel. Féchy: LISA. https://www.immagic.com/eLibrary/ARCHIVES/GENERAL/LISA/L030625P.pdf.

Gerlach, Johanna. 2015. *Improving statistical machine translation of informal language. A rule-based pre-editing approach for french forums*. Doctoral thesis. University of Geneva. https://archive-ouverte.unige.ch/unige:73226.

Ghiara, Silvia. 2018. *El lenguaje controlado. La eficacia y el ahorro de las palabras sencillas*. https://qabiria.com/es/recursos/blog/lenguaje-controlado.

Google. 2020. *Writing for a global audience. Google developer documentation style guide*. https://developers.google.com/style/translation.

Hiraoka, Yusuke & Masaru Yamada. 2019. Pre-editing plus neural machine translation for subtitling: effective pre-editing rules for subtitling of TED talks. In *Proceedings of machine translation summit XVII: translator, project and user tracks*, 64–72. Dublin: European Association for Machine Translation. https://aclanthology.org/W19-6710.

Kenny, Dorothy. 2022. Human and machine translation. In Dorothy Kenny (ed.), *Machine translation for everyone: Empowering users in the age of artificial intelligence*, 23–49. Berlin: Language Science Press. DOI: 10.5281/zenodo.6759976.

Marzouk, Shaimaa & Silvia Hansen-Schirra. 2019. Evaluation of the impact of controlled language on neural machine translation compared to other MT architectures. *Machine Translation* 33. 179–203. DOI: 10.1007/s10590-019-09233-w.

Maylath, Bruce. 1997. Writing globally: Teaching the technical writing student to prepare documents for translation. *Journal of Business and Technical Communication* 11(3). 339–352.

Miyata, Rei & Atsushi Fujita. 2017. Dissecting human pre-editing toward better use of off-the-shelf machine translation systems. In *Proceedings of the 20th annual conference of the european association for machine translation (EAMT)*, 54–59. https://ufal.mff.cuni.cz/eamt2017/user-project-product-papers/papers/user/EAMT2017_paper_42.pdf.

Miyata, Rei & Atsushi Fujita. 2021. Understanding pre-editing for black-box neural machine translation. In *Proceedings of the 16th conference of the european chapter of the association for computational linguistics*, 1539–1550. https://aclanthology.org/2021.eacl-main.132.pdf.

Moorkens, Joss. 2022. Ethics and machine translation. In Dorothy Kenny (ed.), *Machine translation for everyone: Empowering users in the age of artificial intelligence*, 121–140. Berlin: Language Science Press. DOI: 10.5281/zenodo.6759984.

Navarro, Fernando A. 2008. La anglización del español: Mucho más allá de bypass, piercing, test, airbag, container y spa. In Luis González & Pollux Hernúñez (eds.), *Traducción: Contacto y contagio. Actas del III congreso internacional « el español, lengua de traducción ». 12-14 July 2006*, 213–132. Puebla: ESLEtRA. https://cvc.cervantes.es/lengua/esletra/pdf/03/017_navarro.pdf.

O'Brien, Sharon. 2003. Controlling controlled English. An analysis of several controlled language rule sets. In *Controlled language translation*. Dublin City University. 15-17 May 2003. EAMT/CLAW. https://aclanthology.org/2003.eamt-1.12.pdf.

O'Brien, Sharon. 2022. How to deal with errors in machine translation: Postediting. In Dorothy Kenny (ed.), *Machine translation for everyone: Empowering users in the age of artificial intelligence*, 105–120. Berlin: Language Science Press. DOI: 10.5281/zenodo.6759982.

Olohan, Maeve. 2015. *Scientific and technical translation*. London: Routledge.

Pérez-Ortiz, Juan Antonio, Mikel L. Forcada & Felipe Sánchez-Martínez. 2022. How neural machine translation works. In Dorothy Kenny (ed.), *Machine translation for everyone: Empowering users in the age of artificial intelligence*, 141–164. Berlin: Language Science Press. DOI: 10.5281/zenodo.6760020.

Ramírez-Sánchez, Gema. 2022. Custom machine translation. In Dorothy Kenny (ed.), *Machine translation for everyone: Empowering users in the age of artificial intelligence*, 165–186. Berlin: Language Science Press. DOI: 10.5281/zenodo.6760022.

Rossi, Caroline & Alice Carré. 2022. How to choose a suitable neural machine translation solution: Evaluation of MT quality. In Dorothy Kenny (ed.), *Machine translation for everyone: Empowering users in the age of artificial intelligence*, 51–79. Berlin: Language Science Press. DOI: 10.5281/zenodo.6759978.

Šarcevic, Susan. 1997. *New approach to legal translation*. The Hague: Kluwer Law International.

Seoane Vicente, Ángel Luis. 2015. *Lenguaje controlado aplicado a la traducción automática de prospectos farmacéuticos*. handle.net/10045/53587. Doctoral Thesis. URI: http://hdl.

Seretan, Violeta, Pierrette Bouillon & Johanna Gerlach. 2014. A large-scale evaluation of pre-editing strategies for improving user-generated content translation. In *Proceedings of the 9th edition of the language resources and evaluation conference (LREC)*, 1793–1799. http://www.lrec-conf.org/proceedings/lrec2014/pdf/676_Paper.pdf.

Chapter 5

How to deal with errors in machine translation: Post-editing

Sharon O'Brien

Dublin City University

Machine Translation output can be incorrect, containing errors that need to be fixed, especially if the text is destined for publication and if it is important that it contains no errors. The task of identifying and fixing these errors is called *post-editing* (PE). In this chapter, I provide an overview of the PE process, drawing on both academic and industry sources. I explain how PE is generally divided into *light* and *full* PE, and describe standard guidelines for each type, homing in on issues that arise in the application of this classification. The chapter also surveys the various types of interface used in PE (including word processing and spreadsheet software, and professional computer-aided translation tools), and modes of interaction (traditional, adaptive or interactive). Finally, concepts and tools used by researchers into PE are described, and particular focus is put on the measurement of temporal, technical and cognitive effort.

1 Definition

Machine Translation (MT) is an imperfect technology. For one sentence it might produce an accurate and contextually acceptable translation, but the next sentence might have a serious error in meaning, an omission, an addition, or a stylistic problem. If MT is being used just to obtain the gist of the meaning from a text, there may be no need to fix such errors. However, if MT is being used to create a text for publication or widespread circulation within or outside an organisation, it is usually necessary to fix any errors in the text. The identification of such errors and their revision, or correction, is known as *post-editing*. The term was

Sharon O'Brien. 2022. How to deal with errors in machine translation: Post-editing. In Dorothy Kenny (ed.), *Machine translation for everyone: Empowering users in the age of artificial intelligence*, 105–120. Berlin: Language Science Press. DOI: 10.5281/zenodo.6759982 already used in the early stages of development of MT systems, when technology was somewhat slower, or certainly less instantaneous than it is now. A text would be sent electronically to the MT system, the system would translate, the text would be returned to the sender who would then edit it, post – or after – the automatic translation stage. The term has stuck, and is even used to describe contemporary processes in which error fixing happens at the same time as automatic translation (see §3.1).

Post-editing is a bilingual language processing task. It is typically, though not exclusively, undertaken by experienced professional translators. When a person is engaged in this task, they are usually referred to as a *post-editor*. However, the usefulness of this name is debatable, especially because the professional translator's typical work environment involves the use of a computer-aided translation tool that combines technologies such as translation memory, terminology management and machine translation (see Kenny 2022: §4 [this volume] and §3 below). Within this working environment, the translator might be editing a fuzzy match for one sentence, translating the next sentence, and post-editing the one that follows. Does the translator change from being a revisor, to a translator, to a post-editor for each of these sentences? Not really! Essentially, the task is still all about translation and revision. The main difference lies in the technological input or support the translator is using from one moment to the next.

When post-editing, the translator has to understand the source language sentence and the target language proposal from the MT system. They have to then identify any errors, devise a strategy for fixing them, and implement those revisions. Fundamentally, post-editing is a revision task.

MT systems can produce a variety of error types, ranging from grammatical errors, to syntactic errors, to unnecessary additions or omissions, to errors in lexical or terminological choice, errors in collocation or style. The type and number of errors that might exist in a text produced by an MT system will vary depending on many factors, such as the language pair and direction, the content type, and the data or techniques used to train the MT engine.

Here are just a few examples in English of some of these error types and their fixes.

(1) Grammatical error
  a. The cat is very protective of her kittens. She scratches anyone *which* tries to touch them.
  b. The cat is very protective of her kittens. She scratches anyone *who* tries to touch them.

(2) Lexical error

    a. The cat is very protective of her *pups*. She scratches anyone who tries to touch them.

    b. The cat is very protective of her *kittens*. She scratches anyone who tries to touch them.

(3) Syntactic error

    a. The new-born cygnets on the lake *swam*.

    b. The new-born cygnets *swam* on the lake.

(4) Collocation error

    a. The house had no *flowing water*.

    b. The house had no *running water*.

2 Levels of post-editing and guidelines

One of the main objectives of MT is to enable more information to be translated between more languages, but to achieve this more rapidly than is possible through translation unaided by MT and, indeed, at a lower cost. These objectives have led to a distinction between different levels of post-editing, mainly characterised as *light post-editing* or *full post-editing*.

Light post-editing is understood to mean that only essential fixes should be implemented and that this should be done rapidly. Full post-editing, on the other hand, means that all errors in the MT output should be fixed, and this is expected to take more time when compared with "light" post-editing. For both levels, it is generally expected that the translation can be produced faster than translation without computer-assisted translation tools. The International Standards Organisation (ISO) has produced a standard for post-editing known as "ISO 18857:2017" (ISO 2017). In this standard light post-editing is described as the "process of post-editing to obtain a merely comprehensible text without any attempt to produce a product comparable to a product obtained by human translation" (p.2). Full post-editing is defined as the "process of post-editing to obtain a product comparable to a product obtained by human translation" (ibid.).

These definitions are, however, conceptually problematic. In the first instance, it is difficult to articulate what exactly the differences are between the two, except in the very general way we have described them above. What, exactly, is an "essential" fix? This might differ from one organisation to the next, depending on requirements. What does "merely comprehensible" mean and how would that be measured? And can light post-editing really be done without *any attempt* to produce something comparable to human translation? Furthermore, it is unclear how much longer full post-editing would take compared with light post-editing. Such questions prompted the translation industry to describe these levels more formally. For example, the Translation Automation User Society (TAUS) created guidelines suggesting that full post-editing would include stylistic changes, whereas light post-editing would not.

The TAUS guidelines (TAUS 2010) for light and full post-editing are listed in Table 1, where comparable guidelines appear side by side, and an empty cell indicates that there is no comparable guideline in one set of guidelines:

According to the ISO18857 standard (p.6), the objectives of post-editing are to ensure:

- Comprehensibility of the post-edited output;

- Correspondence of source language content and target language content;

- Compliance with post-editing requirements and specifications defined by the TSP.

where "TSP" stands for "translation service provider" and is defined as a "language service provider that delivers translation services" (p.4).

These objectives can be attained by ensuring that the following criteria are met (p.6):

- Terminology/lexical consistency, as well as compliance with domain terminology;

- Use of standard syntax, spelling, punctuation, diacritics, special symbols and abbreviations and other orthographical conventions of the target language;

- Compliance with any applicable standards;

- Correct formatting;

- Suitability for the target audience and for the purpose of the target language content;

- Compliance with client-TSP agreements.

Table 1: The TAUS post-editing guidelines.

Light post-editing	Full post-editing
Aim for semantically correct translation.	Aim for grammatically, syntactically and semantically correct translation.
	Ensure that key terminology is correctly translated and that untranslated terms belong to the client's list of "Do Not Translate" terms.
Ensure that no information has been accidentally added or omitted.	Ensure that no information has been accidentally added or omitted.
Edit any offensive, inappropriate or culturally unacceptable content.	Edit any offensive, inappropriate or culturally unacceptable content.
Use as much of the raw MT output as possible.	Use as much of the raw MT output as possible.
Basic rules regarding spelling apply.	Apply basic rules regarding spelling, punctuation and hyphenation.
No need to implement corrections that are of a stylistic nature only.	
No need to restructure sentences solely to improve the natural flow of the text.	
	Ensure that formatting is correct.

There are overlaps between the two sets of guidelines, though they prioritise different aspects of the task. Taken together, they represent typical guidelines for post-editing. The TAUS guidelines encourage as much re-use of raw MT output as is practical, whereas the ISO guidelines focus more on agreements, standards and suitability for the target audience. The notion of reusing as much of the raw MT output as is possible is an essential aspect of the post-editing task. It is very easy for a translator to simply ignore the MT output, delete it and translate the source sentence directly. In fact, many translators are tempted to do this because they believe that they can produce a better translation and that it will take less time than post-editing. While the first belief was certainly true some time ago, the development of neural machine translation has, in general, increased the quality of MT to such an extent that raw output is now much more useful and usable. The idea that translation would take less time than post-editing is, on the other hand, open to debate. Studies have shown that post-editing can certainly be faster than translation, even if translators think that they are faster (e.g. Guerberof Arenas 2014). Being able to rapidly assess the output from an MT system, decide if it is usable, and what edits are required is something that can be honed with practice.

Levels of post-editing are conceptually linked with levels of quality, though as will be shown in the examples below this linkage is problematic. Light post-editing is seen to be linked with "good enough quality", or text that is "merely comprehensible", i.e. text that should be accurately translated, but that does not necessarily have to flow very naturally or be stylistically sophisticated. On the other hand, full post-editing is linked with "quality similar or equal to human translation". Here again, we run into some difficulty because the inherent assumption is that "human translation" is *always* of a high standard, something that is frankly not always the case.

To better understand the complex, and sometimes confusing, relationship between levels of post-editing and levels of quality, let us look at an example:

(5)   a.   In a new report on the quality of teaching practice, inspectors said pre-school teachers could be *training* to integrate languages such as French, German and Polish in early *learn* settings.

    b.   In a new report on the quality of teaching practice, inspectors said pre-school teachers could be *trained* to integrate languages such as French, German and Polish in early *learning* settings.

The two errors in (a) are quickly fixed to render sentence (b). On the one hand, we could say that we have edited (a) *lightly*; we implemented two rapid edits. However, if we were to follow the light post-editing guidelines, we probably would not implement any edits at all. Implementation of "full post-editing" guidelines would mean that the two errors must be fixed to produce a translation that is semantically, syntactically and grammatically correct. So, with these two rapid edits, have we engaged in light or full post-editing?

Let us take a look at another example.

(6)   a.   In addition, it *reiterates the instinct* of modern *language* into the primary school curriculum *as a fitting step*.

b. In addition, it says *re-instating* modern *languages* to the primary
    school curriculum *would be a timely move.*[1]

Sentence (a) is rather unclear and so significant editing is required to make it
at least semantically correct. Fundamentally, the level of editing depends on the
starting point (the quality of each sentence proposed by the MT system) and the
targeted quality. The post-editor will pivot between quick edits and more significant edits depending on each sentence and the ultimate quality objective. What
is most important here is that the final text has a coherent quality, regardless of
what the starting point is for each sentence, and that the quality meets with the
translation commissioner's and end users' expectations.

One final issue with the concepts of light and full post-editing is that professional translators generally do not want to agree to produce "merely comprehensible" quality, and no commissioner of translation is really willing to admit that
they opted *only* for a light edit.

It is important to know about these concepts and the guidelines that come with
them. However, as is hopefully evident, they are not without their challenges.

3 Post-editing interfaces

At a basic level, post-editing can be done in any text editor where the source text
is visible and the "raw" MT output can be revised. This could even be a spreadsheet, with the source text in one column and the MT output in an adjacent one.
These days, however, professional translation is typically done using computer-
aided translation (CAT) environments, especially translation memory (TM) tools.
As indicated by Kenny (2022: §4 [this volume]), translation memory is a database
that stores segments of texts that have been previously translated. A TM tool is
the software application that is used to access, edit and update the text in this
database. MT, as is evident from the other chapters in this book, is a different
type of technology, though the two are inevitably linked because contemporary
data-driven MT systems typically use the data stored in TMs as an important input for machine learning. Additionally, seeing as TM tools are so commonly used
by translators in their daily work, MT technology is now linked to, if not completely embedded in, TM tools such as Trados Studio, MQM, MateCat, to name
but a few. From a practical perspective, this means that post-editing is frequently
carried out in a TM editing environment.

---

[1]https://www.irishtimes.com/news/education/foreign-languages-could-be-taught-in-
preschool-and-primary-department-1.4270886

There are different ways in which MT can be embedded in a TM environment. For example, the MT system might be called on by the translator if there is no useful match offered from the TM. Alternatively, the translator could customise their TM tool settings to ensure that an MT suggestion is presented automatically when a specific set of conditions are met (for example, when no match is found in the TM).

It is generally accepted that, if the TM is well-maintained and kept up to date, an exact match from the TM database is more valuable to the translator than one from the MT system because the latter might contain errors whereas the former (ideally) should not. It used to also be assumed in industry circles that a "fuzzy match" from the TM of 75% similarity or higher was better than an MT suggestion, for the same reason. MT has, however, become more advanced recently and the suggestions may be very useful to a translator, possibly even more so than a 75% match from the TM. Thus, depending on the TM, the MT system, the language pair and the topic, a translator might customise their TM tool settings so that they see both TM matches and MT suggestions at the same time. In fact, they could even opt to have suggestions from multiple MT systems presented simultaneously. The translator can select the suggestion that they deem to be most useful and edit it as required.

The benefit of using TM/MT integration is that the translator gets more choice and assistance with the translation process. There are some challenges too. With this set up, a lot of information is presented to the translator, which means that they have to process all of this information (the TM match and its match value, the MT suggestion(s), possibly also terminology, and meta data such as who created the TM match and when etc. (see Teixeira & O'Brien 2017), while making a decision on which match to work with and what needs to be revised from a linguistic perspective. This can lead to a high cognitive demand and even overload, and possibly explains why some translators report that post-editing is more demanding and tiring than other forms of translation and revision.

A further challenge with this mixed interface is presented by the post-editing guidelines mentioned above. The translator needs to keep those guidelines in mind when they are working with an MT suggestion, but if they are working with a match from the TM, then they are dealing with a translation generated by a translator (as opposed to an MT system) and so are no longer officially "post-editing". This mix of post-editing, revising and translating potentially makes the task quite complex and we should also acknowledge that the task is typically done under pressure of time too!

3.1 Traditional, adaptive and interactive post-editing

Above, we have outlined the typical interface used for post-editing in a traditional translation setting using a TM tool, with the MT match appearing as a static suggestion that can be selected and edited or discarded in favour of a TM match or full translation of the source sentence. As with all technologies, new inventions appear and we now have some variations on the default, traditional set up. Two such innovations are adaptive MT and interactive MT.

Adaptive MT is a feature developed by TM/MT integrators whereby the MT system learns *in real time* from the edits implemented by the translator. This tackles one of the weaknesses of MT that translators previously found frustrating, i.e. they would fix an error generated by the MT system, but the system would not learn from their revisions. Therefore, if the same sentence occurred again later on, the post-editor had to fix the error again. The integration with translation memory tackled this problem to some extent: Once a sentence was fixed in a TM environment, it would be saved to the TM database. If the same sentence reoccurred later on, it would be presented to the translator as an exact match from the TM database. However, outside that TM environment with that exact database, the MT system would reproduce the error. With adaptive MT, the MT system "learns" from the edit and, theoretically, should adapt so that the same error is not produced by the MT system again. An example of a tool where this feature has been implemented is Trados Studio.

Interactive MT can be seen as a special form of adaptive MT. Whereas the default way of working with MT is as described above, where the MT system pre-translates the entire segment and it is then presented in full to the translator, interactive MT reacts to each decision the translator makes word by word, phrase by phrase. As the translator accepts or confirms a word, the MT system adjusts the output in real time. This is a considerably different way of interacting with MT output, but it is similar to the concept of predictive texting, to which many people have become accustomed. Lilt is an example of a tool where this is one of the primary features. In fact, Lilt is positioned explicitly as an adaptive *and* interactive interface.[2] (For other examples of interactive MT, see Torregrosa Rivero 2018.)

Interactive MT calls into question the term "post-editing". As explained earlier, this term came into use many decades ago when the editing was always done *after* the full text had been translated by the MT system and returned to the requester. With the interactive mode, the machine translation happens in real time, changing as the translator makes decisions in the current moment. As

---

[2]https://lilt.com, last accessed June 2022

a result, the prefix "post" seems irrelevant. "Interactive MT" is a more accurate term. As happens in many domains, the term "post-editing" is now well established so it may not disappear soon, but it will probably become defunct as time goes by. The task itself – interacting with and fixing MT output – is less likely to become defunct in the near future.

3.2 Research interfaces

Above I described the different mainstream interfaces used for post-editing, as well as the modes of interaction. There are many other interfaces one can use, but the features are essentially the same. As post-editing is a relatively new task for professional translators, there has been a significant amount of interest in it from a research perspective. Research has focused on the types of edits that are typically implemented, on measuring whether the task takes less time than translation, the quality produced, and, not least, on the cognitive processes involved.

To capture data on these topics, researchers have developed their own interfaces for post-editing. The main motivations for doing so are that commercial tools can be too expensive for research projects, their features are relatively sophisticated, sometimes actually acting as a hindrance to the research objectives, or they cannot be controlled enough for experimental research conditions. Examples of two research tools developed for post-editing experiments are Casmacat and Translog. Casmacat was developed as part of an EU-funded research project.[3] The aim of this project was to build the next generation translator's workbench using interactive and adaptive machine translation and to build models of the cognitive processes involved in interactive MT. Translog was initially developed for research into translation processes by the Copenhagen Business School. Translog II is a more recent version of the tool that enables research into translation and post-editing.[4] Both of these tools can be integrated with technologies that are very useful for research purposes, e.g. key logging, where the keyboard activity is recorded, and eye tracking, which records eye movements and cognitive load during the translation or post-editing process. The use of these tools has helped us better understand post-editing as a task. Nonetheless, while they are really useful for research purposes, they are considerably pared down in terms of features compared with standard commercial TM tools, and so can provide only limited understanding of the task as it is performed in real production environments.

---

[3]Co-funded by the European Union under the Seventh Framework Programme Project 287576 (ICT-2011.4.2) - http://www.casmacat.eu

[4]https://sites.google.com/site/centretranslationinnovation/translog-ii?authuser=0

4 Measuring post-editing effort

When technology advances, it moves from the lab to the public domain, where it is tested for usefulness. Initially, this can act as a disruptor – processes used and accepted for years are disturbed, which, in turn, understandably leads to questions, worry, or irritation. When we are used to doing a task one way, we find it difficult to quickly embrace a new way of doing it. Moreover, if the technology creates new problems for us, we are not likely to embrace it fully. This is the case with MT and post-editing for professional purposes. Consequently, there has been much interest in measuring the effort involved in post-editing to verify, or debunk, the claim that it is "faster" than translating without such automation.

A vast amount of research has been produced in the past fifteen years or so to investigate this question (Koponen 2016). There are too many studies to mention individually here. However, one of the seminal texts on the topic deserves mention because it set the standard for measuring post-editing effort. That text was written in German by Hans-Peter Krings, with the English translation appearing in 2001 (Krings 2001). Krings investigated the effort involved in post-editing compared with translation. He did so at a time when MT produced much lower quality output than it does nowadays and his experimental set-up was necessarily naïve, given the era in which it was conducted: the tasks were done on paper and he used a camera to record the process. What is most important about Krings' study is not his set up nor his findings, but that he argued for the measurement of effort across *three dimensions* – temporal, technical and cognitive.

All too often, measurement of PE effort focuses only on the temporal dimension, i.e. how long does the task take in comparison with another task. Time is, of course, one of the most important aspects, especially in a commercial environment. Time is relatively easy to measure too, so it tends to be the main focus when commercial organisations wish to measure PE effort.

Krings' work, however, demonstrates that the other two dimensions also need to be considered. Technical effort measures keyboard and mouse actions, i.e. how many words or parts of words are deleted, added, how many phrases are selected, cut and pasted to another location in the text, etc. Translog, mentioned above, is one tool that enables keyboard logging. As PE *is* textual revision, understanding the effort involved in the mechanical changes implemented is important. Not only that, but this kind of revision – which involves deletion, re-typing, copying and pasting – requires a lot of keyboard and mouse usage, which is physically tiring and can even lead to strain in the hands and wrists. On the other hand, if the MT output is relatively good, MT can reduce the amount of typing a translator has to do.

Apart from keyboard logging, technical effort is also measured using what is called *edit distance* metrics. Put simply, edit distance counts the minimum number of operations required to transform one string of text into another. An "operation" could be deletion of a word, insertion of a word, or movement of a word or phrase to another location. There are several metrics for measuring edit distance, each of which counts the operations slightly differently. One basic metric is called the *Levenshtein distance*. It counts the minimum number of character insertions, deletions or substitutions needed to change to transform one word, phrase or sentence into another.

For example: Take the word *drink* and the word *drunk*. How many characters have to change to transform one into the other? One: 'i' is substituted by 'u'. Let us make this a bit more complex: if we transform the phrase "He drinks" into "He is drinking", the Levenshtein distance is 6. (Insert 'i', 's' and one space character after 'He'; substitute 'i' for 's' at the end of 'drinks' and insert 'n' and 'g'.)[5] More sophisticated edit distance measures can be deployed and one that is often used to measure PE edit distance is called *TER*, or the *Translation Edit Rate* (Snover et al. 2006). This can be measured on a scale of 0–1 or 0% to 100%. The lower the score, the lower the PE effort. For example, a score of 30% means, approximately, that 30% of the raw MT output was edited to create the post-edited version of a text string. Challenges exist regarding how best to calculate edit distance and consequently there are several different approaches, with different metrics being proposed on a regular basis.

Temporal and technical effort are relatively easy to measure. Measuring the third dimension – cognitive effort – is much more complex. Cognitive effort refers to hidden cognitive processes such as reading, understanding, comparing source language meaning to that of the MT output, decision making, while taking into account the guidelines and expectations, and monitoring the text as it is revised. These processes take place in the brain and cannot be seen or measured directly. Nonetheless, cognitive effort is still an important aspect to consider. Post-editing is sometimes reported as being more demanding a task than translation without MT as an aid. This is probably due to the list of processes mentioned above and also to the fact that it is a relatively new task for some. Even if translators can produce text faster with MT, they may feel more tired than they would do if they were to produce the translation themselves. Working faster suits commercial production, but not if it results in translator burnout, and that is why cognitive demand is important to consider when measuring PE effort.

But how can we measure cognitive effort? In fact, this is a question for anyone who seeks to measure cognitive effort for any task. Sometimes the effort can be

---

[5]These alculations can be done online using, for example, https://planetcalc.com/1721/.

estimated by asking the person who performs the task to "think aloud" as they work. By doing this, they can highlight cognitive difficulties they encounter. Of course, thinking aloud as you work interferes with and slows down the task itself, so there are disadvantages to this technique. An alternative approach is to record the task on the computer screen as it unfolds, then to replay that as a video when the task is completed, and ask the task performer to retrospectively discuss the problems they encountered. This has the advantage of not slowing down the task itself, but it has the disadvantage that the person may not remember all of the issues they encountered. Finally, researchers have attempted to measure cognitive effort in post-editing using eye tracking, a technology that records where the eyes fall on the screen, as well as how long the eyes rest on parts of the text (called *fixation duration*), and even the *pupil dilation*, a measurement of pupil size. These are known to be good measures of cognitive effort. Yet, the challenges are obvious: you need expensive eye tracking technology, sophisticated knowledge in how to use it and interpret the data it produces, and you need to control the data collection environment so that users do not move their heads too much, or the light does not change substantially because this affects the pupil size, and so on. Since measuring cognitive effort is a considerable challenge, understandably few include it when they measure PE effort. Nonetheless, it is important to recognise cognitive effort as an essential component of the effort involved in post-editing.

There is a final note to add here on measuring PE effort. The amount of effort should indirectly tell us something about the quality of the output produced by a specific MT system, for a language pair and topic. Therefore, we can use PE effort as a form of MT quality evaluation. The lower the quality from the MT system, the more changes and time will be required. MT quality can be measured in other ways, by, for example, identifying, classifying and counting the number of errors produced. This is a useful form of MT quality evaluation but taking the PE effort into consideration is potentially even more informative because it reveals how easy or difficult it is to work with the MT output to produce a defined level of quality.

5 Post-editor profiles and training

What makes a good post-editor? And what kind of training should be provided? As MT has become more of a mainstream technology, these are two questions that have preoccupied those in the language industry as well as in academia (see, for example, Nitzke & Hansen-Schirra 2021).

Taking the first question, a common suggestion is that to be a good post-editor, one first has to be a good translator. Intuitively we know that some people are great translators but not great revisors and vice versa. By deduction then, some will be good post-editors and others not.

But what does it mean to be a good post-editor? This question has received some attention already. de Almeida & O'Brien (2010), for example, suggest that a good post-editor has:

1. The ability to identify issues in the raw MT output that need to be addressed and to fix them appropriately;

2. The ability to carry out the post-editing task with reasonable speed, so as to meet the expectations of daily productivity for this type of activity;

3. The ability to adhere to the guidelines, so as to minimise the number of "preferential" changes, or changes that are not strictly speaking necessary, and which are normally outside the scope of PE.

It could be argued that point (1) means that the post-editor must first have mastered translation skills. Points (2) and (3) suggest that a post-editor needs to be able to work quickly and to adhere to guidelines, resisting the temptation to over-edit. Ultimately, being a "good" post-editor is closely linked with an individual's attitude towards MT as a technology (see Guerberof Arenas 2013 for a deeper discussion). If a translator dislikes MT as a technology, he or she will possibly be tempted to delete or ignore every MT suggestion. Assuming this in turn leads to more time being required for the translation task, as well as a higher cost for the commissioner, then that person cannot be classified as a "good" post-editor, though, again, much depends on the context and the quality produced by the MT system in the first instance.

As for the second question, there has been a growing focus on training in the past decade. As MT was slowly integrated into other CAT tools and translation production processes, professional translators needed training in the form of continuous professional development, e.g. workshops dedicated to learning about MT and post-editing. Over time, MT and PE have been incorporated into translator training programmes in universities. There are many different approaches to this training. Some universities offer entire stand-alone courses on post-editing, some incorporate it into revision courses, and others weave it into translation technology courses (see O'Brien & Vázquez 2019).

A core focus of this training is ensuring that translation students understand the most recent approaches to MT, its strengths and its limitations, how to evaluate it and how to post-edit. Importantly, understanding when and how MT ought to be used has become central to training, both for translation students and for those who are not trained in translation (see Bowker & Ciro (2019) for a discussion of "MT literacy").

References

Bowker, Lynne & Jairo Buitrago Ciro. 2019. *Machine translation and global research.* Bingley: Emerald Publishing.

de Almeida, Gisele & Sharon O'Brien. 2010. Analysing post-editing performance. Correlations with years of translation experience. In *Eamt 2010. Proceedings of the 14th annual conference of the European Association for Machine Translation.* EAMT. http://www.mt-archive.info/10/EAMT-2010-Almeida.pdf.

Guerberof Arenas, Ana. 2013. What do professional translators think about post-editing? *Journal of Specialised Translation* 19. 75–95. https://www.jostrans.org/issue19/art_guerberof.php.

Guerberof Arenas, Ana. 2014. Correlations between productivity and quality when post-editing in a professional context. *Machine Translation* 28. 165–186.

ISO. 2017. *ISO 18857:2017. Translation services – post-editing of machine translation output: Requirements.* https://www.iso.org/standard/62970.html.

Kenny, Dorothy. 2022. Human and machine translation. In Dorothy Kenny (ed.), *Machine translation for everyone: Empowering users in the age of artificial intelligence,* 23–49. Berlin: Language Science Press. DOI: 10.5281/zenodo.6759976.

Koponen, Maarit. 2016. Is machine translation post-editing worth the effort? A survey of research into post-editing and effort. *The Journal of Specialised Translation* 25. 131–148. https://www.jostrans.org/issue25/art_koponen.pdf.

Krings, Hans P. 2001. *Repairing texts: empirical investigations of machine translation post-editing processes.* Ohio: Kent State University Press.

Nitzke, Jean & Silvia Hansen-Schirra. 2021. *A short guide to post-editing.* (Translation and Multilingual Natural Language Processing 16). Berlin: Language Science Press. DOI: 10.5281/zenodo.5646896.

O'Brien, Sharon & Silvia Rodríguez Vázquez. 2019. Translation and technology. In Sara Laviosa & Maria González-Davies (eds.), *Routledge handbook of translation and education,* 264–277. London: Routledge.

Snover, Matthew, Bonnie Dorr, Rich Schwartz, Linnea Micciulla & John Makhoul. 2006. A study of translation edit rate with targeted human annotation. In *Proceedings of the 7th conference of the Association for Machine Translation in the Americas: Technical papers,* 223–231. Cambridge, Massachusetts: Association for Machine Translation in the Americas. https://aclanthology.org/2006.amta-papers.25/.

TAUS. 2010. *MT post-editing guidelines.* https : / / www . taus . net / academy / best - practices / postedit - best - practices / machine - translation - post - editing - guidelines.

Teixeira, Carlos S. C. & Sharon O'Brien. 2017. Investigating the cognitive ergonomic aspects of translation tools in a workplace setting. *Translation Spaces* 6(1). 79–103.

Torregrosa Rivero, Daniel. 2018. *Black-box interactive translation prediction.* PhD Thesis. Alicante: University of Alicante. https://rua.ua.es/dspace/bitstream/ 10045/77110/1/thesis_daniel_torregrosa_rivero.pdf.

Chapter 6

Ethics and machine translation

Joss Moorkens

Dublin City University

Neural machine translation (MT) can facilitate communication in a way that surpasses previous MT paradigms, but there are also consequences of its use. As with the development of any technology, MT is not ethically neutral, but rather reflects the values of those behind its development. In this chapter, we consider the ethical issues around MT, beginning with data gathering and reuse and looking at how MT fits with the values and codes of the translator. If machines and systems reflect value systems, can they be explicitly "good" and remove bias from their output? What is the contribution of MT to discussions of sustainability and diversity? Rather than promoting an approach that involves following a set of instructions to implement a technology unthinkingly, this chapter highlights the importance of a conscious decision-making process when designing a data-driven MT workflow.

1 What do we mean by ethics?

The field of Ethics examines morality, good and evil, right and wrong, and addresses questions about how best to live. The earliest surviving texts on this topic originated in Egypt, Babylonia, and India. Greek philosophers such as Socrates introduced the notion of the "good life", one that is worthy and admirable. Aristotle made this a little more concrete by identifying a set of virtues that, when practised, would allow human beings to flourish. These virtues are still abstract, and are not always helpful when deciding whether an action is right or wrong. Subsequently, philosophers and ethicists have suggested ways to decide on a right or moral course of action, based, for example, on the probability of providing the best result for the majority, or by only acting on good or pure motives.

A problem is that what is well-motivated or produces the happiest result for one group may not necessarily produce an equally positive result for another.

Joss Moorkens. 2022. Ethics and machine translation. In Dorothy Kenny (ed.), *Machine translation for everyone: Empowering users in the age of artificial intelligence*, 121–140. Berlin: Language Science Press. DOI: 10.5281/zenodo.6759984

There is a tension between the idea that an action can be universally good and moral, such as upholding justice or truthfulness, and the position that values may differ depending on the person or group under examination. There have been many suggestions for ways of untangling whether an action is ethical or unethical based on agency, relationships, or a surrounding narrative. This is where theoretical ethics moves into applied ethics, in trying to guide how we should act in a given situation.

Applied ethics in a working situation will often involve a set of codes or standards to guide professional behaviour. If these codes are too restrictive, they may hamper potential progress or societal benefits. Rigid codes could also cause difficulties as ethical decisions are rarely binary and choices may be governed by the unique scenario and pressures brought to bear on the person making that choice. For this reason, different fields of applied ethics have sprung up to consider common problems and dilemmas within their particular context. This chapter will draw on the fields most relevant to machine translation (MT) including computer and information ethics and data ethics when discussing the ethical use of MT by humans in system development. §3 on the ethical use of MT in professional workflows will draw on business ethics and the growing literature on translation ethics. §4 on computers as ethical agents will draw on machine ethics and computer and information ethics. The final sections will draw on more recent diverse work on ethics and artificial intelligence when looking at sustainability and diversity.

Ethics is a growing area of interest in technology in general, as technology becomes an increasingly integral part of all of our lives and many regions move towards ubiquitous computing. We need to be aware of the impact of the choices we make when we design, implement, or use technology. There is an assumption often expressed that technology is ethically neutral and that bias may be introduced only in our use of that technology. However, the consensus among ethicists and philosophers of science is that technology is not ethically neutral, but rather reflects the values of the designer. These values govern the problem addressed by the technology, the decision to create the technology, the method of implementation, its intended users, the references or training data used, the processing of that data, the location and security of data storage, and the limits to access to the technology based perhaps on cost or geographical location.

The speed and scale of technological development means that regulation is inevitably a step or two behind and we are thus reliant on ethical behaviour on the part of engineers and developers. We rely, to a greater or lesser extent, on large technology companies with political power and wealth to act in our collective best interests, but a series of reports and revelations in recent years have demonstrated that our confidence in these companies is sometimes misplaced. While technology opens up access to new avenues and benefits, it also exposes the public to risk. By discussing some of the choices and risks inherent in the development and use of MT systems in this chapter, I hope to guide users in making informed and ethical decisions. The focus throughout is mostly (but not entirely) on MT for dissemination, where MT output is not the final step in production.

2 The ethical use of MT by humans in MT system development

2.1 Case studies of data use

This section looks at legal and ethical issues regarding the use of translation data in MT system development. As Pérez-Ortiz et al. (2022 [this volume]) attest, data-driven MT and particularly neural MT (NMT) requires a lot of data for training.[1] While it may be perfectly legal to reuse translation data for training MT systems, is it ethical? It may be helpful to introduce some of the issues to be discussed in this section by considering the following examples.

Translator A has freely signed a contract with their regular employer to carry out a translation on a freelance basis using a proprietary web-based platform, giving explicit permission for their translation data to be reused for MT training. The employer trains MT systems using the data from Translator A and others. In time, NMT quality improves for Translator A's language pair to the extent that the company moves its translation work to post-editing and imposes a unilateral 30% discount on their per-word payment rate. This discount is applied on the basis that productivity has generally improved by roughly 30%, visible to the company from the translation activity data gathered via the translation platform. In order to raise revenue, the company decides to sell MT services externally. This includes some work for an arms manufacturer.

Translator B is opposed to MT as a matter of principle. B accepts work for a company that expects translators to submit their translation memory with translated target texts, which they will repurpose for future human translation. Translator B is not aware that the work has been automatically assigned by an automated project management system, but there is no translation brief and no direct communication with the company. Translator B is also not aware that the company will soon be acquired by a large conglomerate who will use all available

---

[1]*Data* refers to recorded information in any form, usually stored digitally, and when data are available in huge volumes and processed at scale, we talk of *big data*.

data for MT training and offer it for sale. The data should have all personal information removed before being shared (see §2.5), but this information is retained by accident when the data are uploaded to one purchaser. The company tries to keep this quiet so as to avoid liability.

What ethical issues can you identify in these two scenarios? What would change if the employers or translators made different ethical decisions? In the following subsections, we look at data ownership, permissions, distribution, privacy, and legal frameworks for data sharing. These subsections will, it is hoped, help guide your thinking about the above questions.

2.2 Data ownership

The commonly-used metaphor of data as oil suggests that big data is naturally occurring, whereas in reality it was originally created by humans. The exponential growth in data produced in recent years has meant that there is now more data available for MT training and more demand for translation than ever before, far more than is possible for human translators to produce. MT training data are usually stored in the form of parallel or aligned bilingual segments of text that have been translated by humans, often in translation memories (although MT output is also sometimes used for MT training). The source of this translation data is likely to be shared in public repositories, such as the European Commission's Directorate-General for Translation data, which can be "re-used and disseminated, free of charge... both for commercial and non-commercial purposes" (Steinberger et al. 2012: 457), privately held repositories of translation data, or parallel data crawled from the web.

The Berne Convention, first enacted in 1886, forms the legal basis of copyright for translations, considering them to be derivative works that "shall be protected as original works without prejudice to the copyright in the original work" (Article 2, World Intellectual Property Organization 1979). The convention grants the author of an original work the exclusive right to authorize a translation, although it fails to define "original work" or "originality", allowing for different interpretations in different jurisdictions. Troussel & Debussche (2014) believe that an argument could be made for originality in a creative translation, although this has yet to be tested in courts. The authors further believe that ownership rights to a translation memory database may be asserted where there has been "a substantial investment in either the obtaining, verification or presentation of the contents", according to the European Database Directive (European Parliament 1996: Article 7). In practice, translation memories are usually sent to the client, whether or not there is a contractual agreement in place for waiving any claim of ownership on the part of the translator.

At scale, big translation data has become a valuable resource for MT and machine learning system training (Moorkens & Lewis 2019a). This does not mean that translators receive any secondary payment however, and the granular reuse in MT training means that the source of training data is usually not identifiable. This is also true of data gathered by webcrawling for parallel texts. Translators A and B in our case study probably have little option other than to hand over their translation data and to accept the consequences, especially considering that most translators work on a freelance basis, and thus have limited scope for argument with their employers. It is reasonable to argue that a more equitable system of data ownership would contribute to the sustainability of the translation industry (see also §5).

2.3 Permission to use data

In some jurisdictions, it is considered that the employer who pays for a translation is the rightful owner, whereas in others, ownership may be transferred, granting permission for reuse. We might assume that there is "a degree of collegiality at play among those translators who favour resource sharing" with fellow translators, even with those who they do not know (Moorkens & Lewis 2019b: 8). However, the acceptance of this reuse for human translation may be eroded when translation data are instead used for training MT systems, especially among translators who believe that progress of MT technology is not in their best interests. Some translation contracts may explicitly state that translation data will be reused within human or machine translation workflows, but it is rare for translators to control how their work is reused. There is also no evidence of permission being sought or granted for reuse of webcrawled data.

This means that Translators A and B will contribute towards future projects, the purpose and end use of which will be opaque to them. Translator A may be ethically opposed to working for the arms manufacturing company, but will nonetheless be an unknowing participant in their work. This opacity is a problem faced more generally by those whose data are collected and reused, along with those who contribute work towards large technology projects without the opportunity to ask the questions "What is the final application and use of the products of my work?" and "Am I content or ashamed to have contributed to this use?" (see Moorkens 2020, Weizenbaum 1986).

When data are created during translation, depending on the format for recording and exchange, a number of attributes are recorded. These usually include a name or ID for the translator (see §2.5), the date and time of creation, language codes, software used, and a project ID. This information is useful for deciding when and where to reuse the data based on the translator, the project, or the creation date. Translator activity data, including more detailed timings, editing actions, and records of individual keystrokes may also be recorded, particularly when a proprietary web-based platform is used, as in Translator A's project. Such data can be useful for monitoring translators' work, but is commonly removed for MT training so that only parallel sentence pairs are used. Once any possible identifying metadata (data about data) are removed, preferences for future use or reuse cannot be recorded and individual contributions cannot be measured, even if there is a retrospective change to agreements that means that contributions should earn a royalty. On the other hand, this will improve anonymization of translation data, which is important if the data are to be shared or exchanged.

2.4 Data distribution

In the early days of translation memory sharing, Topping (2000) wrote that, of individual translators, localization agencies and localization customers, only translators felt that it was ethical to share memories. This view seems quaint when we have companies in 2021 whose business model is shaped around amassing and reselling data for MT and other machine learning purposes.[2] This business model works, as the amount of training data and the level of care in curation of this data will make an impact on both the quality and value of an NMT system.

As mentioned in §2.2, certain datasets can be made freely available and distributed through projects such as Opus, the open parallel corpus (http://opus. nlpl.eu, Tiedemann 2012), due to their licensing agreements or because they are covered by the European Union (EU) directive (2003/98/EC) on the re-use of public sector information. This does not necessarily mean that translators have expressly given permission for all possible forms of reuse, but they are aware that the data will be shared with the general public.

Data may otherwise be distributed on the basis of agreements between companies, or due to one company being acquired by another, which is common within the language service industry (Moorkens 2020). It may be bought and sold or donated for research or philanthropic purposes, all without the necessity for approval from the data creator. This is perfectly legal as long as the data cannot be classed as personal data, in which case restrictions apply.

---

[2]Please see the introduction to this volume for more on machine learning. For the purposes of this chapter, we understand machine learning as a use of computers to achieve an end by inference from big data rather than from input of an explicit command.

2.5 Privacy, personal data

If data can render an individual identifiable, it can be considered personal data. This includes translation memories with a named or coded (pseudonymized) creator. Within the EU, the General Data Protection Regulation (GDPR)[3] has restricted the sharing and reuse of personal data since 2018, providing guidelines for national legislation that would impose heavy fines in the case of a data breach. This has had the effect of increasing cybersecurity and limiting the use of servers in non-EU locations. Any secondary use of personal data must be covered by the permissions given for the original use, with some exceptions for research purposes. There are a number of other national regulations outside of the EU that govern the use of personal data.

Companies should report any data breach, but there have been many media reports of breaches being covered up. One reason to do so is to avoid GDPR fines (of up to €20 million or 4% of annual turnover, whichever is the greater, according to Article 83 of the Regulation), but companies may also wish to avoid negative publicity, loss of consumer confidence, and loss of stock market value, in the case of publicly-traded companies. Ideally, transparency would lead to greater public trust in an organization, but the problem of data security in large organizations is not always well understood, with their sheer size presenting a data protection difficulty. What is more, not all data breaches are equal, as they can be due to "ethical hackers" who are employed by the organization to identify cybersecurity vulnerabilities or who identify vulnerabilities to protect the public, or malicious hackers who intend to access data for their own gain.

Once personal attributes are removed and data are anonymized, personal data becomes (just) data, and shareable.[4] Of course, even without the metadata, some data may be recognizable if its content or style is identifiable or if biometric data could be used to link to an individual. If data are shared or pooled, data from an individual or group may be used to make inferences, for example about attributes that are carefully protected by the GDPR such as race or sexuality. As these inferences are made on the basis of combining data rather than being explicitly contained in any single data set, they are not usually covered by the GDPR (Wachter & Mittelstadt 2019). This presents a risk to "group privacy", where a group may be discriminated against due to the content of data that does not identify any individual (Floridi & Taddeo 2016).

---

[3]EU Regulation 2016/679, available from https://eur-lex.europa.eu/legal-content/EN/TXT/HTML/?uri=CELEX:32016R0679&from=EN

[4]There are a number of ongoing efforts to automate anonymization for translation data at the time of writing, but this is difficult to do reliably.

Translators A and B, for example, could have their translation data aggregated with other personal data, allowing a third party to make inferences about them individually or as members of a group. The use of web-based platforms for translation is increasingly common, giving translators less control of their translation data and allowing surveillance of work activities. If personal circumstances lead to a temporary downturn in productivity or translation quality as gauged via translator activity data gleaned from the work platform, that could negatively affect their prospects for future employment. If identifiable translation activity data for an individual that encodes this downturn is shared outside of a single organization, that could have far-reaching consequences for that individual. This does not necessarily mean that it is unethical to monitor quality or productivity. An agency or company needs to be able to stand over their translations. However, by automating employment decisions or communication, as is the case with project management in the example of Translator B, a company will leave the translator with no opportunity to explain translation choices or to build a long-term relationship based on trust. There is no guarantee of ethical behaviour on the part of the translator or user of a platform at the best of times, but when relationships are purely transactional, research has shown that trust and the assumption of good faith on both sides are particularly undermined, with knock-on effects on satisfaction and performance (Whipple & Nyaga 2010).

2.6 Ethics in MT evaluation

Rossi & Carré (2022 [this volume]) look at methods of human and automatic MT evaluation. There are a number of ethical issues related to MT evaluation that are worth raising here. Most MT systems' output is evaluated automatically during training and again afterwards for a quick, easy, and cost-effective measure of quality. In competitive shared tasks, where development teams pit their systems against one another, either automatic or crowd evaluation tends to be used. Based on these evaluations, output may be considered to have reached parity with human translation quality if a segment-level crowd rating or automatic evaluation achieves the same score as a "reference" human-translated target text. If the evaluation score for MT surpasses that of the human reference, it is considered "super-human" output.

This language is problematic, especially when disseminated more widely in research publications and marketing materials, which in turn may be reported in news media, giving the impression that MT produces perfect quality output without risk and that human translators are no longer necessary. However, automatic evaluation metrics tend to show little correlation with human judgment and there are several problems with crowd evaluation, in which anonymous and presumably untrained internet users rank or rate segments of sequential translated material. Freitag et al. (2021) found that expert (professional translator) evaluators produced markedly different results to crowd workers when carrying out a detailed error analysis with access to full source and target documents, and demonstrated a clear preference for human rather than MT output. Additionally, there are issues with crowd work related to poor rates of pay, labour conditions, opaque user rating systems, and use of humans (crowd workers) as research participants without oversight or ethical review. Nonetheless, published results based on automatic evaluation and crowd work are almost always reported cursorily, devaluing human translation and creating an unrealistic and uncritical perception of MT among the general public, including translation clients. This perception increases the likelihood of MT being introduced into professional workflows.

3 The ethical use of MT in professional workflows

3.1 Translation stakeholders

The case studies presented in §2.1 prompt us to think not just about ethics and MT system development, but also about the ethical use of MT in professional workflows. For example, the company who engages Translator A makes a unilateral decision to move translation production to post-editing, when ideally the introduction of MT into a workflow would be based on consultation and agreed by all stakeholders. The stakeholders in the use cases in §2.1 are the translation agency or language service provider, comprising a number of internal roles, and the freelance translators. In addition, the translation client should be aware that MT will be used as part of the translation process and cognizant of the attendant benefits and risks (see §3.2). Almost all research on post-editing productivity has shown a boost in output when compared with translation from scratch or using translation memory. However, the orthodoxy is that the use of translation automation should relate to the shelf-life and level of risk attached to the translated text, and the client relies on translation agency expertise in choosing an appropriate and cost-effective workflow. The end user relies on the client to provide them with a text that does not expose them to unexpected risk. In addition, Pym (2012) suggests that, when even a low-risk target text is made less comprehensible by poor quality MT, the translation may conform to the needs of the client (who reduces costs by applying light or full post-editing) but will require extra effort on the part of the end reader.

Translation software developers are also important stakeholders in the use of MT in workflows, and the values and related design decisions mentioned for technology developers in §1 also apply to them. A translation tool in use can re-shape activities and their meaning. Interaction with MT may be via interactive MT, where MT is used for autosuggest and edited dynamically, or post-edited, appearing as an extra translation suggestion or automatically propagated within the target text window. A tool can focus on usability, for example incorporating familiar keyboard shortcuts, providing an uncluttered interface, and maximiz-ing customizability. Translation activity data (see §2.3), if collected, can be made transparent to users so that they can see what is being collected and use it them-selves if they wish. Alternatively, translators could work within a disempowering platform, accepting jobs as soon as they appear, with no visibility of data gather-ing and a very limited user interface, and have their performance rated with no option for feedback or discussion.

Translators have the option to accept or not accept work offered to them based on the text domain and working conditions. For those who are not aware of the variable ways that MT may be used within professional workflows, the decision to accept or not accept work may be difficult, particularly if the agency has not been transparent. It is also important that translators are transparent in their use of tools, particularly MT, so that agreed confidentiality arrangements are not breached, and risk is not introduced for other stakeholders (or themselves, as may be seen in §3.2) without their knowledge. For translators, the use of a *code of ethics*, a set of rules to guide ethical behaviour, falls under the rubric of deontolog-ical ethics. While such codes are associated with a narrow interpretation of the role of ethics in translation, they are nonetheless useful for decision-making.[5] As with many other professional organizations, translators' associations often pro-vide such a code to encourage professional conduct, impartiality, honesty, and respect for confidential material. These codes also promote trust on the part of current and potential clients. At the time of writing, a review of many of these codes found no explicit mention of MT, even though (as we have just seen) the decision as to whether or not to make use of MT in a translation project may be an ethical one. Chesterman (2001), who has written widely about ethics and trust in translation, suggests a general ethics of service, focusing on loyalty to the terms and quality requirements of the client, to the source text and its author(s), and to the target text reader.

The use of MT in translation production does not necessarily entail a loss of quality, and the cost and effort of human translation is not appropriate for all

---

[5]Lambert (2018) and others propose that the assumption of neutrality in translation, central to many Codes of Ethics, is just as flawed as it is for technology.

types of texts, particularly those with a short shelf-life that present little risk. However, for critical texts in which a mistranslation introduces risk, the use of MT must be considered carefully and subject to review. There is some evidence that certain project managers do not want to know or prefer to turn a blind eye when their translators use MT (Sakamoto 2019), but there may be good reasons for translation clients to be aware of MT use and to stipulate in contracts whether or not it may be used.

3.2 Risk and liability

Translation contracts may attribute ownership of translation data or give permission for retention of a translation memory to the translator or client, as described in §2.2., Canfora & Ottmann (2020) introduce two other contractual areas relevant to the use of MT: liability and confidentiality.

Translators may be found to be in breach of contract due to negligence or failing in their duty of care to a client. Liability can only refer to human behaviour, which means that a person must bear responsibility for an injury or loss related to an error introduced by MT in a translation process. Liability aside, the fact that MT might introduce a risk to end users is an ethical problem. Raw MT should never be used for safety-critical content. Current translation and post-editing standards do not mention liability or risks to end users.

The ISO translation standard does, however, stress the importance of "safe and confidential handling [...] of all relevant data and documents" (ISO 2015, 3.2.a). Users of free online MT systems grant service providers the right to use the data entered for online translation, and there have been instances where confidential and sensitive material has been made available through unthinking use of free online MT. This cybersecurity risk introduced by such MT systems is why Canfora & Ottmann (2020) feel that subscription MT services that do not retain data are a better option, and ideally recommend that companies use closed platforms where server architectures are not open to the public – or choose not to outsource translation work at all in order to protect confidentiality. Freelance translators, for their part, might object to the loss of control over translation data and translator activity data that a closed platform entails, as discussed in Sections 2 and 3.1.

The ISO standard for MT post-editing (ISO 2017) makes no mention of confidentiality or risks to data security, which is rather surprising considering that the process necessarily entails the use of MT, introducing the associated risks. Trust is a key part of risk reduction, as standards, guidelines, and contracts are only of value if the translator feels that they are in a trust partnership, without which they may rationalize unethical behaviour (see, for example, Abdallah 2010).

Aside from concerns about risk, translators and users may not wish to use MT due to the processes described in §2 or due to the impact of artificial intelligence (AI) on the world of work and sustainability. The following section examines the latter point with respect to NMT.

4 Sustainability

4.1 Payment, conditions, job satisfaction among translators/post-editors

Translation is a highly skilled task, but portions of the workflow have been automated (to an extent) in the examples of Translators A and B, with automatic job assignment, the imposition of post-editing, and the repurposing of translation data for tasks that the translators may not expect. There is growing consensus that AI will have a major impact on work in many areas previously considered to be immune from automation. While this might not directly cause higher unemployment rates, the changes could affect economic returns, work organization, and skills management in ways that are difficult to predict. These are considerations for the future in many industries, but in translation the impacts are well underway for a couple of reasons. Firstly, MT post-editing has been the fastest-growing area of the translation market since 2010 or so, predating the shift from statistical to neural MT. Stockpiling of translation data has been commonplace since the advent of translation memory tools in the early 1990s, although the collection of translation activity data for monitoring and automation is relatively recent. Secondly, the largely freelance workforce means that translators have flexibility and autonomy, but work on a project-by-project timeframe. This has created a disparity of power, whereby translators have little say in processes and conditions that can be changed unilaterally by agencies and employers from one project to the next. The effect of the disparity of power is apparent from the discussions regarding data in §2. As the pace of mergers and acquisitions has increased, creating large publicly-traded translation conglomerates, the disconnect has grown between those making decisions on business operations and freelance workers doing translation, post-editing, revision, annotation, review, subtitling, or another of the vast and growing array of roles that engage directly with texts. Suggestions from the industry to automate project management and to use blockchain to attribute authorship or contribution are not likely to improve this situation. More generally, the translation industry has not historically shown strong leadership on ethics and sustainability, as discussed by Moorkens & Rocchi (2021).

The early view of translation technology, as expressed by Kay in 1980, was that the translator should remain in control with technology assisting with work that is mechanical and routine, and possibly boring (Kay 1980). What we have seen instead for many translators is that their work has gradually been circumscribed. Some translators have seen their work reduced to quality checks, annotation, or the correction of repetitive errors in mixed-quality MT output. In the latter case, the MT output may even have been decomposed to individual sentences that lack any accompanying context, with some automatically passed and others marked for review.

Some translators enjoy post-editing and, even with discounts applied (as in the case in the first case study in §2), find the work worthwhile and lucrative. However, there is a balance to be struck between short-term efficiency and long-term gains for all stakeholders in a technologized translation process.

Workers find satisfaction in doing work that has meaning, in mastering their task, and in working with supportive colleagues. They are motivated by a sense of achievement and recognition for that achievement. If this is not a consideration in translation production, better workers will leave and there will be a shortage of skilled translators and/or post-editors. Such a shortage would affect reliable access to multilingual information and the gathering of high-quality bilingual data on which MT training relies. Docherty et al. (2008: 4) consider that a sustainable work system must satisfy the needs of many rather than few stakeholders, and that instead of focusing exclusively on "short-term, static efficiencies such as productivity and profitability; we must also focus on long-term, dynamic efficiencies such as learning and innovation". UN Sustainable Development Goal (SDG) 8 is to provide decent work and economic growth, but environmental sustainability, as addressed by SDGs 13 and 15, is also relevant to MT.

4.2 Environmental concerns

It might reasonably be argued that there is a contradiction between setting a goal for economic growth and for environmental sustainability. Cronin (2017) makes this point particularly about the growth dependency of the localization industry. The ICT industry, on which MT relies, requires the mining of rare metals and has a reputation for poor recycling and polluting. Neural MT is particularly resource intensive, requiring powerful GPUs (Graphical Processing Units) for training and large amounts of power. Strubell et al. (2019) estimate that training for one large transformer neural network model will produce almost five times the CO2 output of a car (including fuel) during its full lifetime.[6] However, most training instances are far less resource-intensive than the one reported in this paper. Furthermore, while hardware becomes more powerful and costly to engineer and produce, optimization of power consumption and the potential to run massive amounts of parallel processes mean that the power required for training is dropping. Nonetheless, it remains the case that training an NMT system is costly and requires a good deal of power. How that impinges on the environment will depend on the source of that power. There is currently no agreed benchmark for power consumption when publishing details of MT systems, although some have been proposed in the context of suggestions for sustainable AI development. The point made strongly by Van Wynsberghe (2021) is that without a focus on sustainability in the development and deployment of AI (and, by extension, NMT), AI development itself will not be sustainable.

5 Diversity

5.1 Among developers and users

The cost and power requirements are a huge barrier to entry into NMT development. The data requirements meant that early systems had to use publicly available data (see §2), usually creating systems for major European languages. It comes as no surprise then, that initial published work on NMT was conducted mostly by well-resourced academic research groups in North America and Europe. This has changed somewhat for two main reasons. Firstly, large technology companies have thrown their weight behind research efforts in NMT, building very well-resourced teams that lead the way in optimizing MT systems between major languages. This means that many academic research groups struggle to compete in major European languages and have moved to the more "niche" area of low-resource and minority languages. Secondly, the ability to create *synthetic* parallel data by machine-translating monolingual data from the intended target language into the intended source language[7] has led to a jump in quality for under-resourced language pairs. Thus the Fifth Conference on Machine Translation (WMT20) includes translation in Inuktitut and Tamil to and from English. However, another way to improve quality for low-resource languages is to build large multilingual systems, which are usually the preserve of the large commercial teams.

---

[6]We note also that only the largest companies can afford the costs of training such large-scale models.

[7]MT researchers call this process "back-translation". It is not to be confused with "back-translation" used as a glossing technique in standard translation studies sources such as Baker (2018).

There has been no survey of the diversity of MT research teams. A search of papers will find a reasonable amount of research published on MT using Simplified Chinese, Bengali, and Hindi – languages with huge numbers of speakers, but ones that are non-European and, in the cases of Bengali and Hindi, historically under-resourced. It is probably less likely that a great deal of diversity will be found among the leaders of these research teams and those who set the research agenda. In discussions of bias outside of MT, such a lack of diversity has been highlighted as a problem that has contributed to a number of well-publicized errors and blind spots in systems that use machine learning, such as facial recognition tools intended to identify likely criminals that pick out disproportionately high numbers of ethnic minorities.

In their article on the societal impact of MT, Vieira et al. (2020: 13) find that inappropriate use of MT can cause harm to vulnerable people in medical and legal use cases reviewed. They find that it can exacerbate inequality, given the "disproportionate availability of data and resources for a relatively small number of the world's languages", combined with a lack of MT literacy among those deploying MT. On the other hand, there is also a benefit in democratizing communication, as more and more under-resourced languages are being catered for in free online MT systems. At the time of writing, Google Translate covers 109 languages, including such under-resourced examples as Chichewa, Scots Gaelic, Uyghur, and Tatar.

5.2 As reflected in MT outputs

In 2016, Jones calculated that, of over 6,000 non-endangered languages, only 1% were catered for by any sort of MT. This situation has improved a little due to the research efforts mentioned in §5.1, and as evinced by the growing number of languages covered by Baidu and Google. However, this takes place in a world where information tends to flow from well- to poorly-resourced languages. Because MT has been shown to exert source language interference to a greater degree than human translation (see Toral 2019), the worry is that poorly-resourced languages will be impoverished in the long run.

This could be the case for all machine-translated languages, especially if a shortage of new human-translated data means that MT systems struggle to keep up with contemporary language. Vanmassenhove et al. (2019) illustrate how lexical diversity is lost when NMT engines are trained up to the point of so-called convergence,[8] suggesting that if training was stopped at an earlier juncture, the NMT output produced would be less standardized and more lexically diverse.

---

[8] The point at which iterative NMT system training is stopped, as automatic evaluation scores show no improvement in output quality. See §7.2.

Vanmassenhove (2019) shows that this standardization of output presents an algorithmic bias that exacerbates existing gender bias in training data, whereby a noun, or other form, is most commonly associated with one or other gender (in binary gender systems), and the less common gender is standardized out of the output data. This can result in output that emphasizes societal bias, with genders assigned inconsistently, even within a single segment. The following section reflects on contemporary efforts to neutralize biased output and the broader role of computers as implicit ethical agents.

6 Computers as ethical agents

Mainstream discussions of ethics in AI are concerned with safety and expanding machine autonomy and the application of the technology to a greater number of tasks. Machine ethics, meanwhile, is distinguished by the fact that it sees "the machine" as a subject with *agency* (that is, a willingness and ability to act) rather than as an object. A small but growing body of research in MT is concerned with bias (see §5.2) and risk, expanding discussions to include the values inherent in MT and AI more generally (see §5.1). This leads to the notion of computers as implicit ethical agents, whereby ethical decisions are implicit in their design. While efforts are being made in this regard, we regularly see biased or discriminatory output shared online from scenarios that were not easily predictable for developers. The stories of unintended consequences of technology, particularly AI, when intelligence appears to be demonstrated by machines, have sparked a series of books and articles that demonstrate unethical uses of that technology.

The problematic aspect of the technology may involve data gathering, the algorithm used to inductively extract patterns from the data, or the nature of the data itself. The consequences of technology may also be intended, whereby the *affordances* of the technology, i.e. the uses and interactions suggested by the tool, nudge the user towards acting in a way that has negative repercussions for them or for others.

The research focus in the small amount of research on bias in NMT has been exclusively on gender bias rather than on other attributes such as race or sexuality, and a number of solutions have been proposed to "de-bias" the MT output. Suggestions for the correct use of gender and the removal of gender bias in NMT output have included the use of gender tags, similar to those that may be used for politeness and register; de-biasing word embeddings; and treating gender bias similarly to domain adaptation for NMT, using transfer learning on a small gender-balanced dataset (Tomalin et al. 2021). In 2020, Google rolled out a system whereby, given certain languages, for every male-gendered output, an almost identical female-gendered output (and vice versa) is created. The user can then evaluate the different options and choose which one to use. This, of course, assumes a binary view of gender, but has improved the quality of Google's gender-specific translations overall (Johnson 2020).

The future may see computers act as explicit ethical agents, with the ability to process information about each situation and to autonomously determine the best or most ethical course of action. Technology has not yet reached that level of sophistication, which is one reason why machine creations cannot claim copyright and machines cannot be held liable for loss or injury. Even if or when this happens, we cannot assume that a computer will act ethically. We have established that technology is not benign. While its use can bring great personal and societal benefits, there are risks and consequences that may not have been considered before the technology was deployed.

There is no doubt that the availability of free online MT has aided communication for many, but the seamless interfaces and improving output may lead end users to assume that its use is harmless (and it usually will be). The professional translation workflow stakeholders in the use cases in §2.1 can be assumed to have expertise in language technology, but this is not true of the general public, who might expect the same level of coherence and comprehensibility in a machine translation that they would find in a (good) human translation. They may not even be aware that they are reading a machine translated text, and even if the output were to be labelled as MT-generated, they are unlikely to be aware of the risks of mistranslation.

7 Summary

As MT quality improves, the technology facilitates more communication either directly or as part of a translation workflow. However, there are ethical concerns to be considered by MT developers, translation buyers, translation agencies, translators, and consumers of translation. As with all technologies, neither MT development nor MT output should be considered neutral, but rather as promulgating the perspective of the developers or the translators who created the training data, in the tools for interaction with MT and in the output text. Uncritical reporting of positive MT evaluation results minimizes public awareness of risk and bias in MT output while potentially devaluing the work of human translators. Readers may find it useful to consider the issues raised in this chapter when working with and using MT, and reflecting on how the related processes fit with their own values, purposes, and principles.

Ethical considerations as laid out in this chapter begin with the source of translation and translator data, ownership, permissions, copyright, and mode of distribution. The ethical use of MT within professional translation workflows may depend on the attitudes of all stakeholders, rules of confidentiality, and the design decisions behind MT platforms. This relates to sustainability, modes of interaction with MT, and the degree of autonomy and ownership of the process allowed for translators. The methods by which we can ensure diversity and de-bias MT systems and data are perhaps least developed, and will no doubt require further discussion and adjustment over time.

References

Abdallah, Kristiina. 2010. Translator's agency in production networks. In Tuija Kinnunen & Kaisa Koskinen (eds.), *Translator's agency*, 11–46. Tampere: Tampere University Press.

Baker, Mona. 2018. *In other words*. London: Routledge.

Canfora, Carmen & Angelika Ottmann. 2020. Risks in neural machine translation. *Translation Spaces* 9(1). 58–77.

Chesterman, Andrew. 2001. Proposal for a hieronymic oath. *The Translator* 7(2). 139–154. DOI: 10.6509.2001.10799097.

Cronin, Michael. 2017. *Eco-translation: Translation and ecology in the age of the anthropocene*. London: Routledge.

Docherty, Peter, Mari Kira & A. B. (Rami) Shari. 2008. What the world needs now is sustainable work systems. In Peter Docherty, Mari Kira & A. B. (Rami) Shari (eds.), *Creating sustainable work systems: Developing social sustainability*, 1–22. London: Routledge.

European Parliament. 1996. *Directive 96/9/EC of the European Parliament and of the Council of 11 March 1996 on the legal protection of databases*. https://eur-lex.europa.eu/legal-content/EN/ALL/?uri=CELEX:31996L0009.

Floridi, Luciano & Mariarosaria Taddeo. 2016. *What is data ethics?* DOI: 10.1098/rsta.2016.0360.

Freitag, Markus, George Foster, David Grangier, Viresh Ratnakar, Qijun Tan & Wolfgang Macherey. 2021. Experts, errors, and context: a large-scale study of human evaluation for machine translation. *Transactions of the Association for Computational Linguistics* 9. 1460–1474. DOI: 10.1162/tacl_a_00437.

ISO. 2015. *ISO 17100:2015. Translation services – requirements for translation services*. https://www.iso.org/standard/59149.html.

ISO. 2017. *ISO 18857:2017. Translation services – post-editing of machine translation output: Requirements*. https://www.iso.org/standard/62970.html.

Johnson, Marvin. 2020. *A scalable approach to reducing gender bias in Google Translate*. https://ai.googleblog.com/2020/04/a-scalable-approach-to-reducing-gender.html (20 May, 2020).

Kay, Martin. 1980. *The proper place of men and machines in language translation* (Report CSL-80-11). Palo Alto, CA: Xerox Corporation.

Lambert, Joseph. 2018. How ethical are codes of ethics? Using illusions of neutrality to sell translations. *Journal of Specialised Translation* 30. 269–290. https://www.jostrans.org/issue30/art_lambert.php.

Moorkens, Joss. 2020. "A tiny cog in a large machine": Digital Taylorism in the translation industry. *Translation Spaces* 9(1). 12–34.

Moorkens, Joss & David Lewis. 2019a. Copyright and the reuse of translation as data. In Minako O'Hagan (ed.), *The Routledge handbook of translation and technology*, 469–481. London: Routledge.

Moorkens, Joss & David Lewis. 2019b. Research questions and a proposal for the future governance of translation data. *Journal of Specialised Translation* 32. 2–25.

Moorkens, Joss & Martha Rocchi. 2021. Ethics in the translation industry. In Kaisa Koskinen & Nike K. Pokorn (eds.), *The Routledge handbook of translation and ethics*, 320–337. London: Routledge.

Pérez-Ortiz, Juan Antonio, Mikel L. Forcada & Felipe Sánchez-Martínez. 2022. How neural machine translation works. In Dorothy Kenny (ed.), *Machine translation for everyone: Empowering users in the age of artificial intelligence*, 141–164. Berlin: Language Science Press. DOI: 10.5281/zenodo.6760020.

Pym, Anthony. 2012. *On translator ethics: principles for mediation between cultures*. Amsterdam: John Benjamins.

Rossi, Caroline & Alice Carré. 2022. How to choose a suitable neural machine translation solution: Evaluation of MT quality. In Dorothy Kenny (ed.), *Machine translation for everyone: Empowering users in the age of artificial intelligence*, 51–79. Berlin: Language Science Press. DOI: 10.5281/zenodo.6759978.

Sakamoto, Akiko. 2019. Unintended consequences of translation technologies: from project managers' perspectives. *Perspectives* 27(1). 58–73.

Steinberger, Ralf, Andreas Eisele, Szymon Klocek, Spyridon Pilos & Patrick Schlüter. 2012. DGT-TM: a freely available translation memory in 22 languages. In *Proceedings of the 8th international conference on language resources and evaluation (LREC 2012)*. ELRA. https://www.aclweb.org/anthology/L12-1481/.

Strubell, Emma, Ananda Ganesh & Andrew McCallum. 2019. *Energy and policy considerations for deep learning in NLP*. https://aclanthology.org/P19-1355.pdf.

Tiedemann, Jörg. 2012. *Parallel data, tools and interfaces in OPUS*. In Proceedings of the 8th International Conference on Language Resources & Evaluation (LREC 2012). 2214-2218. Luxembourg: ELRA. http://www.lrec-conf.org/proceedings/lrec2012/pdf/463_Paper.pdf.

Tomalin, Marcus, Bill Byrne, Shauna Concannon, Danielle Saunders & Stefanie Ullmann. 2021. *The practical ethics of bias reduction in machine translation. Why domain adaptation is better than data debiasing*. 419–433. DOI: 10.1007/s10676-021-09583-1.

Topping, Suzanne. 2000. Sharing translation database information: Considerations for developing an ethical and viable exchange of data. *Multilingual* 11(5). 59–61.

Toral, Antonio. 2019. Post-editese: An exacerbated translationese. In *Proceedings of machine translation summit XVII*, 273–281. EAMT. https://www.aclweb.org/anthology/W19-6627/.

Troussel, Jean-Christophe & Julien Debussche. 2014. *Translation and intellectual property rights*. Luxembourg: Publications Office of the European Union.

Van Wynsberghe, Aimee. 2021. Sustainable AI: AI for sustainability and the sustainability of AI. *AI and Ethics* 1. 213–218. DOI: 10.1007/s43681-021-00043-6.

Vanmassenhove, Eva. 2019. *On the integration of linguistic features into statistical and neural Machine translation*. PhD Thesis. Dublin City University.

Vanmassenhove, Eva, Dimitar Shterionov & Andy Way. 2019. Lost in translation: Loss and decay of linguistic richness in machine translation. In *Proceedings of machine translation summit XVII: Research track*. Dublin: EAMT, 222–232. https://www.aclweb.org/anthology/W19-6622.pdf.

Vieira, Lucas Nunes, Minako O'Hagan & Carol O'Sullivan. 2020. Understanding the societal impacts of machine translation: A critical review of the literature on medical and legal use cases. *Information, Communication & Society* 24(11). 1515–1532. DOI: 10.118X.2020.1776370.

Wachter, Sandra & Brent Mittelstadt. 2019. A right to reasonable inferences: Rethinking data protection law in the age of big data and AI. *Columbia Business Law Review* 2019(2). 1–130.

Weizenbaum, Joseph. 1986. Not without us. *Computers and Society* 16. 2–7.

Whipple, Daniel F. Lynch, Judith M. & Gilbert N. Nyaga. 2010. A buyer's perspective on collaborative versus transactional relationships. *Industrial Marketing Management* 39(3). 507–518. DOI: 10.1016/j.indmarman.2008.11.008.

World Intellectual Property Organization. 1979. *Berne convention for the protection of literary and artistic works*. (as amended on September 18, 1979). Geneva: WIPO. http://www.wipo.int/wipolex/en/details.jsp?id=12214.

Chapter 7

How neural machine translation works

Juan Antonio Pérez-Ortiz

Universitat d'Alacant, Spain

Mikel L. Forcada

Universitat d'Alacant, Spain

Felipe Sánchez-Martínez

Universitat d'Alacant, Spain

This chapter presents the main principles behind neural machine translation systems. We introduce, one by one, key concepts used to describe these systems, so that the reader achieves a comprehensive view of their inner workings and possibilities. These concepts include: neural networks, learning algorithms, word embeddings, attention, and the encoder–decoder architecture.

1 Introduction

The first thing you should know about neural machine translation (NMT) is that it considers translation as a task involving operations on numbers performed by mathematical systems called *artificial neural networks*: these systems take a sentence and transform it into a series of numbers. They add some more numbers here (usually, thousands or millions of them), multiply by other numbers there, perform a few additional, relatively simple, mathematical operations, and eventually output a translation of the original sentence into another language.

Maybe you have always considered translation from a different perspective: as an intellectual task that involves cognitive processes which can barely be explicitly enumerated and which take place in some deep areas of the human brain.

Juan Antonio Pérez-Ortiz, Mikel L. Forcada & Felipe Sánchez-Martínez. 2022. How neural machine translation works. In Dorothy Kenny (ed.), *Machine translation for everyone: Empowering users in the age of artificial intelligence*, 141–164. Berlin: Language Science Press. DOI: 10.5281/zenodo.6760020

And you are indeed right! But the approximation currently carried out by computers follows a completely different path: millions of mathematical operations are performed in a fraction of a second to obtain a translation which may sometimes be labelled as adequate and may sometimes not. And it turns out that the percentage of times they happen to be adequate has dramatically in the last few years. But, historically, artificial neural networks were devised as a simplified model of how *natural neural networks* such as our brains work, and the cognitive processes carried out in it are also the result of distributed neural computation processes which are not that different from the mathematical operations mentioned above.

This chapter will teach you the key elements of NMT technology. We will start off by pointing out the connection between how translation could be carried out in a human brain and how an NMT system undertakes it. This will help us to introduce the basic concepts needed to get a comprehensive overview of the principles of *machine learning* and *artificial neural networks*, which constitute two of the cornerstones of NMT. After that, we will discuss the essential principles of *non-contextual word embeddings*, a computerised representation of words with many interesting properties that, when combined through a mechanism known as *attention*, will produce the so-called *contextual word embeddings*, a key factor in the realisation of NMT. All these ingredients will allow us to present an overall picture of the inner workings of the two most used NMT models, namely, the *transformer* and the *recurrent* models. The chapter wraps up by introducing a series of secondary themes that will improve your knowledge on how these systems run behind the scenes.

2 An imperfect analogy between human translation and NMT

To simplify the discussion a bit, let us make the radical approximation that translating a text is equivalent to translating each of its sentences independently of each other. Let us now assume for a minute that translating a sentence is a two-step process: the translator first determines the *interpretation* or *meaning* of the whole source sentence and then produces in one go a sentence that allows more or less the same interpretation, but is now written in the target language. But every day translators encounter sentences that they have never seen before, such as "The pencil slipped from my hand, stood up, and started talking to me", and can still translate them: how is that possible? Linguistics has formulated the answer to this question as a principle, the *principle of semantic compositionality*:

we *build* the interpretation of each sentence by combining the individual interpretations of its component words, and the order in which they are combined is
dictated by the syntactic structure of the sentence in which words form phrases,
phrases form larger phrases, until one gets to the whole sentence. A translator
would then analyse this interpretation and perform the inverse procedure, but
in the target language. Of course, translators do not always process sentences as
a whole, particularly when they are long, and they may take shortcuts to avoid
building interpretations of whole sentences, but let us stick to this simplification
for a while.

NMT works in a similar way. When translating a sentence, during the *encoding* phase, the system assigns a neural *representation*, or *embedding*, to each
source-text word in isolation. These neural representations are then combined
to produce a similar representation, but this time at sentence level. As they are
combined, individual representations are also modified according to their context; one could consider this a contextualised representation of interpretation
or meaning. Then, in the *decoding* phase, the sentence-level representations are
unravelled step by step to predict, one by one, the words in the target sentence.
The *encoder* and the *decoder* performing these two phases are artificial neural
networks interconnected into a single composite neural network.

As in the case of translators, current neural architectures do not really work
by considering the whole source sentence when producing each target word, but
rather have learned to pay *attention* to the relevant source words and the target
words already produced when they do so.

In the remaining sections of this chapter we will describe in more detail the
nature of these representations, the structure of the artificial neural networks
(which we may simply call "neural networks" from now on) that build and transform them by selectively paying attention to what is important, and the ways
in which these artificial neural networks can be *trained* to do this task using
translation examples.

3 Artificial neural networks

To make sense of NMT, one needs to consider in more detail the artificial neural
networks (Goodfellow et al. 2016) that perform it: what they are made of, how
they work and how they are trained.

The name *neural* clearly invokes neurons and the way in which the nervous
systems of animals, and particularly people's brains, work. Artificial neural networks are indeed made up of thousands or millions of artificial units that resem-
ble neurons whose *activation* (that is, how *excited* or *inhibited* they are) depends

on the signals they receive from other neurons and the strength of the connections carrying these signals.

3.1 Artificial neurons

Artificial neurons are the main building blocks of artificial neural networks. These artificial neurons (we will simply call them *neurons* from now on) may be seen as operating in two steps when updating their state or activation. Let us imagine the simple situation in Figure 1 in which we study how the activation of neuron S_4 is updated in response to stimuli received from neurons S_1, S_2, and S_3.

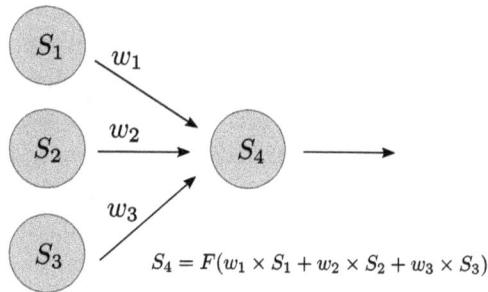

$$S_4 = F(w_1 \times S_1 + w_2 \times S_2 + w_3 \times S_3)$$

Figure 1: Updating the state S_4 of artificial neuron 4 in response to stimuli received from neurons 1, 2 and 3.

In the first step, the activations of neurons S_1, S_2 and S_3, all of them connected to neuron S_4, are added, but first each one is multiplied by a *weight* (w_1, w_2 and w_3) representing the strength of their connections; these weights determine how their activations are turned into actual stimuli for neuron S_4. Weights may be positive or negative. For instance, if weight w_2 is positive and the activation of S_2 is high, it will contribute to exciting neuron S_4 (a positive stimulus); if, however, w_2 is negative, it will contribute to inhibiting neuron S_4 (a negative stimulus). In general terms, neurons connected through positive weights tend to be simultaneously excited or inhibited, while neurons connected through negative weights tend to be in opposite states. Coming back to neuron S_4, if we add the stimuli coming from each neuron, we get a *net stimulus*:

$$x = w_1 \times S_1 + w_2 \times S_2 + w_3 \times S_3. \tag{1}$$

The net stimulus x can take any possible value, negative or positive, but it is not the activation of neuron S_4 yet. In the second step, neuron S_4 *reacts* to this stimulus. In the example, when the stimulus is intermediate, that is, not too positive or too negative, the neuron S_4 is very sensitive to it. However, when stimuli get large (no matter if positive or negative), changes in their values have a lesser impact on the output, as the neuron is respectively largely inhibited or largely excited.

In the example, neuron S_4 is such that its activation is bound between -1 and $+1$. Figure 2 represents how neuron S_4 reacts to the stimulus in equation 1. The reaction is represented with a function $F(...)$, called the *activation function*, which is applied to the stimulus; the result is the activation of S_4:

$$S_4 = F(x) = F(w_1 \times S_1 + w_2 \times S_2 + w_3 \times S_3). \qquad (2)$$

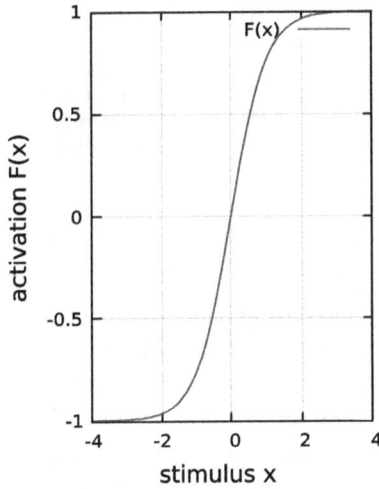

Figure 2: How a neuron reacts to the total stimulus received.

As can be seen, for values around 0 in the horizontal axis the reaction is proportional to the stimulus, but for large positive or negative stimuli, when the neuron is very inhibited or very excited, the reaction is much smaller. For this kind of neuron, the actual extreme values of -1 and $+1$ are never reached, no matter how strong the total stimulus is. As said above, neuron S_4 in our example is a specific type of neuron with an activation that varies between -1 and $+1$. There are other kinds of activation functions with different ranges, but exploring them is out of the scope of this chapter.

3.2 From neurons to networks

Neurons like the one discussed in the previous section may be connected to form an artificial neural network that performs a specific computational task, to solve

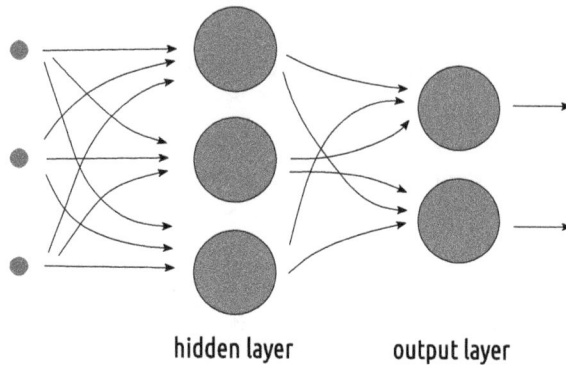

hidden layer   output layer

Figure 3: An artificial neural network with three three hidden neurons and two output neurons. Each connection has a weight not shown in the diagram. The three input neurons on the left are represented by smaller circles to emphasise the idea that they directly emit the values of the external input, but, unlike regular neurons, they do not compute a stimulus or react to it via an activation function.

a specific problem. In a network, some neurons receive external stimuli which act as *inputs* to the network (much as our eyes are connected to our brain and feed it with images) and represent an instance of the problem to be solved; some neurons, known as *hidden neurons*, receive stimuli only from other neurons; and finally, some neurons, known as *output neurons* represent the solution to the problem (a bit like the signals sent to the muscles of one of your hands to move it in a specific way). Figure 3 shows an example of such a neural network with five neurons; the network takes three inputs, which are fed to three hidden neurons, which in turn stimulate two output neurons.

When building a neural network to solve a specific problem, one first needs to determine its *architecture*: how many neurons it has, how they are connected, which neurons receive external inputs and which neurons are designated as output neurons; but the actual computation performed depends on the weights of all of the connections in the network. How these weights are arrived at is explained in Section 3.5. Suffice it to say here, that one nice feature of artificial neural networks is that they may be *trained* to perform a task from examples, that is, their weights may be set to specific values by observing a set of solved examples, each one made up of the values of input signals representing the problems, and the values of the desired output activations representing the solutions.

3.3 Layers of neurons

Imagine that you are an absolute beginner and want to learn some basic techniques to paint landscapes in oils. A manual might teach you a step-by-step over-simplified method with, for example, these four stages: drawing (a rough composition is sketched in), colour distribution, drawing refinement, and finish (when the final touches are made). The point here is not the number of stages or the particular characteristics of each of them, but the fact that the whole process flows in an incremental manner in such a way that the output of one step becomes the input to the next one. Each step refines the previous outcome: the outcome of the second step (colour distribution) is more of an actual landscape painting than the outcome of the first one (drawing) and, similarly, the outcome of the fourth stage (finish) can be conceptually considered as a better painting than those resulting from any of the previous steps.

It turns out that neural computation benefits from a similar step-by-step incremental process. Back in the sixties, researchers discovered that by including multiple layers of neurons more complex tasks could be tackled. Each layer in a multilayer neural network refines the output of the previous layer and takes a bigger or smaller step towards the ultimate solution. The resulting architecture would be similar to that in Figure 3 but with a number of additional hidden layers. One can clearly see this layered structure in the simple network in Figure 3: computation, performed by two layers, takes place in two steps.

A model made of neurons organised in layers is referred to as a *layered neural network*. In spite of theoretical results proving that a two-layer network has enough computational power to perform virtually any task (Hornik 1991), in the real world, the computational power of neural networks appears to be correlated with the number of layers; models with more than a few layers are often labelled as *deep neural networks* and the corresponding training algorithms are known as *deep-learning algorithms*.

As an example of the complexity that these deep models may reach, GPT-3 (Brown et al. 2020), one of the largest neural networks released in 2020 in the field of natural language generation, has 96 layers with tens of thousands of neurons each, which results in around 175,000 million weights to be learned by the training algorithm. Supercomputers were used to train the GPT-3 system, a process that can take several weeks or even months, but it has been estimated that learning the weights for such a model with a single powerful gaming desktop personal computer would have taken more than 350 years.[1]

---

[1]"OpenAI's GPT-3 language model: A technical overview" (2020). Retrieved from https://lambdalabs.com/blog/demystifying-gpt-3.

3.4 Neural machine translation

If we manage to represent a source sentence as a set of inputs to a neural network, and we can interpret the neural network's outputs as a target sentence, we have a *neural machine translation* (NMT) system. NMT first processes the words in the source sentence. Each time a source word is ingested by the encoder part of the neural network, the activations of sets of specific neurons in the network change. When the whole source sentence has been processed, the decoder part of the network starts its work. It has been trained to provide, step by step, a probability score for each possible target word in the translation, given the target words it has already output. This is similar to how predictive keyboards in contemporary smartphones work, but, as we will see, word predictions in NMT also depend on the source sentence, as they are meant to be a translation of it.

NMT systems are deep neural networks with architectures that will be discussed later in section 6. They have thousands of neurons and millions of weights (or many more) which have to be trained by providing examples taken from a parallel corpus containing millions of source sentences and their translations. Mathematical representations of the words in a given sentence in the source language are fed as inputs to the neural network and the words in the corresponding target-language sentence are used to represent the desired output. As you might expect, training a large network in reasonable time is computationally demanding: one needs very powerful, specialised number-crunching hardware to train the network by showing it the examples over and over again. On each iteration, small changes are made to the weights in the network to improve its prediction of target words.

3.5 Training neural networks

Training a neural network is the process of determining the weight of the connections between its neurons so that, given a *training set* of input–output examples, it produces an actual output which is as close as possible to that in the relevant example.

Training starts with a set of random weights or with weights taken from a neural network solving a similar task. During training weights are modified in such a way that the value of an error function (also known as a *loss function*), which measures how much actual outputs deviate from the desired outputs, is made as small as possible. *Training algorithms* (also called *learning algorithms*) repeatedly compute small corrections (updates) to weights until the error function is minimal or small enough for all examples in the training set, or a certain performance is observed in a different *development set*, which has been reserved or "held out" for this purpose (see Section 7.2). The technical details of the training algorithm are beyond the scope of this chapter; let us just say that it is usually based on computing how much the error function varies when each weight is varied by a fixed but very small amount (the *gradient* of the error function), and then varying each weight a bit in the direction in which it reduces the error function.[2] This type of training is called *gradient descent*; it is not guaranteed to find the very best weights, but it is likely that good candidates will be found. The intensity of these weight variations is regulated by a parameter called the *learning rate*; this learning rate is usually higher in the first steps of the training algorithm, but its magnitude is made progressively smaller as the weights get closer to their final values. Note that training neural networks is quite laborious: many examples are necessary and they need to be presented many times to learn. This is often due to limitations of the training algorithms, however, rather than to the lack of capacity of a specific neural network to represent the solution to a problem.

Once the weights are determined, training stops (see Section 7.2) and the neural network can be used to obtain the outputs for new inputs which are not included among the examples used during training.

3.6 Generalisation in neural networks

Generalisation is a fundamental cognitive process for humans and animals. It allows us to use what we learned in the past in new situations which can be regarded as similar but not identical to the situation in which learning originally took place. A person does not need to relearn how to drive when entering a new street or driving a new car. Similarly, generalisation happens when an organism which already responds to a certain stimulus in a particular way responds to similar stimuli in similar ways. Generalisation is also key to language learning: young children soon learn to say sentences they have never heard before.

Neural networks may ideally generalise in the context of machine translation by producing similar outputs when fed with similar inputs, independently of whether they were included in the training set or not. One feature of neural networks is the *smoothness* of the computations, meaning that if the input values are slightly changed, the result of the formulas will not vary significantly.

In a broad sense, in order to achieve generalisation, similar sentences should get similar representations, and as sentence representations will be obtained from word representations, we may conclude that representing similar words

---

[2]Some of you may recognise here the mathematical concept of *derivative of a function*.

with similar numbers is a precondition for generalisation in neural language processing.

The next section will delve into how we can end up with a convenient list of neural representations for the words in a sentence that benefits from the smoothness of neural networks so that, after training, the system is able to generalise properly to sentences it has not seen before.

4 Word embeddings as vector representation of words

In the previous section we noted that neurons are usually arranged in layers in such a way that the output of the neurons of one layer becomes the input to the neurons of the following one. Interestingly, the output of the set of neurons in a given layer constitutes a representation of the information they are processing at that stage.

In the field of natural language processing, and as indicated above, the information processed by neural networks is made up of words, and their representations within the network are usually referred to as *embeddings* (Mikolov et al. 2013). What makes these embeddings really useful is that those words with similar meanings or that usually co-occur in the same contexts end up having similar embeddings. In order to better understand this, take a piece of paper and draw a square with sides of about 10 centimetres. Now, take the words in the following list and put them all on the square by following a criterion that places words which are closer in meaning nearer each other than words with less related meanings. If this concept of meaning closeness seems imprecise to you, you may place the words based on their frequency of co-occurrence in sentences or paragraphs. The words are: *restaurant, red, garden, fountain, flower, tomato, balloon, waiters, knife, flowers, menu, cooked, chromosome* and *consistently*. Do this before reading on.

The restriction imposed by means of the criterion of word meaning proximity implies that you have not been able to freely distribute the words on the square. Probably, you have decided to group words such as *restaurant, menu* and *waiters*, on the one hand, and words such as *garden, flower* and *fountain*, on the other hand. There are, however, some doubtful cases: *red* is clearly a neighbour of *tomato*, but it should be close to *flower* as well; a compromise solution would be to put it somewhere in between, a little bit closer to *tomato* than to *flower* if we acknowledge that *red* is not as essential to flowers as it is to tomatoes.

You may have noticed some clusters in your design: an island representing the semantic field of restaurants and related things, and another island around the idea of gardens and orchards. There are some outliers on the list, especially the word *consistently*, which seems in principle disconnected from the rest of words, forcing us to put it as far as possible from all of them. *Chromosome* is another isolated word, but as flowers and waiters use chromosomes to carry their genetic information, it may be put somewhere in the middle of the line between these words but at the same time not very close to *red*. See Figure 4 for a possible solution that may not match yours exactly.[3]

In order to assign mathematical codes to the words in our list, let's assign coordinates to each word to reflect its position on the square. As we are in a two-dimensional space, we need two coordinates for each word: the first coordinate is a number that represents the distance to the left vertical side of the square; the second coordinate is a number that represents the distance to the bottom horizontal side of the square. The word *restaurant* could be assigned, for example, the two numbers 0.25 and 1.1, and the word *menu* the numbers 0.6 and 1.3, close to *restaurant* as seen in Figure 4. These coordinate values can be represented using *vector notation*, which simply consists of writing the numbers as a comma-separated list of values between brackets. The vectors corresponding to *restaurant* and *menu* would therefore be $[0.25, 1.1]$ and $[0.6, 1.3]$, respectively. Each of these vectors represents a possible word embedding for these two words.

Although it may not be completely obvious, considering embeddings made up of two numbers instead of a single number boosts the possibilities of solving the problem of placing words closer or farther apart as we have more freedom to satisfy all the restrictions. In fact, moving from two dimensions to a higher number of dimensions increases these possibilities even more. A five-dimensional representation of a word could be, for example, $[2.34, 1.67, 4.81, 3.01, 5.61]$. NMT systems consider embeddings with hundreds of dimensions, and the input sentence to be translated is represented by a collection of these vast word embeddings.

Word embeddings are learned using the very same algorithm used to learn the weights of the neural network presented in Section 3.5. In fact, both the weights and the embeddings are learned at the same time. Bearing in mind that the input layer of a neural network involved in NMT usually consists of the embeddings of the words in the input sentence, there is no need to limit ourselves to fixed vectors. Instead, their values can be repeatedly updated during training in such a way that the value of the error function is minimised.

---

[3]We have deliberately placed Figure 4 a few pages on, so that you do not see it before you attempt the exercise.

4.1 Generalisation

As already discussed, for the network to be able to properly *generalise*, that is, to be able to learn to translate and be capable of translating sentences never seen before, similar sentences should get similar representations. As sentence representations are obtained from word embeddings, we may conclude that representing similar words with similar numbers is a precondition for generalisation in neural natural language processing. Following our example, words such as *poured, rained, pouring* or *raining* should ideally share similar embeddings as all of them are semantically similar; the codes for *pouring* and *raining* should also be closer to words such as *driving* since the three of them are gerunds and may appear in similar contexts; *poured* and *rained* should be neighbours as well because both of them are past tenses. This is why we usually need many dimensions: we want words to be close to each other in different ways or for different reasons, simultaneously.

4.2 Geometric properties of word embeddings

Word embeddings exhibit interesting properties that demonstrate that they represent semantic characteristics (or something related to semantics) of words. As already explained, the embedding of a word consists of several real numbers, usually hundreds or thousands of them, and each of these numbers seems to capture a certain aspect of the meaning of a word. For example, the word embedding for *Dublin* should capture several semantic-related aspects of it: a city, the capital of Ireland, the place for the headquarters in Europe of several multinational companies, etc.

Thanks to this specialisation of the different dimensions of the embeddings, we can perform some arithmetic operations with the embeddings and obtain meaningful results. These operations are simply additions and subtractions that are straightforward to compute. Adding (or subtracting) two embeddings simply consists of adding (or subtracting) the components of the vectors one by one; for example, $[1.24, 2.56, 5.23] + [0.12, 1.12, 0.01] = [1.36, 3.68, 5.24]$. Below are two examples of arithmetic operations with meaningful results performed on embeddings that NMT systems usually learn:

$$[king] - [man] + [woman] \simeq [queen]$$
$$[Dublin] - [Ireland] + [France] \simeq [Paris]$$

where the square brackets refer to the embedding of a word, and with $\simeq$ we mean that the resulting embedding after the operation is close to the embedding of the

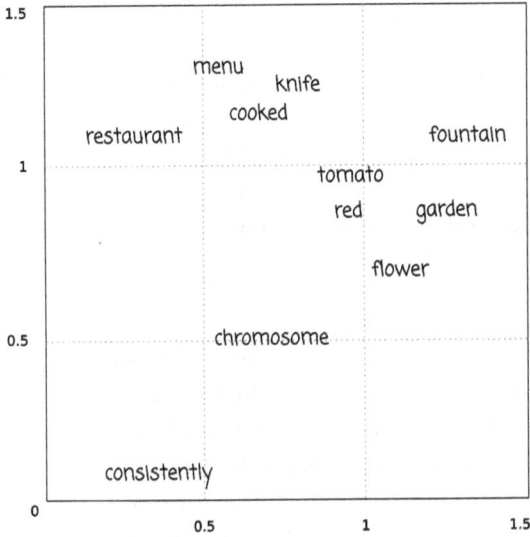

Figure 4: Placement of words in a two-dimensional area in such a way that related words are positioned close to each other, but far from words they have less in common with.

word on the right-hand side of the example. This can be interpreted as indicating that *king* is to *man* what *queen* is to *woman*, a male or female monarch; and *Dublin* is to *Ireland* what *Paris* is to *France*, the capital of a country.

5 Contextual word embeddings through attention

Words do not always have the same meaning in every sentence. The embedding of the word *letter*, for example, should not be the same when the word refers to a character of an alphabet or when it refers to a document addressed to another person. In fact, it may even be interesting for an NMT system to represent the word with different embeddings depending on whether it refers to a love letter or a complaint letter. The embeddings we introduced before are *non-contextual*: they were computed by considering words that usually co-occur in sentences but without taking into consideration the different meanings words may have.

In the NMT arena, *attention* plays an important role as it allows the neural network to compute *contextual word embeddings*, that is, vector representations of the words in a sentence computed in such a way that the representation obtained for a word is adapted to its meaning in each particular sentence. Attention is, once again, a concept which is implemented by means of mathematical operations conveniently learned by a training algorithm. In our context, attention is similar, to the situation in which we pay attention to something or someone in our everyday lives.

By conveniently using attention to concentrate on some words in the sentence, the embedding vector corresponding to the word *season*, for example, will differ between the sentences in examples 1 and 2 below:

1. The first episode will pick up right where the previous season left off.

2. Summer is the hottest season of the whole year.

In principle, it may sound as if the purpose of contextual word embeddings is that the different meanings of a word get different representations, but, while this will be usually true, the idea goes beyond this. The contextual word embeddings for *season* in the sentences "Winter is the coldest season of the year in polar and temperate zones", "Summer is the hottest season of the whole year" and even "Of the whole year, summer is the hottest season" will all be different, although presumably closer to each other than the representation of *season* in "The first episode will pick up right where the previous season left off". These divergences result from the fact that the words in the sentences or the order in which they are placed differ. Remarkably, the two instances of *the* in each of our examples will get two different contextual vectors because the context of each instance is also different.

How are contextual embeddings mathematically computed through attention? Given the sentence in example 2 above ("Summer is the hottest season of the whole year."), the procedure starts by obtaining the non-contextual word embeddings that were introduced in Section 4. As the sentence has nine words, the result is a collection of nine vectors which are the ingredients for the next step. Now, in order to compute the contextual word embedding for the word *season* in the sentence, an attention vector is mathematically produced by the neural network. This attention vector will have nine percentages representing the degree of attention that needs to be paid to each of the words in the sentence in order to obtain the representation of the word *season*. The element at a certain position in the vector corresponds to the attention to the word at that position in the sentence. For example, an attention vector $[25\%, 8\%, 10\%, 15\%, 25\%, 8\%, 2\%, 0\%, 7\%]$ would indicate that in order to compute a contextual vector representation of the word *season* in the running sentence, the word embeddings for *summer* and *season* will be equally highly relevant (together, they receive fifty percent of the total attention), which makes sense as they are semantically connected to the concept of a meteorological season. Notice that the preceding determiner gets some attention too (10%), which may be explained by the fact that it helps to label *season* as a noun. The contribution of the verb (8%) to the contextual embedding may also be described in terms of its contribution to marking the number of *season* as singular. Note that the percentages always add up to 100%.

Determining how the attention vector is used in order to obtain a new embedding that combines the original non-contextual embeddings to get a new embedding is beyond the scope of this chapter. Suffice to say that the procedure involves a specific sequence of mathematical operations and that the resulting embedding will be located somewhere in between the original embeddings.

Following our running example, nine different attention vectors will be computed for this sentence (one for each word) and then applied to the original non-contextual embeddings in order to obtain a collection of nine new embeddings, each one corresponding to a different word in the sentence. These new embeddings may be considered as contextual embeddings as they are influenced to different degrees by the rest of the words in the sentence.

5.1 Many attention layers, better than one

Previously, in Section 3.3 of this chapter, we discussed the benefits of successively refining neural computations by exploiting models with different layers. Consequently, it will come as no great surprise that in order to obtain more precise representations, the contextual embeddings just obtained may be combined with new attention vectors to obtain yet another new embedding for each word. As a real-life example, Turing Natural Language Generation (T-NLG), another of the largest language models published in 2020, has 78 attention layers that successively polish embeddings of 4,256 dimensions.[4] Recall that these representations, which are learned by applying many consecutive layers, are known as *deep* representations.

5.2 Many heads, better than one

There is no reason to restrict ourselves to a single attention vector for each word in each layer. For example, given the sentence "My grandpa baked bread in his oven daily", it could be interesting to have an embedding for *oven* which has the flavour of *grandpa* to reflect that this oven belongs to an older person, and a different embedding for *oven* with the flavour of *bread* to reflect what has been

---

[4]"Turing-NLG: A 17-billion-parameter language model by Microsoft", 2020. Retrieved from https://www.microsoft.com/en-us/research/blog/turing-nlg-a-17-billion-parameter-language-model-by-microsoft/

cooked in it. A single attention vector would have to mix both flavours in a single embedding containing too much heterogeneous information that could affect negatively the search for a translation for the word represented by the embedding. For this reason, some NMT systems obtain different attentions for each word in each layer and use them to compute a number of different embeddings for each word. Each of these embeddings is said to be computed by a different *head*. T-NLG has 28 attention heads in each layer. Therefore, its last layer produces 28 different 4,256-dimensional embeddings for each word.

5.3 Contextual word embeddings in natural language processing

Embeddings are the cornerstone of NMT but they have also proved to be useful in many other natural language processing applications such as sentiment analysis and automatic summarisation. As an illustration, systems that automatically classify as positive or negative the sentences in a text containing a product review may work by first computing a collection of deep contextual embeddings for each word in the sentence and then feeding these embeddings to a much simpler neural network that will compute a number between 0 and 1 indicating the degree of positiveness of the sentence (for example, 0.95 will indicate a decidedly positive sentence, 0.2 a negative sentence, and 0.51 a neutral sentence). These systems are usually trained with a corpus of sentences manually tagged by humans. The part of the model that computes the embeddings is not necessarily trained for a particular corpus as *pre-trained* models already trained with millions of sentences are freely available for many languages.

6 Neural machine translation, at last

At this point, you are hopefully in a good position to understand how NMT works, even if we describe its fundamentals in only a few sentences as we do next. We will focus on two architectures: those of so-called transformer and recurrent neural networks.

6.1 Transformer: Attention-based encoder–decoder

Put simply, a transformer NMT system is composed of a module that computes contextual word embeddings for each word in the source input sentence and a second module which successively predicts each word in the target sentence. The former module is called an *encoder* and the latter module is known as a *decoder*. For predicting the words in the target language, the decoder pays attention to

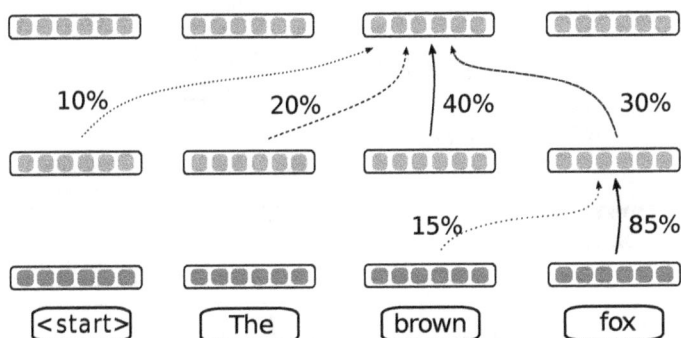

Figure 5: The encoder of a transformer-based neural machine translation system. The symbol *start* is usually prefixed to explicitly mark the beginning of the sentence. The diagram also shows that first-layer embeddings for *brown* and *fox* contribute to different degrees to obtain the embedding for *fox* in the second layer; similarly, the embedding for *brown* in the last layer integrates information from all the embeddings in the second layer using different degrees of attention.

the embeddings of all the words in the source sentence as well as to the embeddings of the target words already generated. The whole architecture is called a *transformer* (Vaswani et al. 2017). Figure 5 shows an example of a three-layered encoder and the degrees of attention considered in order to compute an embedding in the second layer and in the third one. Figure 6 depicts this encoder in an extended diagram that also includes the decoder so that it represents the whole transformer architecture.

A parallel corpus is used by the learning algorithm to obtain a set of weights, embeddings and attention vectors for the transformer such that the training data can be reproduced up to a certain degree and the system is able to generalise beyond the sentences in the training set.

For example, assume that a transformer with one single head per layer is used to translate the sentence "My grandpa baked bread in his oven daily" into Spanish. The encoder first produces a collection of eight embedding vectors. The decoder then computes an 8-dimensional attention vector such as [60%, 10%, 0%, 0%,

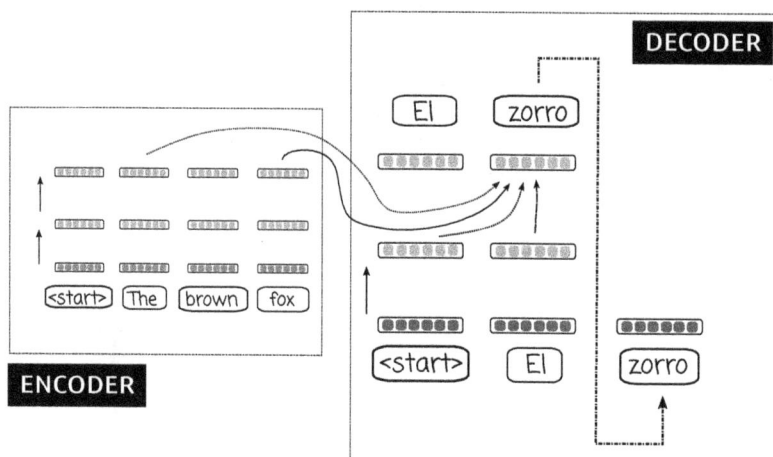

Figure 6: A complete transformer-based neural machine translation system translating a sentence. An enlarged version of the encoder can be seen in Figure 5. Note how the prediction of *zorro* is obtained by paying attention to the embeddings of the previous target words but also to the embeddings corresponding to some of the input words coming from the last layer of the encoder.

0%, 30%, 0%, 0%] and uses it to obtain a flavour of the source sentence that allows it to obtain an embedding for the first word in the target sentence. Let us assume that the system correctly generates the Spanish word *mi*. The decoder will then compute a 9-dimensional attention vector such as [50%, 10%, 0%, 0%, 0%, 20%, 0%, 0%, 20%] (the last percentage corresponds to the attention paid to the first word in the target sentence) and use it to obtain an embedding for the second word in the target sentence. The procedure will continue until the decoder generates a special token that marks the end of the sentence.

The output of the decoder at each step is not exactly an estimation of the embedding of the next word. Actually, an additional layer is added at the end of the decoder to compute a vector of probabilities or likelihoods for each word in the target-language vocabulary. Section 7.3 will discuss how these probabilities can be used in order to obtain the sequence of words that result in the target-language sentence.

6.2 Recurrent architectures

The transformer, as presented in the previous section, is the model used in most current commercial NMT systems, but alternative neural models exist. Another top model is the *recurrent* encoder–decoder model (Bahdanau et al. 2015). Similarly to transformer-based models, there is an encoder that produces a collection

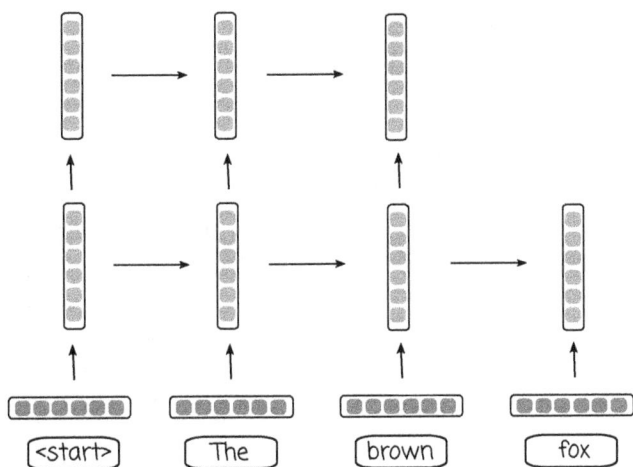

Figure 7: Left-to-right submodel of the encoder of a recurrent neural machine translation system, just after processed "<start> The brown" and when about to processs "fox".

of embeddings for the words in the input sentence and a decoder that uses attention to compute embeddings for each target word by integrating the information from the input words and the already generated target words. The encoder and decoder in the recurrent model, however, compute the contextual word embeddings in a local manner in such a way that the embeddings for the fifth encoded word, for example, are based on the embeddings of the four first words, on the one hand, and the embeddings of the next words, on the other hand. This is achieved by traversing the input sentence from left to right and from right to left; see Figure 7 for a diagram of this model showing only left-to-right processing.

It is worth noting that the mathematical model used imposes some restrictions on the relevance given to the words around the word for which the contextual word embeddings are computed (in our example the fifth one), resulting in a mechanism that specially focuses on the nearest words and tends to ignore the representations of distant words. Similarly to the transformer, a final layer at the end of the decoder computes a vector that gives the probability of each target-language word being the word at the corresponding position in the output sentence. Forcada (2017) describes in more detail the recurrent encoder–decoder model and also discusses the kind of outputs that NMT produces.

7 Additional settings

7.1 Words and sub-words

According to what has been presented in this chapter, independently of whether a transformer or a recurrent model is used, an embedding is obtained for each word after training. Does this mean that we end up having an embedding for every possible word in the language? Not really. Languages, specially those which are highly inflected or agglutinative, may easily have hundreds of thousands or even millions of different word forms. In order to understand why this poses a challenge for NMT systems you should know that the number of word embeddings (which is referred as the *vocabulary*) conditions the number of weights in the neural network and that large neural networks often struggle to generalise to unseen data. The size of the vocabulary could be reduced by considering only those word forms present in the training corpus but this usually still implies considering a substantial number of words and raises a new issue: when training is finished and the NMT system undertakes the translation of new sentences containing words not in the training set, these unseen words will make the model perform clumsily and lose accuracy as every unknown word is assigned a single non-contextual embedding reserved for this situation.

The solution engineers came up with is to split words into so-called *sub-word units*. Ideally, these units should make linguistic sense and carry some components of meaning; for instance, splitting *demystifying* as *de-* + *-myst-* + *-ify-* + *-ing* surely makes more linguistic sense (and is therefore likely to be more helpful when it comes to performing machine translation) than splitting it as *dem-* + *-ystif-* + *-yi-* + *-ng*. But performing a linguistically sound splitting requires the existence of a set of splitting rules and procedures for the language in question, a resource that may not be available for many languages.

A commonly-used workaround is to automatically learn splitting rules by inspecting large texts, such as one containing all the source or all the target sentences in the training set. A popular approach[5] is called *byte-pair encoding* (BPE) (Sennrich et al. 2016), and starts with letter-sized units which are joined into two-letter, three-letter, etc. units when they appear frequently in the corpus.[6] Byte-pair encoding would probably identify a frequent *-ing* suffix in many verb

---

[5]There are more advanced methods such as *SentencePiece* (Kudo & Richardson 2018), which treats the whole text as a sequence of characters and performs word division (*tokenization*) and sub-word division in one fell swoop.

[6]Byte-pair encoding was originally a text compression algorithm: frequent letter (*byte*) sequences would be stored once and replaced by short codes to reduce the total storage needed.

forms (*marching, considering*) and chop it off, even for unseen forms (such as *bart-simpsoning*); *-ing* would then be turned into a contextual embedding carrying its atomic meaning.

7.2 Stopping criteria and metrics

As mentioned in section 3.5, in addition to a large training corpus, a small *development corpus* is usually held out and not used for training. The purpose of this corpus is to monitor the performance of the NMT system while it is being trained, to decide, for instance, when training should stop. Training tries to minimise an error function (or, in NMT, actually maximise the probability of the target sentences in the training corpus). One possible problem that may occur is that training too deep on the training corpus hurts generalisation as the neural network ends up *memorising* the example translations too much. This is where the development corpus comes into play: after a certain number of iterations or steps of the training algorithm, the source sentences in the development corpus are translated with the neural network and the output is automatically compared to the desired target sentences in the corpus using simple approximate automatic evaluation metrics (see Rossi & Carré 2022 [this volume]), the most common of which is BLEU (Papineni et al. 2002). BLEU measures how many one-word, two-word, three-word and four-word sequences in the output are found in the reference, and computes a score that varies from 0 (no match) to 100% (all stretches found). If, during training, BLEU on the development set starts to signal a degradation of performance, training may be stopped, or the current set of weights may be stored and training then continued for a while to see if BLEU improves again. Of course, there are many other automatic evaluation metrics which can take the place of BLEU in this process.

7.3 Beam search

The decoder in NMT systems produces the output sentence sequentially, one target word at a time, as explained in Sections 6.1 and 6.2. At each time step, the neural network produces a probability or likelihood (a value between 0 and 100%) for every single word in the target vocabulary. One way of using this information is to pick the most likely target word and output it, ignoring other possibilities. It is worthwhile noting that, in doing so, we are completely determining the ensuing steps taken by the NMT system as the current prediction is given as input to the decoder in the next step (see, for example, the word *zorro* in Figure 6). One possible way to explore more possibilities is to consider, for instance, the three most likely words, and *clone* the system into three systems, each of which would be determined respectively by each of the three choices, and see how they fare. But one cannot do this indefinitely, as one would triplicate the number of systems translating the sentence at each step, and their number would grow exponentially. To avoid that, only a certain number of systems are allowed to *survive*, namely those obtaining the best value in an approximate calculation of the probability of the full sentence that would be produced. This is usually called *beam search* and is a common approximation in other probabilistic models of human language processing such as speech recognition.

8 Conclusions

To train an NMT system, one needs thousands or even millions of examples of source sentence–target sentence pairs. For many language pairs, many domains and many text genres, such resources do not exist, which constrains many specific applications, but for well-resourced languages, general-purpose NMT is a reality and is very widely used, not only by translators. Moreover, scientific advances in approaches such as multilingual models or unsupervised NMT have recently started to produce promising results in low-resource scenarios.[7]

This chapter has introduced – and provided technical details of – the key elements in NMT systems, and explored how they interact in the two currently most popular architectures, namely transformer-based and recurrent neural networks. Research activity in the area is so intense at the time of writing that proposals for new models arise almost every month. Transformers are currently the paradigm of choice if enough parallel corpora are available for training, because they require shorter training times and allow subtle quality improvements in comparison to recurrent neural networks, but the picture may change dramatically at any time.

---

[7]A *multilingual model* is a single neural network that is trained to translate between many different language pairs so that *knowledge* from well-resourced languages may be *transferred* to low-resourced ones. Interestingly, multilingual models bring the possibility of *zero-shot translation* (Ko et al. 2021) in which a system may be able to translate with reasonable quality, for example, between Spanish and Upper Sorbian using a multilingual model trained on German–Upper Sorbian and Spanish–German corpora, even when no Spanish–Upper Sorbian parallel corpus is available. *Unsupervised NMT* goes a step further by learning NMT systems from monolingual corpora only.

References

Bahdanau, Dzmitry, Kyunghyun Cho & Yoshua Bengio. 2015. Neural machine translation by jointly learning to align and translate. In Yoshua Bengio & Yann LeCun (eds.), *3rd International Conference on Learning Representations, ICLR 2015*. DOI: 10.48550/arXiv.1409.0473.

Brown, Tom B., Benjamin Mann, Nick Ryder, Melanie Subbiah, Jared Kaplan, Prafulla Dhariwal, Arvind Neelakantan, Pranav Shyam, Girish Sastry, Amanda Askell, Sandhini Agarwal, Ariel Herbert-Voss, Gretchen Krueger, Tom Henighan, Rewon Child, Aditya Ramesh, Daniel Ziegler, Jeffrey Wu, Clemens Winter, Dario Amodei, Christopher Hesse, Mark Chen, Eric Sigler, Mateusz Litwin, Scott Gray, Benjamin Chess, Jack Clark, Christopher Berner, Sam McCandlish, Alec Radford, Ilya Sutskever & Dario Amodei. 2020. Language models are few-shot learners. *CoRR* abs/2005.14165. https://arxiv.org/abs/2005.14165.

Forcada, Mikel. 2017. Making sense of neural machine translation. *Translation Spaces* 6(2). 291–309.

Goodfellow, Ian, Yoshua Bengio & Aaron Courville. 2016. *Deep learning*. Cambridge, MA: MIT Press.

Hornik, Kurt. 1991. Approximation capabilities of multilayer feedforward networks. *Neural Networks* 4(2). 251–257.

Ko, Wei-Jen, Ahmed El-Kishky, Adithya Renduchintala, Vishrav Chaudhary, Naman Goyal, Francisco Guzmán, Pascale Fung, Philipp Koehn & Mona Diab. 2021. Adapting high-resource NMT models to translate low-resource related languages without parallel data. In *Proceedings of the 59th annual meeting of the Association for Computational Linguistics and the 11th International Joint Conference on Natural Language Processing*, 802–812.

Kudo, Taku & John Richardson. 2018. SentencePiece: A simple and language independent subword tokenizer and detokenizer for neural text processing. In *Proceedings of the 2018 Conference on Empirical Methods in Natural Language Processing: System Demonstrations*, 66–71. Brussels, Belgium: Association for Computational Linguistics.

Mikolov, Tomas, Ilya Sutskever, Kai Chen, Greg Corrado & Jeffrey Dean. 2013. Distributed representations of words and phrases and their compositionality. In *Advances in Neural Information Processing Systems 30*, 3111–3119.

Papineni, Kishore, Salim Roukos, Todd Ward & Wei-Jing Zhu. 2002. BLEU: A method for automatic evaluation of machine translation. In *Proceedings of the 40th Annual Meeting of the Association for Computational Linguistics*, 311–318.

Philadelphia, Pennsylvania, USA: Association for Computational Linguistics. DOI: 10.3115/1073083.1073135.

Rossi, Caroline & Alice Carré. 2022. How to choose a suitable neural machine translation solution: Evaluation of MT quality. In Dorothy Kenny (ed.), *Machine translation for everyone: Empowering users in the age of artificial intelligence*, 51–79. Berlin: Language Science Press. DOI: 10.5281/zenodo.6759978.

Sennrich, Rico, Barry Haddow & Alexandra Birch. 2016. Neural Machine translation of rare words with subword units. In *Proceedings of the 54th Annual Meeting of the Association for Computational Linguistics*, 1715–1725. Berlin: Association for Computational Linguistics.

Vaswani, Ashish, Noam Shazeer, Niki Parmar, Jakob Uszkoreit, Llion Jones, Aidan N Gomez, Łukasz Kaiser & Illia Polosukhin. 2017. Attention is all you need. In *Advances in Neural Information Processing Systems 30*, 5998–6008.

Chapter 8

Custom machine translation

Gema Ramírez-Sánchez

Prompsit Language Engineering

> This chapter gives an overview of the theoretical and practical implications of customizing machine translation (MT) to make it fit for a particular purpose. The chapter is written for readers who have just a basic knowledge of MT, but experts who are seeking new ways of explaining MT to non-experts may also find it useful. The MT paradigm assumed in the chapter is that of neural MT.

1 Introduction

1.1 Generic machine translation

Most casual users of machine translation (MT) undoubtedly rely on *generic* MT, that is, MT based on engines trained to cover a wide range of topics, styles and genres, and not specialized in any particular domain.

While generic engines may be perfectly suitable for general-purpose usage, they may become less useful for texts that use a narrow range of vocabulary, or have very particular, characteristic styles, or are constrained by the conventions of a particular genre. This typically applies to texts associated with highly specialized domains such as law or medicine, but such constraints are also a feature of texts that we encounter in every-day life. Recipes, for example, have typical structures and vocabulary that differentiate them from other "every-day" texts like consumer guides. You hardly ever find questions in recipes, but these are frequent in consumer guides. Both types of text are often translated into other languages, either for casual use (think of a search engine translating something like "how can I make chocolate cookies?", or "what type of light bulb is recommended to save energy?"), or for professional use (think of a publisher translating a recipe book, or a manufacturer translating technical specifications for a

Gema Ramírez-Sánchez. 2022. Custom machine translation. In Dorothy Kenny (ed.), *Machine translation for everyone: Empowering users in the age of artificial intelligence*, 165–186. Berlin: Language Science Press. DOI: 10.5281/zenodo.6760022 consumer product). In the following paragraphs, I use examples from a recipe (for apple crumble) and a consumer guide (for a type of light bulb) to see how generic MT engines cope when faced with the specific terminology used in these two every-day genres.

Recipes are frequently divided into three parts: title, ingredients and instructions. For generic MT, a simple recipe title can already be a struggle. Table 1 shows how three generic MT systems cope with the term *apple crumble* in Spanish, French and Italian. MT1 works well for French and Italian, but not Spanish; MT2 does not work well in any target language; and MT3 translates adequately into French, but poorly into Spanish and Italian.

Table 1: Machine Translation of a recipe title: apple crumble.

	MT1	MT2	MT3
Spanish	migas de manzana 'crumbs of apple'	se desmorona la manzana 'the apple falls apart'	Desmoronamiento de la manzana 'falling apart of the apple'
French	crumble aux pommes 'apple crumble'	Crumble d'apple 'crumble of apple'	Crumble aux pommes 'apple crumble'
Italian	Crumble di mele 'apple crumble'	La mela si sbriciola 'the apple crumbles'	Crumble di mela 'crumble of apple'

Don't worry if you are not fluent in Spanish, French or Italian. Just do a similar test yourself by translating *apple crumble* into a language you know using your favourite online MT service. You'll probably see translations related to 'collapsing apples' or 'apples that fall apart' like we see in some of the examples in Table 1. Other translations, namely *crumble aux pommes* and *Crumble di mele*, are good (which is why we have glossed them in Table 1 simply as 'apple crumble'). How the MT engine copes depends on the data used to train the engines. Special steps may also be taken to feed engines with the correct terminology during training or as a post-translation step. But, without built-in treatment of specialized terminology, what we get from system MT2 is fairly typical of what we can expect from generic MT.

Now let's dive into the intriguing world of light bulbs. A huge variety of specialized information is available to consumers eager to learn about the many types of light bulbs on the market. So, imagine you are a non-native speaker of English living in an English-speaking country; a light goes out, and your neighbour offers to give you a twisted fluorescent lamp. You offer your best smile in exchange, as you are not sure what the neighbour means exactly. Using your phone, you check the translations provided by some generic MT systems. They provide the translations reproduced in Table 2.

Table 2: Machine Translation of a type of light bulb: twisted fluorescent lamp.

	MT1	MT2	MT3	Should be
Spanish	Lámpara fluorescente retorcida	Lámpara fluorescente retorcida	Lámpara fluorescente retorcida	Bombilla fluorescente en espiral
French	Lampe fluorescente torsadée	Lampe fluorescente tordue	Lampe fluorescente torsadée	Ampoule spirale fluorescente
Italian	Lampada fluorescente contorta	Lampada fluorescente contorto	Lampada fluorescente attorcigliata	Lampadina fluorescente spirale

After reading this, you expect your neighbour to give you a funny-shaped standard lamp or table lamp. Where are you getting this idea from? Oh, ambiguity: none of the engines provides a word meaning *light bulb* as a translation for *lamp*. All of them go for the other meaning of *lamp*, where the word stands for the whole piece of *lighting equipment*.

Generic MT got it wrong, but a custom MT engine should be able to get it right. But what is custom MT? The next section should give you an idea.

2 Custom machine translation

Custom MT, as opposed to generic MT, is MT that is designed to fit a specific purpose.

Imagine you work for a company that produces a big car brand. Like other manufacturers in the automotive sector, your company will produce lots of technical and user manuals as well as marketing material in dozens of languages.

Anything that helps your company improve communication with its internal staff, train car salespeople, or convince buyers, is deemed a key activity, and in a multilingual environment like this one, MT can be very helpful. Your company thus uses MT to produce the first draft of nearly all its translations. Reviewers, known as post-editors (see O'Brien 2022 [this volume]), then improve these drafts.

Your company starts out on its MT journey using a generic MT system and improving the output through post-editing. Soon, the post-editors begin to realize that they need to fix the same terminology, genre and style mistakes over and over again: this is not very appealing or efficient. Your company then remembers that it has been producing translations for decades, and wonders whether it could use these existing translations to somehow improve the process.

The answer is yes. But how? First, by including its own past translations as training data, your company allows the MT engine to learn from them. That is, it uses its own training data to create a custom MT engine. The custom engine produces draft translations which are much closer to the company's past translations and have far fewer errors in terminology and style, and the post-editors are happier.

But are things really as simple as that? Well, yes, but only if you have a sufficient amount of data (millions of translated sentences) which is in the right format (aligned parallel data; see Kenny 2022 [this volume]), is internally consistent (otherwise be prepared for inconsistent output), and is in the desired language pair or pairs. You also need engineers or external providers to train the system and integrate it into the company's translation workflow, as well as the right hardware and software. All this just to start with. Then you need a retraining plan if you want to take advantage of the next translations that will be produced: this can be on-the-fly if you work with adaptive MT, every six hours if you have crazy production numbers, every six months or once a year if you just want to keep the system up-to-date and consistent.

So maybe "simple" is not the word, and you might ask whether all the effort will be worth it? Let's set reasonable expectations.

2.1 What can we expect from custom machine translation?

Once the preserve of MT experts, custom MT is now commonly encountered by all sorts of users. It is even shown to us raw, without any revision, and is performed on-the-fly when we click a "get a translation" button. We see it on online hotel booking websites, online technical support for specialized software, job vacancy listings, teachers' messages in educational apps, etc.

As general users, our main goal is usually to understand information we have retrieved from somewhere, often a website. In such cases, we might expect that custom MT will, at the very least, do a better job in outputting accurate terminology and idioms than generic MT would; and we might also expect better adherence to text style.

For example, if we are looking for information about nursing homes on a website, we expect *home* to be translated to communicate the sense 'main page' on the navigation menu but 'institution where people are cared for' in the website content. If we are looking at a baseball website, there should be no confusion between the 'main page', 'base' or 'team's own grounds' senses of *home*. In other contexts, *home* should be not translated at all; for example, when it is part of a brand name. Better management of specific translations for specific contexts is something that we can expect from custom MT.

For language professionals, other, seemingly small, details take on particular importance. They appreciate when their custom MT engine outputs the right upper and lower case forms of words, or can cope with formatting conventions like bulleted lists, or renders numbers appropriately. When these phenomena are not handled correctly (as in Table 3), post-editors need to review the output of the MT engine carefully and correct these "little" mistakes, which is both irritating and time-consuming. Adherence to textual conventions and style is also something expected in a professional environment.

Table 3: Machine translation output details matter

Input	Output: generic MT		
English	Spanish	French	Italian

Given sufficient effort and the right resources, custom MT is capable of outputting text without the kinds of error in Table 3. Among the resources required are suitable human resources, which I address in the next section.

2.2 Who customizes machine translation?

As you will learn from this short section, MT is a truly interdisciplinary field in which computer engineers work alongside linguists.

Back in the days when linguistically-aware, rule-based MT was state-of-the-art, both engineers and linguists had an active role in building systems: the linguists wrote the grammatical rules and dictionaries, and the engineers wrote the computer programs that implemented the rules.

Later on, in statistical MT times, engineers took almost full responsibility for the process. Linguists were occasionally involved in output evaluation, but hardly ever in error analysis and never in defining action points to improve the machine translated output.

The technology was still reliant on human translators, however, as they provided the translations that fed the translation models.[1] But I can confirm that, in the heyday of statistical MT, linguists were more or less excluded from the actual building of the systems.

Nowadays, little by little, linguistics-savvy engineers have started to pay attention not only to tweaking parameters and hardware or automatic evaluation metrics, but also to the quality of the translations produced by their systems, at a very fine-grained level. At the same time, technology-savvy linguists have started to get involved in assessing and curating the data needed to train engines, in playing with training kits, in evaluating systems, and in defining a strategy not only to improve them but also to integrate them into the translation workflows of client companies.

The ideal situation given the nature of the task is collaboration between professionals from the two fields, professionals who are interested in learning about and contributing to each other's areas. This is particularly effective for custom MT where the need to tune systems to a particular domain means that there are significant benefits to be gained from linguists assessing the usefulness of the training data, taking control over (or at least understanding) the strategy followed during the training process, and analyzing the output. Custom MT also benefits from engineers understanding the specifics of the texts and the languages they are working with in order to be creative in finding solutions to advance and solve the main issues present in the output: is a new module or a pre- or post-processing step needed to cope with rich morphology, product names or alphanumeric codes, for example?

Training for linguists and engineers in the more technical or linguistic aspects of MT is becoming more and more usual in educational environments, but it is still predominant in professional contexts, where needs arise in a more dynamic way.

Before concluding this section, it is worth mentioning another group of people, who are increasingly contributing to MT customization, but who may or may not be covered by the term *linguists* used above, namely *translators*. In this chapter I mainly cover custom MT as an off-line activity which requires human intervention and which happens only from time to time. However, it is worth noting that

---

[1]Keep this in mind next time you hear that "machine translation is achieving human parity *without human intervention*". So, what about the texts used to train the engines?

in some current settings, namely those involving so-called "adaptive" MT (see O'Brien 2022 [this volume]), customization may also happen in real-time (or at least much faster and more frequently than in other settings). In such scenarios, translators and their translations are becoming the cornerstone for custom MT where customization actually means real-time user mimicking. New translations are integrated automatically into already proficient systems as the translator delivers new parallel sentences (source-target pairs), and preferred translations are made available to translators as they work.

3 How to customize a machine translation engine

3.1 An allegory

Imagine that you land on a new planet – no life found, but there is an extraordinary library with plenty of written texts in what seem to be a number of different languages: some texts are in one language (L1), some in another language (L2), some appear to be bilingual texts (L1-L2). But there is no grammar book, no orthography book, no organized linguistic knowledge; no clue as to how these languages work at all. Just texts with plenty of sentences, pairs of sentences and more sentences.

By chance, you also find lists of L1-L2 word correspondences. Also, while inspecting the texts, you observe that some of them are marked with a particular stamp, others are marked with a different stamp, and yet others do not have any stamp at all.[2] You feel lucky: all these texts are probably the only knowledge about the lost life on this newly discovered planet.

But no! Wait! As you leave the library, you discover that there is still life on this planet: two of its inhabitants are staring at you in a hostile way but you also notice that they look at each other in an even more inimical way. After some time, you discover that their lack of friendliness is due to a key factor: they don't understand one another; one is an L1 speaker, the other an L2 speaker and they did not know about the library. You need to help them! As a polyglot, you've done this before, and you have no option: you will teach them translation from L1 to L2 and the other way round.

How will you do this? By trying to learn about the languages individually first and then diving into how to translate between them? (This will take too long.) Or by going directly to the bilingual texts and lists? (This seems more promising.)

---

[2]For the purposes of this analogy, each different stamp represents a different domain, and texts with no stamp can be considered as non-domain specific.

You might start with the list of words and observe further relationships between other words, phrases and longer chunks. Or you could use the fact that texts can be classified into those with stamps and those without stamps. You could, for example, start grouping together texts carrying similar stamps. Or you could use all the texts at the same time. A myriad of possibilities is open to you to start learning from data about translation between L1 and L2.

At this point, when an MT system is learning how to translate, it is in the same situation as you are on this mission: you both have texts, bilingual (and monolingual), maybe also terminology lists, but nothing else. These are the only sources to learn from, but there are different ways of carrying out the learning process.

Back on your newly discovered planet, you first open your mind and try to learn from what you can observe in the bilingual L1-L2 texts. You use the lists already compiled to check if your assumptions are right and then try to build on these assumptions by forming new assumptions. You soon move from words to longer chunks. At this point you don't pay attention to whether a text is stamped or not; you try to use all resources together as a whole.

In a similar way, to build a first MT system, one usually starts by concatenating, or stringing together, all bilingual data, regardless of the different domains they come from, and by performing initial training using the default software settings.

After a first effort, you start getting messages from the L1 speaker and translating them into the L2. Then you show your translated messages to the L2 speaker to validate them. And then you repeat the process working the other way round. You keep improving your knowledge as you interpret the expressions on the L1 and L2 speakers' faces. Sometimes they laugh, but most of the time they nod their heads, and sometimes they even look as if they get it. You learn from their feedback and keep going.

In MT development, evaluation is not usually based on human (or extraterrestrial) assessment. Rather, we use automatic metrics to compute quality scores based on a comparison of the machine's output with translations already produced by professional translators (see Rossi & Carré 2022 [this volume]). In most cases, the more similar the machine output is to the human translation, the better it is deemed to be. If the automatic metrics suggest that things are OK, and a quick inspection of the output suggests that it does not present any major issues, the system can be considered as a functional baseline. Otherwise, we keep training, maybe adding some pre-processing or post-processing. After each round of training, we check our automatic metrics. When the scores are as good as we think we can get them, we stop training.

Back on the newly discovered planet, as you progress in your learning process, you discover that there is more than one translation for some words in the same language combination, but that correspondents are consistent across texts marked with the same stamp. So you decide to separate the texts by their stamps and to compile specific correspondences in separate lists. You start further inspecting non-stamped texts and then move to stamped ones. Stamped texts look a bit different to non-stamped ones: for example, sentences tend to be very long in some stamped texts while in non-stamped texts they are very short.

Given this situation, depending on how much data we have and the final goal of the system, we could train an MT engine using only texts that share the same stamp (and where the stamp represents a domain). Our in-domain system could use both generic and domain-specific texts or just domain-specific ones. And we will definitely make the most of state-of-the-art MT techniques to make the system as domain-aware as possible. This is exactly what customization is about: playing with data and techniques. In what follows we explain each of these approaches in basic terms. A more comprehensive survey of *domain adaptation* in neural MT is provided by Saunders (2021).

3.2 Customization through data

MT can be adapted to fit a specific purpose by using specific texts: we can build a very good MT system for mobile phone descriptions provided that we have a sufficient number of texts that describe mobile phones and that they are translated into the language we want to target. We can also use monolingual texts or bilingual vocabulary lists that are specific to the domain in question. This is what we call *in-domain data*. The ideal situation is to have access to bilingual in-domain data in the form of parallel sentences.[3]

3.2.1 How much data do we need?

It is difficult to say how much data is enough. For generic MT, the answer would be take as much as you can get, then maybe filter it based on qualitative factors, discarding, for example, very repetitive sentences (where there is not much to learn from), very ugly sentences (e.g. ones made up mostly of numbers), or very long sentences (which are too difficult to learn from). For custom MT, the answer could be the same, but this time also taking into account that in-domain

---

[3]Pairs of source-target sentences that are translations of each other, and are ideally ordered as they appeared in the texts they came from, to take advantage of the co-text in recent sentences (see Kenny 2022 [this volume]).

data needs to represent a generous proportion of the whole training data set, otherwise our system will not be able to learn how to produce in-domain translations.

The unspecific measure "a generous proportion" is used here on purpose as we know that it is very rare to have enough in-domain data to train a system. After all, we will need at least several million sentence pairs; maybe less than for generic MT, but still a lot. So, we normally end up mixing the available in-domain data with generic or out-of-domain data.

Depending on the language combination, when adding the available in-domain data to the out-of-domain data as the first step in customizing an MT system, we are usually faced with one of two very different scenarios: we either have too much data or too little data. When it comes to data, size matters.

3.2.1.1 A "too much" data scenario

A scenario in which we have too much data can lead us to impractical situations in which we need an unreasonable amount of time and number of servers up and running to train systems. It is difficult to give a precise figure, so let's say that you have too much data when you realize that with less data, you get the same results and, as a bonus, you need fewer computational resources and less time to achieve them. (For more details on how developers use metrics such as BLEU to tell if an engine has stopped learning, see Pérez-Ortiz et al. (2022 [this volume]), especially 7.2).

In custom MT, the available in-domain data is prioritized and we use all of it. For the out-of-domain data, however, we will need to select a subset of the available parallel sentences. Data selection is normally performed using the in-domain data as a model of what we want. Selection can be done automatically in many different ways, for example by:

- Scoring the out-of-domain sentences by textual, semantic or syntactic similarity to the in-domain ones

- Grouping the out-of-domain data by the topics discovered in the in-domain data

- Re-classifying the out-of-domain sentences as in-domain based on examples of what would be very good or very bad in-domain sentences

3.2.1.2 A "too little" data scenario

In the opposite "too little" data scenario, we could compromise the usefulness of the MT system if we do not make an effort to get more data. The system would probably output poorly translated sentences with many untranslated words. We should start with the in-domain data, and try to extend it as much as possible. This extension can be done by integrating more already existing data (if available) or by creating it. We can get as-is or made-to-measure data for free or consider purchasing it. Automatic data extension strategies include:

- Getting additional bilingual data by crawling multilingual websites for the targeted languages in general, or paying specific attention to the vocabulary covered by the in-domain data

- Using additionally available monolingual data, ideally in the target language, and translating it back into the source language with a third-party MT system

- Pivoting through another language, translating monolingual data in two steps: first into the pivot language then into the target/source language of our combination

- Creating new sentences in the source and target languages by automatically composing new ones from the available data (replacing words by synonyms or similar frequency words, using automatic paraphrasing, etc.)

Experience shows that not only bilingual data, but also monolingual and multilingual data, and generic, in-domain and multi-domain data, have all proven useful in helping MT systems to learn (Saunders 2021). What is more, tiny amounts of data are starting to be taken into account in adaptive or incremental MT scenarios (see O'Brien 2022 [this volume]). The landscape is changing fast but one thing is certain: provided that there is some data, there is a chance for learning, and MT will make the most of it.

3.2.2 Data quality

Data quality also plays a role in the customization of MT systems, impacting directly on the quality of the final output. This has become a topic of interest particularly with the rise of neural MT (see Kenny 2022 [this volume] and Pérez-Ortiz et al. 2022 [this volume]), as studies show that it is very sensitive to noise in the training data (Khayrallah & Koehn 2018). Most of the work done to overcome this problem consists in filtering out noise using a mix of patterns and rules to remove obvious noise, scoring sentences for quality, and classifying them to discriminate between high-quality and low-quality content. It also includes the removal of duplicates (Khayrallah & Koehn 2018).

3.2.3 Data organization

Finally, data organization is also becoming a topic of interest (Mohiuddin et al. 2022). Some studies organize training data using sentences with similar length to improve training and translation speed. Others feed the models with sentences from more simple to more complex to improve quality. Others use documents instead of shuffled sentences to take advantage of the wider textual context, in order to get improved MT outputs.

3.3 Customization through techniques

Once we have compiled and cleaned all the data we can get our hands on to train an in-domain MT system, how do we use these data? What type of system architecture is best for our purposes? Do we have different options to constrain the output? This is what customization through techniques is all about. The techniques in question may have to do with modifying the architecture of the network, adjusting parameters during training or combining different systems during training or translation time (also called inference).

Below I review some of the most popular techniques to get domain-specific MT. Koehn (2020: Ch. 13) provides a more detailed discussion.

3.3.1 Self-taught systems

In the self-taught systems approach, we would use first only the generic data to train a system. Then, taking this system as a starting point, we would perform a second training pass using only the in-domain data. This would result in a fine-tuned system with some general knowledge of the languages and a very specific knowledge of the in-domain vocabulary, structures, etc.

3.3.2 Coached systems

Besides training the MT system using generic and in-domain data, one can also use language models trained ideally on in-domain texts in the target language, but at the very least good quality monolingual texts. The language model will help in tailoring the output towards more in-domain-like language. It is also possible to use domain controllers or discriminators to label training data at word, sentence or even embedding level. This technique consists in identifying precisely what in the generic data is closer to or further from the in-domain data and use this information during training.

3.3.3 Partnering systems

Some systems are based on ensembles of several components (e.g. domain-specific sub-networks) or even full systems. They combine their knowledge to produce better output together than individually.

4 Customization in practice

Theory and practice are frequently two sides of the same coin. This section gives very practical details on customizing a neural MT engine. It is aimed at beginners and does not assume advanced technical knowledge.

4.1 Available tools

There are already several professional kits for MT customization. These mostly allow users to play with data but not techniques. So while customization through data is well within the reach of a wider range of language professionals, customization through techniques remains the preserve of researchers and developers.

Most MT providers offer remote access to pre-trained generic or domain-specific engines for a given price. Some also offer customization options.[4] When customization is offered, this usually covers:

- Adding your own corpora

- Adding your own terminology

- Training a new model with your data

- Testing the custom model

---

[4]At the time of writing, there are more than 40 providers offering MT services and around 20 provide some customization options. Source: https://inten.to/mt-landscape/, last accessed 26 June 2022.

All this can be done in a semi-automatic way, where a real person takes care of the data and the processes involved, or in an fully automatic way, where customization happens without further human intervention.

There are also MT testing environments designed for teaching language professionals how MT works. These are used in translation technology classrooms or in professional environments as training tools. They usually offer customization options to see what happens when a system is trained with more generic or in-domain data. A good example of such an environment is MutNMT.[5]

4.2 Key factors when defining a strategy

The most important factors that need to be taken into account when defining a custom MT strategy are:

- Language combination

- Domain

- Available data

- Purpose of the system

- Deadline

- Hardware characteristics and availability

Let's take a look at each in turn:

Depending on the language combination, you may decide to work with one or another tool. Morphologically-rich languages, for example, may benefit from pre- or post-processing using a tool designed to support the language in question.

Some domains have very special textual characteristics that might be supported by training kits. For example, a particular training kit might be ideal for dealing with very long or very short sentences, numerical expressions, or proper names, which usually need to be retained in translation. If the domain has other very specific characteristics, they need to be taken into account.

The amount and quality of available data is a key factor in deciding when to go ahead and train a system, or when to try customizing a system using more and/or higher quality data. Also, if there is data beyond parallel sentences that you want to include, it is necessary to make sure that technology will support it.

---

[5] See http://www.multitrainmt.eu/index.php/en/neural-mt-training/mutnmt, last accessed 26 June 2022.

The purpose of most neural MT systems is to produce the best raw output possible, but additional requirements usually need to be met. Before you opt for a particular service provider you might need to consider whether their language models can be accessed remotely or whether you actually need access to them on your own premises. Will the system be used online with concurrent users or as a batch one-at-at-time queued process? Will the system translate text strings? Or does it need to support translation using different file formats? Will it be accessed through an API, web app, or a connector to a third-party tool? And so on.

Deployment of custom MT might require a trade off between quality and meeting a delivery deadline. The best possible system may need more training days than you can afford.

Finally, hardware is also a key component, both for training and for later use of a system in production. Depending on other factors, you may need a service that is available 24/7, and uses several GPUs/CPUs at the same time.

4.3 Getting the right data

Custom MT systems heavily depend on the availability and quality of in-domain parallel data that is similar to the texts we ultimately wish to translate. In 3.2.1, I discussed data sizes and ways to select or extend such data depending on the scenario. Here I cover a very basic question: where can you find the right parallel data for your system?

In the first instance, you might try getting existing parallel data for free: there is a myriad of data repositories that offer free and publicly available bilingual corpora ready to use for MT. Most of these repositories or corpora can be accessed through the OPUS website, which is maintained by the University of Helsinki, and hosts corpora in more than 200 language combinations.[6]

Purchasing parallel data is also an option. (Selling parallel data for MT is a business.) What is on offer varies from very large to very small collections, each with different usage rights, and using different business models and pricing. One of the largest MT-specific data collections is offered by TAUS and covers more than 600 language combinations.[7]

It is also possible to assemble parallel data yourself. Although probably not ideal for assembling large amounts of data, parallel corpora can be created by:

- crawling multilingual websites: if a URL contains bilingual content, you can download such content for a given language pair, and either align it yourself (see Kenny 2022 [this volume] for an example of an aligned text), or use a third-party service to align it.

---

[6] See https://opus.nlpl.eu/index.php, last accessed 26 June 2022.
[7] See https://www.taus.net/, last accessed 26 June 2022.

- aligning your own translated documents: if you have translated documents and their original source texts, you can use standard open-access or proprietary tools to align them at sentence level.[8]

4.4 Getting the data right

Once we've got the right data, we need to prepare it before training our system. This means making sure that we have:

- One text file per language (or language combination): plain text files are the usual food for MT training. One per language is the ideal, although some systems can cope with spreadsheet-type formats that use one column per language, or even TMX files (see Kenny 2022 [this volume]).

- One sentence per line: the text files need to be formatted so that each sentence takes up a single line. This effectively means that each sentence becomes a one-sentence paragraph. Longer or shorter units are not usually allowed,[9] although headings can be treated as if they are sentences.

- One-to-one aligned sentences: independently of the format, every line in the source file needs to correspond to the same line in the target file.

- Clean data: there should be no duplicates, typos, or noisy sentences (e.g. those with only numbers, or that are badly encoded, or not in the language you want, etc.).

- Anonymized data (if necessary): you might need to eliminate any sensitive data, and especially personal data, from your training corpora.

- Organized data: corpora need to be divided into three sets corresponding to the different phases of the training process. These sets are usually named the *training set* (*train* for short), the *validation set* (also *development set* or *dev* for short) and the *test set* (or just *test*).

Some rules of thumb for organizing data are as follows:

- Overlap between the sentences in these three sets must be avoided at all costs. Indeed, if possible, sentences from different sources should be used in each set to guarantee their balance and independence.

---

[8]Free alignment tools include LF Aligner (https://sourceforge.net/projects/aligner/, last accessed 26 June 2022); while well-known paid-for alignment tools include those provided with translation memory tools (see Kenny 2022 [this volume]).

[9]I am assuming here sentences as the training unit, not documents.

- Training sets can vary in size from several thousand to several million sentences, but validation and test sets do not normally exceed 5,000 sentences.

- Training data may contain generic and custom data, but validation and test data should be as in-domain as possible to test the suitability of the trained model for its intended purpose.

- When the training set contains both generic and in-domain data, the proportion of in-domain data needs to be as large as possible, otherwise the model will take most of its knowledge from the generic data.

Thus far, nothing we have mentioned is peculiar to custom engines; all this preparation applies equally to generic and custom MT. The next steps, related to pre-processing, also apply in both scenarios but may vary for particular languages or language combinations:

- Text needs to be tokenized: you need to provide the training process with texts where tokens can be clearly identified. Tokens are the different units into which one can divide a text. They can be words, spaces or punctuation marks, for example. Tokenizing is mostly about identifying word boundaries, and this sometimes involves guessing where a word starts and ends, often using the spaces between written words to guide us. Languages like Thai are not written with spaces between words however, which makes word tokenization challenging. Tokenizers for these languages sometimes simply split sentences into chunks containing seemingly arbitrary sequences of characters. This approach has the advantage of being language independent, even if it has no concept of "units of meaning".

- Text may need to be truecased: we may want our training process to capture the fact that a word spelled with an initial capital letter at the beginning of sentences in our training data (for example, *The*) is the same word as that spelt all in lower case (in this case, *the*) in other sentence positions in the data. We thus use *truecasers* to convert all words except proper names (in languages like English) to lower case.[10] Truecasing only applies to languages that distinguish uppercase and lowercase so it is not applicable to Chinese, Arabic, Hebrew and many others.

---

[10] Note that all nouns in German begin with upper case, and, like proper nouns in English, these should not be truecased.

- Sub-word splitting: depending on the tokenization performed on a text, further splitting of words into sub-words, characters or other chunks of text may apply. This splitting may be based on frequency counts or a linguistically-motivated segmentation that takes into account morphemes, stems, and additional morphological information. This is not always configurable in custom environments as it requires the neural network to be able to cope with special types of input and output, and sometimes only one method is supported in pre- or post-processing.

So, what if you have texts that you want to use as training data, but they are not in the right format? Don't worry, because most of the time, tokenization, truecasing and subword splitting – if applicable – are included by default as pre-training, pre-processing (and post-processing) steps in standard training kits. They are mentioned here so that users of these training kits know what's going on. There are also plenty of stand-alone tools you can use to perform these steps. To find these tools, you can go to platforms like Hugging Face[11] or Github,[12] or simply open a search engine and start typing: sentence splitter, sentence aligner, parallel corpus filtering, anonymizer, tokenizer, truecaser, etc. For more refined searches, add the source and target languages. You will discover a whole world of tools.

4.5 Training the custom model

Training an MT model once we have the right data, in the right format, is just a matter of clicking a button in many current training environments. Some environments allow users to tweak a number of parameters to get the best out of the combination of data-training environment and system architecture. Sometimes users are allowed to tweak settings for educational or research purposes.

The most common parameters that can be adjusted by the user before training are as follows:

- *Vocabulary size* specifies the number of different words or sub-words (also called sub-word units, types or word types) allowed in the vocabulary computed from the training corpus.

- *Batch size* is the number of tokens[13] that will be processed together in each training step. This is needed because it is not possible to feed all the data in the training set to the neural network at once.

---

[11]https://huggingface.co/, last accessed 26 June 2022.

[12]https://github.com/, last accessed 26 June 2022.

[13]Batch size in *tokens* (see Rossi & Carré 2022 [this volume]) instead of sentences has become the most used batch type in the last years in order to make batches more similarly sized.

- *Beam size* is the number of translation hypotheses (i.e. translation candidates) that are taken into account when translating a word. Hypotheses are produced during the training process and when the system is actually translating.

- *Duration* refers to the number of epochs allowed in the training process. An *epoch* is a full training pass over all the sentences in the training set. Each epoch comprises all the training steps necessary to see all the data once.[14]

- *Validation frequency* is the number of steps included before each evaluation of the status of the training takes place. Typically, validation cycles happen many times in each epoch.

- *Stopping condition* specifies the maximum number of validation cycles allowed where no improvement of the engine's performance is registered. When this maximum is reached, the training process is ended, regardless of the number of epochs initially set. Improvements can be measured based on any automatic metric, or on a combination of metrics. Common automatic metrics include as BLEU, chrF1 and perplexity.[15]

All of these parameters usually come with default values that developers have set after optimizing the training process for a particular environment.

Once parameters have been set – or the default parameters have been accepted – training proceeds as follows: at each training step, a batch of training data is fed into the neural network, the output for each sentence in the batch is computed, the error loss is computed, weights are updated, and it all starts again! After a predetermined number of training steps (set by the validation frequency), the engine's performance is evaluated, and then training resumes. When further training fails to improve the engine's performance, or the performance starts to degrade, the training stops. There it is, our model!

---

[14]Given the large amounts of data used in NMT, the use of epochs to measure the duration of the training can be impractical. Rather than using epochs, you can use the number of steps, in relation to a particular batch size, to help you measure duration independently of the model, language pair or amount of data.

[15]Perplexity in natural language processing, and more specifically in MT, measures how uncertain a translation model is about predicting the next word when translating. A low perplexity is obtained when the translation model assigns a high probability to each word/token in a given target sentence. For more information on BLEU and chrF1, see Rossi & Carré (2022 [this volume]).

4.6 Testing the custom model

Once we've trained an MT system, we need to test or evaluate it. The many options for testing can be summarized as follows:

- Try it yourself (or ask someone else to try it)! If you know the languages you are working with and the purpose for which the system was trained, and you have the time, just take a bunch of sentences, translate them and take a look at the resulting translation! With the correct tools, you can also inspect not just the one best translation output by the system, but also the list of *n*-best translations considered by it for each sentence.

- Measure it! There are automatic metrics that one can compute to see how the system behaves (see Rossi & Carré 2022 [this volume]). Most metrics are based on comparing the output of the system to a "reference" translation created by a professional (human) translator (see Rossi & Carré 2022 [this volume]). The meaning of these metrics can vary considerably: some are useful for comparing two different systems with each other, but mean very little by themselves. This applies to *n*-gram or character-based metrics such as BLEU (Papineni et al. 2002), METEOR (Denkowski & Lavie 2014) and CHRF1-3 (Popović 2015). Others are useful to see how much work is needed to turn the automatic translation into the professional translation. This applies to post-editing effort-oriented metrics such as WER (Popović & Ney 2007) or TER (Snover et al. 2006). Yet others tell you about the characteristics of the individual texts translated by the system. Textual metrics include those that measure lexical variety or lexical density. Finally, some metrics are used to rank systems, and will tell you whether your system is preferred to others.

- Get feedback from real-life usage! You can assess whether the system is useful in a real setting, professional or casual, taking into account the purpose of the system. Did you train a system to help people write e-mails? If yes, then ask people to write e-mails using it and tell you about their experience. Did you train a system to help people understand recipes? Then ask users to follow recipes translated by your system and give you feedback. Did you train a system to translate legal documents? If so, ask users to use it for their next translation, and report back to you on how they felt about using the system, whether they saved time by using the system, and so on. By gathering this kind of feedback, you will not only be able to judge the current status of your system, but you will also get information that will help you work out how you might improve the system.

Finally, if you have gone to the trouble of creating a custom system, with all the excitement and pain that this might entail, you might want to compare the output of your system with that of a generic system, using any of the relevant testing options above. If your custom system outperforms the generic system, then it is a success. Well done! Otherwise, try to keep having fun!

5 Conclusion

This chapter has provided a brief overview of the customization of MT. Having differentiated between custom MT and generic MT, the chapter stressed the importance of managing expectations when it comes to customization, before introducing the professional roles involved in custom NMT, and asking where MT sits in the translation workflow. Customization through both data and techniques was discussed, and analogies with real-life learning processes were suggested. The chapter concluded with a practical section on tools, customization strategy, data compilation and preparation, training and – finally – testing, in a bid to help readers get hands-on experience of custom MT.

6 Acknowledgments

I would like to thank Dorothy Kenny, Jaume Zaragoza Bernabeu, Carmen Iniesta López, Amelia Arenas Olivares and Maite Heredia Arribas for their time and suggestions on how to improve this text. Thanks also to Reinhard Rapp and Felix Kopecky for their thorough review of this chapter. Any remaining errors are mine alone.

References

Denkowski, Michael & Alon Lavie. 2014. Meteor universal: Language specific translation evaluation for any target language. In *Proceedings of the ninth workshop on Statistical Machine Translation*, 376–380. Baltimore: Association for Computational Linguistics. DOI: 10.3115/v1/W14-3348.

Kenny, Dorothy. 2022. Human and machine translation. In Dorothy Kenny (ed.), *Machine translation for everyone: Empowering users in the age of artificial intelligence*, 23–49. Berlin: Language Science Press. DOI: 10.5281/zenodo.6759976.

Khayrallah, Huda & Philipp Koehn. 2018. On the impact of various types of noise on neural machine translation. In *Proceedings of the 2nd workshop on neural machine translation and generation*, 74–83. Melbourne: Association for Computational Linguistics. https://aclanthology.org/W18-2709.pdf.

Koehn, Philipp. 2020. *Neural Machine Translation*. Cambridge: Cambridge University Press.

Mohiuddin, Tasnim, Philipp Koehn, Vishrav Chaudhary, James Cross, Shruti Bhosale & Shafiq Joty. 2022. *Data selection curriculum for neural machine translation*. DOI: 10.48550/ARXIV.2203.13867.

O'Brien, Sharon. 2022. How to deal with errors in machine translation: Post-editing. In Dorothy Kenny (ed.), *Machine translation for everyone: Empowering users in the age of artificial intelligence*, 105–120. Berlin: Language Science Press. DOI: 10.5281/zenodo.6759982.

Papineni, Kishore, Salim Roukos, Todd Ward & Wei-Jing Zhu. 2002. BLEU: A method for automatic evaluation of machine translation. In *Proceedings of the 40th Annual Meeting of the Association for Computational Linguistics*, 311–318. Philadelphia, Pennsylvania, USA: Association for Computational Linguistics. DOI: 10.3115/1073083.1073135.

Pérez-Ortiz, Juan Antonio, Mikel L. Forcada & Felipe Sánchez-Martínez. 2022. How neural machine translation works. In Dorothy Kenny (ed.), *Machine translation for everyone: Empowering users in the age of artificial intelligence*, 141–164. Berlin: Language Science Press. DOI: 10.5281/zenodo.6760020.

Popović, Maja. 2015. Chrf: Character n-gram f-score for automatic MT evaluation. In *Proceedings of the tenth workshop on statistical machine translation*, 392–395. Association for Computational Linguistics. 10.18653/v1/W15-3049.

Popović, Maja & Hermann Ney. 2007. Word error rates. In *Proceedings of the Second Workshop on Statistical Machine Translation* (StatMT '07), 48–55. Prague, Czech Republic. DOI: 10.3115/1626355.1626362.

Rossi, Caroline & Alice Carré. 2022. How to choose a suitable neural machine translation solution: Evaluation of MT quality. In Dorothy Kenny (ed.), *Machine translation for everyone: Empowering users in the age of artificial intelligence*, 51–79. Berlin: Language Science Press. DOI: 10.5281/zenodo.6759978.

Saunders, Danielle. 2021. Domain adaptation and multi-domain adaptation for neural machine translation: A survey. *CoRR* abs/2104.06951. https://arxiv.org/abs/2104.06951.

Snover, Matthew, Bonnie Dorr, Rich Schwartz, Linnea Micciulla & John Makhoul. 2006. A study of translation edit rate with targeted human annotation. In *Proceedings of the 7th conference of the Association for Machine Translation in the Americas: Technical papers*, 223–231. Cambridge, Massachusetts: Association for Machine Translation in the Americas. https://aclanthology.org/2006.amta-papers.25/.

Chapter 9

Machine translation for language learners

Alice Carré[a], Dorothy Kenny[b], Caroline Rossi[a], Pilar Sánchez-Gijón[c] & Olga Torres-Hostench[c]

[a]Université Grenoble-Alpes [b]Dublin City University [c]Universitat Autònoma de Barcelona

Machine Translation (MT) has been controversial in second and foreign language learning, but the strategic integration of MT might be beneficial to language learning in certain contexts. In this chapter we discuss the conditions in which MT can be useful in language learning, set out digital alternatives to MT, and provide examples of how MT can support language learners.

1 Introduction

Machine translation (MT) has been controversial in second and foreign language learning,[1] with some commentators arguing that it can encourage plagiarism, promote errors or deflect learners from what they should be doing. In some cases, however, MT has been found to help students complete certain tasks, and there appears to be merit in considering MT as just one among many digital resources that contemporary language learners can use. The successful integration of MT into language learning requires us to understand, even at a basic level, how the technology works, how we can judge the quality of its outputs, how those outputs can be improved through intervention either before or after the fact of translation (through pre-editing or post-editing), and what the ethical issues in using

---

[1]Note that we use the generic terms *language learning* and *language learner* in this chapter to cover instances of foreign language learning and second and subsequent language learning. If a student's first language is their L1, then the language learning to which we refer corresponds to their learning of an L2, L3 or L*n*.

Alice Carré, Dorothy Kenny, Caroline Rossi, Pilar Sánchez-Gijón & Olga Torres-Hostench. 2022. Machine translation for language learners. In Dorothy Kenny (ed.), *Machine translation for everyone: Empowering users in the age of artificial intelligence*, 187–207. Berlin: Language Science Press. DOI: 10.5281/zenodo.6760024

MT are, among other factors. These factors, which are often subsumed under the heading of *MT literacy* (Bowker & Ciro 2019) have been covered in depth in Chapters 2 to 6 of this book. Torres-Hostench (2022 [this volume]), meanwhile, presented compelling arguments as to why MT needs to be considered as a vital building block of multilingual societies *alongside* language learning. What has been missing so far is a deeper engagement with the use of MT *within* language learning. In this chapter we aim to complete the jigsaw by addressing precisely this issue. We start by looking at the role of translation in language learning, and then ask whether it is acceptable to use MT for this purpose, and what benefits can be gained by doing so. We go on to suggest contexts in which language learners should or should not use MT, depending on a number of contextual parameters, and given the other, often more appropriate digital resources available to them. Finally, we give practical examples of how MT can be used in language learning contexts.

2 Translation in language learning

Before considering the role of MT in language learning, it is worth remembering that the role translation itself might play in language learning has long been a matter of debate. The much criticized grammar-translation method, in which learners were asked to learn vocabulary and grammar rules before translating sentences out of context, is generally rejected as a narrow pedagogical use of translation, but this rejection is itself based on a very narrow understanding of translation. At the same time, there is renewed interest in what Cook (2010) aptly dubbed TILT (Translation in Language Teaching) and "studies exploring translation in the language classroom have multiplied in the last decade within a variety of disciplines" (Pintado Gutiérrez 2018: 12). Reported benefits include improved "plurilingual, pluricultural and communicative competences" as well as better writing skills, language awareness and control (ibid.: 13). The use of translation in the language classroom has also been shown to reduce anxiety and cognitive load among language learners (Kelly & Bruen 2017). The vibrancy of TILT is exemplified in sources such as Noriega-Sánchez et al. (2021), which presents the latest trends in the integration of translation-related activities in the language curriculum.

3 Machine translation in language learning

3.1 Is it acceptable to use MT in language learning?

Research conducted in the 2010s suggests that MT was, by and large, still taboo in the language classroom at the time. Based on the results of a survey of teachers worldwide, Pym et al. (2013) showed that very few reported working with machine translated texts in their language classes. There also appeared to be a causal link between MT and reluctance to use translation in language teaching, as reported by one informant in the study: in secondary schools the decision not to use translation was often based on "fear of students preferring to rely on machine translation tools" (Pym et al. 2013: 93).

There is, however, a growing realization that the use of Free Online MT (FOMT) is widespread among language learners, regardless of what teachers think, and that the effects of this use are worthy of investigation. Researchers such as Lee (2021) and Jolley & Maimone (2022) review the burgeoning literature on the use of MT in language learning. Among the trends they recognize is the tendency to view the use of MT as cheating. This has led some commentators to write about how MT use could be "detected" in students' L2 writing. When MT quality was generally poor, its use was easily detected in the kind of mistakes that were typical of the technology. Nowadays, researchers now argue that:

> As MT technologies continue to improve, identifying translation "mistakes" will likely become increasingly difficult for language instructors. Instead, it will be the technology's subtle successes, rather than its breakdowns, that will signal MT use. (Ducar & Schocket 2018: 787)

In other words, students will get caught out not because their writing is riddled with errors, but because it is too good for their level. A beginner learner of French who produces a subjunctive verb form that would not normally be encountered until they had reached an advanced stage, for example, might thus be suspected of using MT.

But whether someone is cheating or not depends not on the technology they are using, but on the rules of the game. If learners are forbidden from using MT in their L2 writing, but nonetheless use the technology surreptitiously, then that is cheating. Even if they are not expressly forbidden from using MT, but use it without letting the teacher know, and with the intention of passing the MT output off as their own writing, then this is still a dishonest action that is carried out to gain some kind of advantage. Indeed, the presentation of "someone else's words" as one's own belongs to the category of cheating known as *plagiarism,* a topic that is addressed by Mundt & Groves (2016) in the context of MT use in language learning. A number of studies (e.g. Correa 2011, Clifford & Munné 2013, Ducar & Schocket 2018) show, however, that attitudes to the use of MT in language learning can differ between learners and teachers, or depending on the extent of the use of MT, or a host of other issues, and so the situation may not be as clear cut as it first seems.

If you are learning a language in a formal setting, the best advice is to talk to your teacher, to make sure you understand what does and does not constitute cheating in your particular circumstances. If you are a language teacher, the best advice is to talk to your students to ensure that they know what is expected of them. Either way, the wish to avoid cheating is just one thing that needs to be taken into consideration when deciding whether or not it is acceptable to use MT in a language learning assignment. Other considerations are listed under "situational parameters" in §3 of this chapter, and in Moorkens (2022 [this volume]) on ethics. For now, we limit ourselves to a discussion of the nature of the "advantage" that might be gained in using MT, with or without the approval of a teacher.

3.2 What do you gain by using MT in language learning?

There is some evidence that learners can gain an advantage in the short term by using MT to accomplish particular tasks. In the study reported on by O'Neill (2019), for example, 310 American intermediate-level university students wrote short compositions in French and Spanish, under different conditions, involving the use of: Google Translate with prior training for students; Google Translate without prior student training; an online dictionary with prior training; an online dictionary without prior training; or no technical aid at all. The students who used Google Translate, and had prior training in the use of the tool, scored better than all others on their compositions, followed by those who used an online dictionary, again with prior training. In a post-test conducted about a week later, and a delayed post-test conducted some three to four weeks later, where students no longer had access to the tool in question, the Google Translate + Training group no longer performed better than the other groups. It appears that any advantage they had gained by using the tool was short-lived and dependent on the continued availability of the tool.

In a separate study, Fredholm (2019) tracked lexical diversity in compositions written, over the course of a full school year, by 31 Swedish upper secondary school pupils of Spanish as a foreign language, in which roughly half the pupils used a printed dictionary as a translation tool, and the other half used Google

Translate. He found that use of MT was associated with higher lexical diversity, and hence better performance, as long as students continued to have access to the tool, but once access was removed, the effect vanished. Again, the benefit bestowed by use of MT seemed dependent on the continued availability of the tool.

So does this mean that it is not worthwhile using MT in language learning? Not quite. In both studies, the use of MT did not harm students in the long run; there was simply no difference between students who used MT and students who did not, once the tool was no longer accessible. In the short term, however, the students who used MT did better than the others. So whether you benefit or not from MT use appears to depend on whether you take a short or long term view, and whether you focus on a particular task as an end it itself or on your development as a language learner.

Another lesson from O'Neill's (2019) study is that – in the short term at least – training matters. Learners who are trained, even briefly, in how MT works, write better compositions than those with no training.

3.3 What, exactly, can MT help you with?

We have already seen that the use of MT has been shown to help certain learners write better compositions generally, or write compositions with more diverse vocabulary than other learners. In general, studies that track the effect of MT use on L2 (or L3) written composition tend to focus on learners' use of *vocabulary*, *grammar*, and *syntax*. According to Lee (2021):

> Numerous studies have confirmed that MT helps students reduce ortho-graphic, lexical, and grammatical errors and focus more on content, and as a result, students with MT produce revisions with a greater number of successful edits and a better quality of L2 writing. (Lee 2021: 4)

But it should be noted that individual studies can produce seemingly conflict-ing results. Fredholm (2015), for example, found that Swedish pupils who used FOMT in their written compositions in Spanish made fewer mistakes in spelling and article/noun/adjective agreement, but more mistakes in syntax and in verb conjugation, than pupils who did not use FOMT.

Other studies are interested in learners' *metalinguistic awareness*, defined as:

> the ability to focus attention on language as an object in and of itself, to reflect upon language, and to evaluate it. (Thomas (1988: 531) in Thue Vold 2018: 67)

Enkin & Mejías-Bikandi (2016) propose (but do not test) exercises in which students are presented with machine translations into Spanish of sentences involving "structures of interest" in English, and where contrastive differences mean that MT traditionally has not been very successful. This is the case, for example, with non-finite subordinate clauses that are best translated into Spanish using finite subordinate clauses. The idea is that students can reflect on where the machine goes wrong, thus honing their own metalinguistic, and especially contrastive awareness. The authors note, however, that as MT improves, "materials may need to be updated" (Enkin & Mejías-Bikandi 2016: 145). It is probably fair to say, however, that neural MT engines for language pairs like English-Spanish have already reached such a level of quality that it is no longer reasonable to expect them to translate any given structure of interest incorrectly, as a matter of course, and that the kind of exercise envisaged by these authors needs to be rethought, so that students are encouraged to reflect on the successes, rather than the failures, of MT.

The same observation can be made about studies that rely on learners correcting errors in MT output. Not only can exposure to "bad models" (Niño 2009) be controversial in language learning, but it might also be increasingly difficult to spot errors in contemporary neural MT in the first place (Castilho et al. 2017, Loock & Léchauguette 2021), making post-editing type tasks (see O'Brien 2022 [this volume]) less suitable for use in certain language learning contexts than was previously the case (cf. Zhang & Torres-Hostench 2019).[2]

Thue Vold (2018) reports on another study on metalinguistic awareness. This time learners of French as an L3 in an upper secondary school in Norway had to read two different machine-translated versions of the same text (one translated by Google Translate, the other by Microsoft's Bing Translator), decide which machine translated version was better and explain why. The exact proficiency level of the students was not ascertained, although the author (Thue Vold 2018: 73) intimates that it was unlikely to be above B1 on the Common European Framework of Reference for Languages.[3] Thue Vold concludes that while the use of MT texts to develop learners' metalinguistic awareness has "considerable potential", "training, scaffolding techniques and guidance from the teacher are of paramount importance" (ibid.: 89) as, left to their own devices, learners may not explore fruitful avenues of analysis, and their group conversation may even reinforce misconceptions about language (ibid.).

---

[2]Having said that, recent studies, like that conducted by Loock & Léchauguette (2021), may be more interested in developing MT literacy – rather than metalinguistic awareness per se – among language learners, and *teacher-guided* error analysis of MT output may serve this purpose well.

[3]https://www.coe.int/en/web/common-european-framework-reference-languages

3.4 Tips on using MT in language learning

The jury is still out on the precise benefits of using MT in language learning. It is likely, however, that such benefits depend on a whole host of factors including students' proficiency levels and the text genres used in L2 writing tasks (see Chung & Ahn 2021), as well as the language pair concerned (see §4.1 below). What is increasingly agreed upon in existing research is, however, that:

- Language learners use MT and rather than trying to outlaw its use, it is better to take a nuanced approach, based on an understanding of where MT can be more or less helpful, depending, perhaps, on the extent and context of use.

- Language learners make better use of MT when they have received appropriate training.

- Language learners can generally benefit more from MT if they already have reasonably good proficiency in the foreign language (O'Neill 2012, Resende & Way 2021).

Assuming that we do embrace MT in language-learning contexts there are some basic points that should be noted by both teachers and learners, as they may not be self-evident (see also Bowker 2020).

First, there is more than one option available to learners who wish to use MT. Many learners appear to be aware only of Google Translate (see, for example, Dorst et al. 2022), but there is much to be learned by comparing the outputs of different FOMT systems, such as Bing Translator, DeepL or Baidu.

Second, MT outputs change over time as engines are re-trained or improved by users. This means that systems should not be written off based on a single use. It also means that researchers who use FOMT in their publications should always say exactly when they created the outputs in question, but this is rarely done.

Third, if you are using a FOMT system to create a language-learning exercise, to make a point about the technology, or to help you with a written composition, you should make sure that you give the system a fair chance to succeed. Very slight changes in input can have a big impact on outputs. An example may help here: in a generally very helpful discussion of MT in L2 learning, Ducar & Schocket (2018: 785) present an example of where Google Translate apparently produces a poor output based on "the more frequent and literal meaning of the word milk rather than the intended metaphorical meaning." The example is reproduced here in Figure 1.

About 1,300,000,000 results (0.74 seconds)

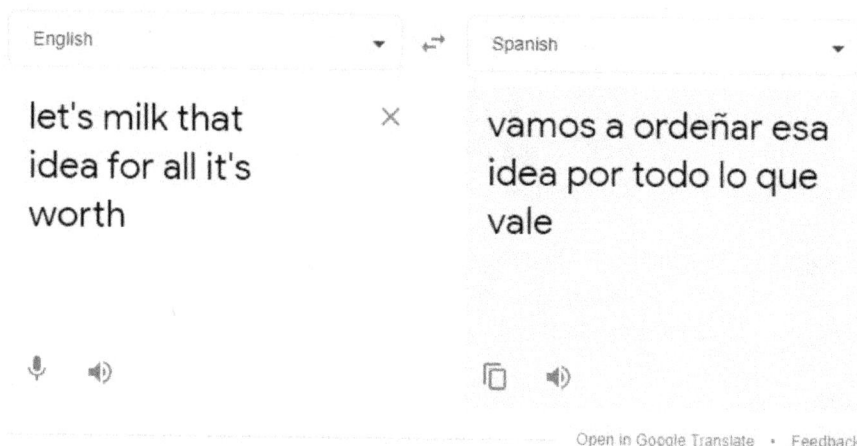

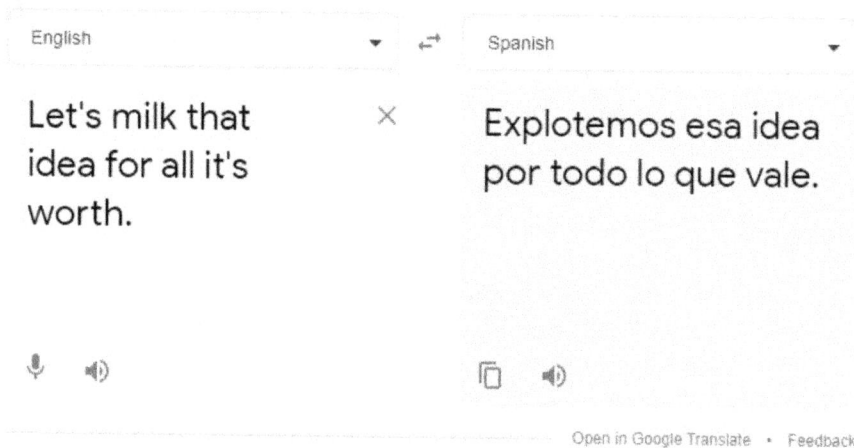

English	⇄	Spanish
let's milk that idea for all it's worth	✕	vamos a ordeñar esa idea por todo lo que vale

Open in Google Translate · Feedback

Figure 1: : input to Google Translate with sentence-initial lower case and no sentence-ending punctuation, produced 19 October 2021

What is notable here is that the input does not have a capital letter at the beginning of the sentence and there is no full stop at the end. If these features of the standard written language are reinstated, however, the output also changes – for the better – as shown in Figure 2.

About 1,300,000,000 results (0.74 seconds)

English	⇄	Spanish
Let's milk that idea for all it's worth.	✕	Explotemos esa idea por todo lo que vale.

Open in Google Translate · Feedback

Figure 2: input to Google Translate with sentence-initial upper case and sentence-ending punctuation, produced 19 October2021

Similar issues have been observed when students copy-paste text into a FOMT window, not realizing that they may have done so in such a way that each line has a line break at the end of it, and what the FOMT thus sees is a series of independent lines, each of which will be translated independently of the others. State-of-the-art MT engines are trained to translate sentences. They work best when they can actually identify and translate full sentences. It is therefore important to make sure that you don't "feed" text full of stray line breaks to the machine.

- Just as the outputs of different MT engines or systems can be fruitfully compared with each other, the usefulness of MT in language learning can be fruitfully compared with the usefulness of competing or complementary tools, such as corpus tools or online dictionaries. The next section elaborates on this point.

4 When to use MT: linguistic and situational parameters

4.1 I get by with a little help

So, if you are learning a foreign language, or dealing with a foreign language that you don't know very well, is MT your best friend? It will appear to be an easy and quick solution, and one that could even help you trick your teacher or addressee into believing that your mastery of the language is quite good, so much so that it is not unusual these days for modern language students to share love stories about free MT engines, acknowledging for instance that the system made them "bilingual for an hour".[4] Can you, however, use MT to improve your foreign language writing, reading, listening and conversation skills? As indicated above, research shows that you need two things for this improvement to happen: first, reasonably good proficiency in the foreign language, and second, sound knowledge of MT and a set of skills now often described as "machine-translation literacy" (Bowker & Ciro 2019), as indicated above. While the former can only be achieved through repeated practice, the principles and advice presented in this section will show you how to develop the latter.

4.2 Language pairs and genres

To begin with, you need to consider that MT may be very good with some language pairs, and less good with others. Indeed, because NMT systems are corpus-

---

[4]This is just one of our students' MT stories: https://mtt.hypotheses.org/our-students-mt-stories

based (as explained in Chapters 2 and 7), they will produce poorer results when too little data is available to train the system. In the examples given in this Section, we use the FR<>EN language pair (looking at translations from French into English as well as from English into French), for which current MT solutions often produce good enough results, but we certainly encourage readers to find examples in their language pairs and compare them with ours.

Genre also makes a difference. You may find for instance that FOMT is better at translating essays than it is at translating poems or the lyrics of your favourite song. This may be because the data used to train the MT system are more similar to the former, and translated songs and poetry are probably quite rare in the training data. Poem and song translation are also particularly demanding: translated poems and songs may have to be recitable or singable. They may require particular rhyming schemes or metres. Although machines can be trained to write and even to translate poetry (Van de Cruys 2018, 2019, 2020), general-purpose FOMT might not be up to the task. It is still an interesting exercise to try it out, however: take a popular song, poem or nursery rhyme in either your L1 or L2. Find a good human translation of it,[5] one that tries to create pleasing rhymes and rhythm in the target language. Now run the original through a FOMT engine and compare the MT with the human translation. The results are likely to encourage you to reflect on what MT does well, and what human translators do wonderfully.

4.3 Ask a linguist

Second, you need to consider your expectations and those of your teacher and/or interlocutor. It's always a good idea to ask them whether MT is an acceptable solution, and whether it might interfere with your learning in ways that could be inappropriate. There might be cases in which the material used by your teacher cannot be put into a FOMT engine, because it contains personal or confidential data (as explained in Moorkens 2022 [this volume]). A language teacher could also tell you that MT will prevent you from learning grammar rules as it partly deprives you of the possibility of actively finding the right structure and phrasing. And if proficient use of grammar is needed to fix MT outputs, you won't necessarily become more proficient as you interact with MT. Quite the opposite: exposure to mistakes or approximations that might go unnoticed by learners could be detrimental. Learning about a foreign language based on repeated exposure to fluent MT outputs might occur, however, in at least some cases: in a recent study, Resende & Way (2021) evidenced implicit learning about syntax

---

[5]You may be able to find published human translations of poems, songs and nursery rhymes online.

from NMT outputs in some of the participants. It remains to be seen whether learners will also be influenced by the errors in the MT. Without good MT literacy and good-enough knowledge of the target language, it is more likely that they simply won't see the mistakes. (See, for example, Loock & Léchauguette 2021.)

Our advice, therefore, is that you should always ask a linguist: your teacher is a good start, as they will have a good idea of your L2 language proficiency and of the good and bad sides of using FOMT for a given language pair in a given context.

4.4 Situational parameters

In order to help language learners to decide when to use MT and when not, Table 1 includes a short list of situations with suggested decision parameters. Our proposal is based on the use of free online NMT solutions. (Note: If the answer to parameter 1 in Table 1 is negative, then don't use MT.)

5 Machine translation and competing digital resources

FOMT is quick and easy to use, and because you can use full texts as inputs, you might be content with what you get and tempted to look no further. But more often than not, MT won't be enough, and in some situations it might even be inappropriate. How does MT compare to other digital resources? Here is a list of four questions that will be discussed in turn in what follows, with a view to shedding light on what MT is, and what it is not. Gathering answers to these questions is a good way of starting a discussion on uses of MT versus other online tools:

- Do you use online dictionaries, and if so, which ones?

- How would you define a corpus?

- Have you used an online corpus before?

- Do you know what a concordance is?

The aim of the series of comparisons presented in what follows is to help L2 learners and foreign-language users in general reach beyond the immediacy of MT. One of the key points that we would like to make with these comparisons is the following: just because they are easy to use and provide you with almost instant translations does not mean that NMT solutions should be the preferred choice all the time.

Table 1: When to use MT and when not

Situation	Decision parameters, ranked by order of importance
Understanding an L2 text	1. No personal or confidential data in the text 2. Quality of the NMT output (which does not have to be perfect, but should be good enough)
Writing an essay in your L2	1. Teacher's agreement 2. No personal or confidential data in your essay 3. Sufficient L2 proficiency (B1 or B2 in CEFR) 4. Quality of the NMT output
Performing a translation assignment	1. Teacher's agreement (unlikely because using MT transforms the assignment from a translation task to a post-editing task) 2. No personal or confidential data in your source text 3. Quality of the NMT output
Getting ready for an oral presentation in your L2	1. Teacher's agreement 2. No personal or confidential data in your presentation 3. Sufficient L2 proficiency (B1 or B2 in CEFR) 4. Quality of the NMT output and availability of good text-to-speech output

5.1 MT versus online dictionaries

Generally speaking, a dictionary is "a book that contains a list of words in alphabetical order and explains their meanings, or gives a word for them in another language" (*Cambridge advanced learner's dictionary and thesaurus*, 2020). The definition further extends to electronic products like online dictionaries or apps, which are usually well-known to language learners. Examples of online dictionaries include more traditional ones like the Oxford English Dictionary,[6] and new forms in which at least part of the information has been crowdsourced, such as Wiktionary[7] or Urban Dictionary.[8]

Whether you have already been using them on a regular basis or not, the question for every user faced with such varied resources is: how can you tell that a dictionary is reliable? Lexicography (the writing of dictionaries) defines best practices and is constantly evolving to take into account the development of new dictionary forms and formats. Many dictionaries are now based on large collections of texts (also known as corpora) that can be used as references, but a lexicographer will never be happy with a mere quote from a corpus. Instead, corpora are often used to check language use and find relevant examples. Before doing so, a lexicographer's job crucially involves finding the relevant entries for a given dictionary, and writing up good definitions. To help you appreciate what this involves, learners' dictionaries are particularly telling because they include a really careful selection of entries, definitions and examples. With most dictionaries now freely available online, it should be easy for you to identify one or two learners' dictionaries and look for words that you have learnt recently or that you particularly like.

Here is another important point: the Linguee website claims to include a dictionary, but what kind of dictionary is it? Distinguishing between corpus-based and corpus-driven dictionaries may help: while corpus-based dictionaries still rely on a lexicographer's intuitions and are built according to the methods of lexicography, corpus-driven dictionaries are based on automatic extractions from a corpus. Linguee includes a corpus-driven, bilingual dictionary that does not provide you with definitions of words or carefully selected examples.

Before looking at online corpora, let us sum up the main differences between an NMT output and a dictionary entry:

---

[6]https://www.oed.com/
[7]https://en.wiktionary.org/, last accessed 20 June 2022.
[8]https://www.urbandictionary.com/, last accessed 20 June 2022.

- Dictionary entries are based on a single word, while you can get an NMT output for as much text as you like. NMT engines are far less useful than dictionaries because their output for an isolated word is often unreliable.[9]

- Dictionaries provide you with definitions, which may be the only reliable way to make sure you have understood the meaning of a word.

- Dictionary entries are based on human intuition and (most of the time) they are designed and/or checked by lexicographers.

- NMT outputs are based on corpora, but they are not exact quotes from the corpora that have been used for training (as explained in Pérez-Ortiz et al. 2022 [this volume]). The next section addresses this difference in more detail.

5.2 MT vs online corpora

At least two definitions are needed before we start explaining the differences between MT and online corpora.

First, a parallel corpus is a collection of source texts aligned with their translations. This parallelism or alignment means that each segment (usually a sentence) appears next to its translation.

A concordancer is the tool that is used to look for data in corpora and to display results. Table 2 contains an example from the Hansard corpus, a parallel corpus (English and French) of debates in the House and Senate of the Canadian Parliament.

Note first that the concordances are displayed as a function of the search: here we have looked for a French phrase, with a translation into English, so French appears first (that is, on the left), even though the source text for this part of the corpus is English (information that is not always displayed when using online corpora). It is also worth saying that bilingual concordancers usually highlight the exact search query (in bold in Table 2) in the source segment. Many also attempt to highlight the part of the target segment that corresponds to the search query, but the identification of such correspondences is based on a kind of probabilistic "guesswork", and is often not completely reliable. We have, in fact, "cleaned up" the target side of Table 2, to make the "equivalent" (see Kenny 2022: §1 [this volume]) parts of the concordance lines clearer. In short, alignment might

---

[9]We say this in the knowledge that language learners and university students in general do, in fact, use FOMT engines very frequently to find translations of single words (see, for example, Jolley & Maimone 2022, Dorst et al. 2022).

be accurate at sentence level, but fine-grained correspondences are not always identified automatically in bilingual or parallel concordancers.

Note also that online concordancers often display the full paragraph or text for each concordance, as shown in Table 2, or links to the relevant part of the corpus.

In contrast, an MT output will provide you with a proposed translation only for the words in your search, with no other contextual elements.

Table 2: Sample concordance lines for *nous allons faire le nécessaire* in the Hansard parallel corpus

French translation	English source text
Nous vous disons que *nous allons faire le nécessaire*, mais aidez-nous à nous assurer que tout le monde respecte les règles. Monsieur le Président, nous avons promis que *nous allions faire le nécessaire* pour ratifier l'accord.	But we're saying, hey, *we'll do it, we'll set it up*, but help us to make sure everybody abides by the rules. Mr. Speaker, we promised that *we were going to do what was required* to ratify the agreement.

Table 3: Sample NMT output for *nous allons faire le nécessaire* (MT by https://www.bing.com/translator, 2021-11-01)

French query	English NMT output
Nous allons faire le nécessaire. Nous allons faire le nécessaire pour ratifier l'accord.	We will do what is necessary. We will take the necessary steps to ratify the agreement.

Table 3 presents a comparison of two queries, the first one being shorter and more ambiguous than the second. It shows that NMT engines are able to adjust to sentence contexts: linked with the explicit mention of an objective (*pour ratifier l'accord*) a different construction is used in the English NMT output, where *faire le nécessaire* becomes *take the necessary steps to*.

Overall, it makes much more sense to use NMT with full sentences (see Kenny 2022: §7 [this volume]) or texts than with isolated words or phrases. When looking for a word, a collocation or a phrase, it might be more efficient and reliable to use a dictionary and/or a corpus, since you will get controlled results. Parallel corpora give you access to a series of translation choices whose context is usually easy to retrieve. MT, on the other hand, outputs results that are based on complex computations from training data that are not always accessible (they are typically hidden in FOMT interfaces). This can make it difficult for users to determine whether a proposed translation is indeed reliable.

6 Error analysis

One of the key skills that is needed to leverage MT for the purposes of second or foreign language learning is a keen awareness of errors. Various activities might be set forth in order to develop this skill, but because proposals are still scarce, we provide readers with one commented example in what follows.[10]

Based on a text and its MT, learners make a list of the types of errors they are able to detect and correct in the language pair in question. They submit the list to their teacher and then receive their teacher's feedback and a second list containing all the errors they hadn't noticed, with additional explanations, suggestions for further improvements and helpful examples. This exercise will be difficult if the target (machine translated) text is in the L2, and we suggest that teachers might start with translation into the mother tongue. While such tasks have been excluded from the language classroom for a long time, as indicated in the earlier part of this chapter, recent proposals integrating translation into situated tasks have been made, with a view to turning the learner into a "self-reflective, interculturally competent and responsible meaning maker in our increasingly multilingual world" (Laviosa 2014: 105).

Table 4 contains an example of an NMT output for a short text translated from English into French.[11] Errors in the NMT output are highlighted in bold and commented on below.[12]

---

[10]Further recent ideas on the integration of MT into language teaching and learning can be found in Vinall & Hellmich (2022).

[11]The text is taken from a textbook for French learners of English (Joyeux 2019:22). In order to turn this activity into a situated task, learners could be asked to provide a good translation to a French person with virtually no knowledge of English (e.g. a visitor to the class on a special occasion). They would need to receive minimal information about MT and about the need to correct the output that has been provided to them.

[12]Error analyses of MT output generally depend on *error typologies*, which list various types of problems that can be found in MT output. These usually incorporate accuracy errors (e.g. the meaning of the target segment is not consistent with that of the source segment) and errors that affect the fluency or well-formedness of the target segment (e.g. errors in grammatical agreement, word order, collocation, etc.). For more information, see Rossi & Carré (2022 [this volume]) on MT evaluation and O'Brien (2022 [this volume]) on post-editing.

Table 4: Sample NMT output for a short textbook excerpt

English source text	French NMT output
Hi there! My teacher asked me to write and tell you what a typical day in my life looked like so I'll do my best to give you an idea! I get up around 7:00 am, I have breakfast (two slices of toast and a cup of tea) then I get ready and put on my uniform. I make my lunch, and I double-check that my bag is packed. I leave my house at around 8:00 am. I've only got a 15-minute walk to school, so I arrive early. I usually chat with my friends, or listen to music with my headphones. Classes begin at 8:45 am.	Bonjour à tous ! Mon professeur m'a demandé de vous écrire et de vous raconter à quoi ressemblait *une journée typique de ma vie*, alors je vais faire de mon mieux *pour vous donner une idée* ! Je me lève vers 7 heures du matin, je prends mon petit déjeuner (deux tranches de pain grillé et une tasse de thé) puis je me prépare et je mets mon uniforme. Je prépare mon déjeuner, et je vérifie que mon sac *est bien emballé*. Je quitte *ma* maison vers 8 heures. *Je n'ai que 15 minutes de marche pour me rendre à l'école, donc j'arrive tôt. J'ai l'habitude* de discuter avec mes amis ou d'écouter de la musique avec mes écouteurs. Les cours commencent à 8h45.

Errors include overly literal translations like *une journée typique de ma vie*. The plural would work best in French and *typique* needs rephrasing: *mes journées de lycéen* (literally: 'my days as a pupil') would be a good solution. As you may note, literal translations are all the more inappropriate as the expression *a typical day* is more or less fixed in the source language. For idioms like *to give you an idea*, you will need to find an idiomatic expression in the target language: something like *pour vous en donner un aperçu*.

Some of the errors are more linked to grammar and language use. Clitic pronouns like *en* would be needed in the French text, and we could for instance improve *donc j'arrive tôt* by turning it into *donc j'y arrive en avance* ('so I arrive in advance'). On the other hand, possessives are used in English even when possession is implicitly retrieved from the rest of the text, in which case the definite is preferred in French (*je quitte la maison* 'I leave the house' rather than 'my house'). Language use also concerns the lexicon, and while it is common in English to refer to manner of motion (*a 15-minute walk to school*), French is usually more neutral (*15 minutes de trajet pour l'école* '15 minutes of journey for the school') with precisions added only if necessary (e.g. *à pied* 'on foot').

There are many more possible examples, but the above will hopefully be enough to show that although the French NMT output looks good enough, with no major grammatical or lexical mistakes, there is still a lot of room for improvement. Finding out what learners can and cannot correct will certainly be illuminating for teachers (see Loock & Léchauguette (2021) on this point).

We encourage readers to get NMT outputs for their own language pair, translating in the first instance into their L1. Activities including NMT outputs in an L2 in situated tasks can be used at a later stage of language learning, especially if the task involves detecting and fixing errors in the output.

7 Conclusions

In this chapter we have presented some of the main findings of research to date into the use of MT in language learning, focusing on more recent sources that take into account the progress made in MT since the arrival on the scene of NMT. We have also offered some basic tips on using MT in language learning, before building on the pragmatic approach to quality evaluation presented in Rossi & Carré (2022 [this volume]), focusing on what it implies for second and foreign language learners. Unlike specialized translators, who may not be given a choice about the tools they use in current translation scenarios, language learners have choices, but they first need to decide whether and when to use MT. To this end, we presented a list of situation-based parameters that can help them make this decision. We also contrasted MT with complementary online tools such as dictionaries and corpora, stressing the relative merits of each. Finally, we proposed activities to harness the potential of NMT and include it in the second or foreign language classroom.

References

Bowker, Lynne. 2020. Machine translation literacy instruction for international business students and business English instructors. *Journal of Business & Finance Librarianship* 25(1-2). 25–43. DOI: 10.1080/0896.1794739.

Bowker, Lynne & Jairo Buitrago Ciro. 2019. *Machine translation and global research*. Bingley: Emerald Publishing.

Cambridge University Press. 2020. *Cambridge advanced learner's dictionary and thesaurus*. https://dictionary.cambridge.org/dictionary/english/.

Castilho, Sheila, Joss Moorkens, Federico Gaspari, Iacer Calixto, John Tinsley & Andy Way. 2017. Is neural machine translation the new state of the art? *The Prague Bulletin of Mathematical Linguistics* 108. 109–120. DOI: 10.1515/pralin-2017-0013.

Chung, Eun Seon & Soojin Ahn. 2021. The effect of using machine translation on linguistic features in L2 writing across proficiency levels and text genres. *Computer Assisted Language Learning.* DOI: 10.1080/09588221.2020.1871029.

Clifford, Lisa Merschel, Joan & Joan Munné. 2013. Surveying the landscape: What is the role of machine translation in language learning? @tic. *Revista D'innovació Educativa* 10. 108–121.

Cook, Guy. 2010. *Translation in language teaching.* Oxford: Oxford University Press.

Correa, Maite. 2011. Academic dishonesty in the second language classroom: Instructors' perspectives. *Modern Journal of Language Teaching Methods* 1(1). 65–79.

Dorst, Lettie, Susana Valdez & Heather Bouman. 2022. Machine translation in the multilingual classroom. *How, when and why do humanities students at a Dutch university use machine translation? Translation and Translanguaging in Multilingual Contexts* 8(1). 49–66. DOI: 10.1075/ttmc.00080.dor.

Ducar, Cynthia & Deborah Houk Schocket. 2018. Machine translation and the l2 classroom: Pedagogical solutions for making peace with google translate. *Foreign Language Annals* 51. 779–795.

Enkin, Elizabeth & Errapel Mejías-Bikandi. 2016. Using online translators in the second language classroom: Ideas for advanced-level Spanish. *LACLIL* 9(1). 138–158. DOI: 10.5294/laclil.2016.9.1.6.

Fredholm, Kent. 2015. Online translation use in Spanish as a foreign language essay writing: Effects on fluency, complexity and accuracy. *Revista Nebrija de Lingüística Aplicada a la Enseñanza de las Lenguas* 18. 7–24.

Fredholm, Kent. 2019. *Effects of google translate on lexical diversity: Vocabulary development among learners of Spanish as a foreign language,* vol. 13. 26378/rn-lael1326300. 98–117. DOI: doi:10.26378/rnlael1326300.

Jolley, Jason R. & Luciane Maimone. 2022. Thirty years of machine translation in language teaching and learning: A review of the literature. *L2 Journal* 14(1). 26–44. http://repositories.cdlib.org/uccllt/l2/vol14/iss1/art2.

Joyeux, Maël. 2019. *Fireworks, anglais.* https://www.lelivrescolaire.fr/.

Kelly, Niamh & Jennifer Bruen. 2017. Using a shared L1 to reduce cognitive overload and anxiety levels in the L2 classroom. *The Language Learning Journal* 45(3). 368–81.

Kenny, Dorothy. 2022. Human and machine translation. In Dorothy Kenny (ed.), *Machine translation for everyone: Empowering users in the age of artificial intelligence*, 23–49. Berlin: Language Science Press. DOI: 10.5281/zenodo.6759976.

Laviosa, Sara. 2014. *Translation and language education: Pedagogic approaches explored.* London/New York: Routledge.

Lee, Sangmin-Michelle. 2021. The effectiveness of machine translation in foreign language education: A systematic review and meta-analysis. *Computer Assisted Language Learning* 33(3). 157–175. https://www.tandfonline.com/doi/full/10.1080/09588221.2021.1901745.

Loock, Rudy & Sophie Léchauguette. 2021. Machine translation literacy and undergraduate students in applied languages: Report on an exploratory study. *Revista Tradumàtica: tecnologies de la traducció* 19. 204–225. DOI: 10.5565/rev/tradumatica.281.

Moorkens, Joss. 2022. Ethics and machine translation. In Dorothy Kenny (ed.), *Machine translation for everyone: Empowering users in the age of artificial intelligence*, 121–140. Berlin: Language Science Press. DOI: 10.5281/zenodo.6759984.

Mundt, Klaus & Michael Groves. 2016. A double-edged sword: The merits and the policy implications of Google Translate in higher education. *European Journal of Higher Education* 6(4). 387–401. DOI: 10.8235.2016.1172248.

Niño, Ana. 2009. Machine translation in foreign language learning: Language learners' and tutors' perceptions of its advantages and disadvantages. *ReCALL* 21(2). 241–258. DOI: 10.1017/S0958344009000172.

Noriega-Sánchez, María, Ángeles Carreres & Lucía Pintado Gutiérrez. 2021. Introduction: Translation and plurilingual approaches to language teaching and learning. *Translation and Translanguaging in Multilingual Contexts* 7(1). 1–16.

O'Brien, Sharon. 2022. How to deal with errors in machine translation: Post-editing. In Dorothy Kenny (ed.), *Machine translation for everyone: Empowering users in the age of artificial intelligence*, 105–120. Berlin: Language Science Press. DOI: 10.5281/zenodo.6759982.

O'Neill, Errol. M. 2012. *The effect of online translators on L2 writing in French.* Unpublished PhD, University of Illinois at Urbana-Champaign. Retrieved from http://hdl.handle.net/2142/34317.

O'Neill, Errol. M. 2019. Training students to use online translators and dictionaries: The impact on second language writing scores. *International Journal of Research Studies in Language Learning* 8(2). 47–65.

Pérez-Ortiz, Juan Antonio, Mikel L. Forcada & Felipe Sánchez-Martínez. 2022. How neural machine translation works. In Dorothy Kenny (ed.), *Machine translation for everyone: Empowering users in the age of artificial intelligence*, 141–164. Berlin: Language Science Press. DOI: 10.5281/zenodo.6760020.

Pintado Gutiérrez, Lucía. 2018. Translation in language teaching, pedagogical translation, and code-switching: Restructuring the boundaries. *The Language Learning Journal* 49(2). 219–239.

Pym, Anthony, Maria del Mar Gutiérrez-Colón Plana & Kirsten Malmkjaer. 2013. *Translation and language learning: The role of translation in the teaching of languages in the European Union*, vol. 3. Luxembourg: Publications Office of the European Union.

Resende, Natália & Andy Way. 2021. Can Google Translate rewire your L2 English processing? *Digital* 1(1). 66–85.

Rossi, Caroline & Alice Carré. 2022. How to choose a suitable neural machine translation solution: Evaluation of MT quality. In Dorothy Kenny (ed.), *Machine translation for everyone: Empowering users in the age of artificial intelligence*, 51–79. Berlin: Language Science Press. DOI: 10.5281/zenodo.6759978.

Thomas, Jacqueline. 1988. The role played by metalinguistic awareness in second and third language learning. *Journal of Multilingual and Multicultural Development* 9(3). 235–246. DOI: 10.1080/01434632.1988.9994334.

Thue Vold, Eva. 2018. Using machine-translated texts to generate L3 learners' metalinguistic talk. In Åsta Haukås, Camilla Bjørke & Magne Dypedahl (eds.), *Metacognition in language learning and teaching*, 67–97. Routledge. DOI: 10.4324/9781351049146.

Torres-Hostench, Olga. 2022. Europe, multilingualism and machine translation. In Dorothy Kenny (ed.), *Machine translation for everyone: Empowering users in the age of artificial intelligence*, 1–21. Berlin: Language Science Press. DOI: 10.5281/zenodo.6759974.

Van de Cruys, Tim. 2018. *Il pleure dans mon processeur multi-cœur*. Poésie automatique. http://www.timvandecruys.be/media/charles2018.pdf.

Van de Cruys, Tim. 2019. *La génération automatique de poésie en français*. Proceedings of TALN 2019. Toulouse. 113–126. https://aclanthology.org/2019.jeptalnrecital-long.8.pdf.

Van de Cruys, Tim. 2020. *Articuler ou trahir*. Translating Europe Workshop. Université Toulouse Jean Jaurès. 7 February 2020. http://timvandecruys.be/media/presentations/pres_tradlit_070220.pdf.

Vinall, Kimberly & Emily Hellmich (eds.). 2022. *Machine translation & language education: Implications for theory, research, & practice*, vol. 14. 1–3. https://escholarship.org/uc/uccllt_l2/14/1.

Zhang, Hong & Olga Torres-Hostench. 2019. Cómo enseñar posedición de traducción automática a una segunda lengua: Una propuesta didáctica para el aprendizaje de lenguas. *Revista Tradumàtica: traducció i tecnologies de la informació i la comunicació* 17. 153–161. DOI: 10.5565/rev/tradumatica.237.

Name index

www.ingramcontent.com/pod-product-compliance
Lightning Source LLC
Chambersburg PA
CBHW080915100426

42812CB00007B/2277

* 9 7 8 3 9 8 5 5 4 0 4 5 7 *